Pelican Books
The Sexual Behaviour of

Michael Schofield took his degree in psychology at
Cambridge University and has since specialized in
social psychology. He has conducted researches
for the British Social Biology Council, the Home
Office and the University of London, and was the
Research Director of the Central Council for
Health Education. He has published many research
reports on social problems and is the author of
Sociological Aspects of Homosexuality, which was
quoted by several M.P.s during the debates on this
subject before the law was changed. Recently he
carried out an educational study for the Nuffield
Foundation, which resulted in a Schools Council
Working Paper entitled *Society and the Young
School Leaver*. This suggests possible developments
in the curriculum of the humanities and social
studies in preparation for the raising of the school-
leaving age. Michael Schofield is also a
member of the Home Office and Ministry of Health
Advisory Committee on Drug Dependence.

The Sexual Behaviour of Young People

Michael Schofield

In collaboration with John Bynner
Patricia Lewis, Peter Massie

Penguin Books

Penguin Books Ltd, Harmondsworth,
Middlesex, England
Penguin Books Australia Ltd, Ringwood,
Victoria, Australia

First published by Longmans 1965
Revised and re-written for Pelican Books 1968
Reprinted 1969
Copyright © Michael Schofield, 1965, 1968

Made and printed in Great Britain by
Cox & Wyman Ltd, London, Reading, and Fakenham
Set in Monotype Times

The Central Council for Health Education

Steering Committee

*Dr J. D. Kershaw, MD, BS, DPH (Chairman)
*Miss C. Barton
 Sir Herbert Broadley, KBE
*Dr A. J. Dalzell-Ward, MRCS, LRCP, DPH, FRSH
 Frank Dawtry, MBE
*The Rev. G. R. Dunstan, MA, FSA
 Dr C. M. Fleming, MA, EdB, PhD
*Dr T. C. N. Gibbens, MBE, MD, DPM
 Professor D. V. Glass, BSc, PhD
 Dr M. E. M. Herford, DSO, MBE, MC
*Professor H. T. Himmelweit, MA, PhD
*Miss D. M. Marshall
*Professor C. A. Moser, BSc
*Dr C. S. Nicol, MD, FRCP
*Dr H. C. Maurice Williams, OBE, MRCS, LRCP, DPH

Ex-officio Members of Committee

Sir W. Allen Daley, MD LLD, FRCP (late President, CCHE)
Councillor J. A. Brown, CBE, JP (Council Member, CCHE)
G. S. Burden, BSc (Econ.) (late Chairman, CCHE)
A. S. Mays, OBE (Hon. Treasurer, CCHE)
Alderman Mrs C. C. Scott, JP (Acting Chairman, CCHE)

Observers

 Dr I. G. Davies, MD, FRCP, DPH (Ministry of Health)
 Dr C. B. Huss, MB, BS, DPH (Department of Education
   and Science)

Members of the Research Sub-Committee

Contents

Note on References   10
Acknowledgements   11
Foreword by Sir Herbert Broadley   13

Part One: The Design of the Research

1. Introduction   19
   A. Aims and Scope   19
   B. The Need for this Research   23
   C. The Teenage Population   25

2. Research Plan   29
   A. Other Researches into Sex Behaviour   29
   B. The Sample Design   31
   C. The Procedure   33
   D. Presentation   36

Part Two: The Extent of Teenage Sexual Activities and Attitudes

3. Incidence   41
   A. Dating   41
   B. Kissing   42
   C. Petting   43
   D. All Sexual Activities   45
   E. Accumulative Incidence   48
   F. Five Stages of Sex   51
   G. Weighted Incidence Figures   55

4. Early Experiences 57

    A. The First Contacts 57
    B. Early Inceptive Behaviour 59
    C. Homosexuality 60
    D. The First Experience of Sexual Intercourse 62
    E. Early Starters 70
    F. Characteristics of the Early Starters 72

5. Frequency 76

    A. The Intensity of Dating 76
    B. Frequency of Inceptive Activities 77
    C. Sexual Intercourse Frequencies 78
    D. Reactions to Sexual Intercourse 79
    E. Boys Compared with Girls 80

6. Knowledge about Sexual Matters 82

    A. Conception 82
    B. Parental Advice about Sex 84
    C. Sex Education at School 86
    D. Birth Control 87
    E. Venereal Disease 93

7. Attitudes 98

    A. The Attitude Inventory 98
    B. Opinions and Beliefs 99
    C. Attitudes to Marriage 102
    D. Attitudes to Sex Education 104
    E. Inhibiting Factors 106
    F. Attitudes to Sex before Marriage 108
    G. Attitudes to Virginity 108

Part Three: The Difference Between Sexually
Experienced Teenagers and Others

8. Family Background 115

    A. Associated Factors 115
    B. Early Background 116
    C. Relations with Parents 119
    D. Home Influence 120
    E. Parental Circumstances and Attitudes 124

9. Education and Work 126
   A. School Record 126
   B. Occupational Record 128

10. Groups 132
   A. Group Membership 132
   B. The Influence of the Group 133
   C. Close Friends 135
   D. Friends as a Source of Information 137

11. Leisure 140
   A. Youth Clubs 140
   B. Other Spare-Time Activities 141
   C. Parties 144
   D. Drinking and Smoking 146
   E. Delinquency 149

12. Personal Factors 152
   A. The Assessment of Personality 152
   B. The Analysis of the Attitude Inventory 154
   C. First Order Factors 156
   D. Second Order Factors 170
   E. Teenage Attitude Structure 177
   F. The Third Order Factors and Sex Experience 181
   G. The Exclusion of Age 185
   H. The Exclusion of Other Variables 189
   I. Sexual Experience and Personality 193

Part Four: Summary and Discussion

13. Profile of the Experienced Teenager 199
   A. Rating Scales 199
   B. Undistinguishable Features 200
   C. Discriminating Features 202
   D. Experienced Girls Compared with Boys 206

14. Validity 209
   A. Sources of Error 209
   B. The Bias Caused by Refusals 210
   C. External Checks 215
   D. Evaluation of the Results 220

15. Questions of Public Concern   223

    A. Premarital Sexual Intercourse   223
    B. Sex Education   224
    C. Illegitimacy   227
    D. Venereal Disease   229
    E. Restraints and Controls   232

Part Five: Appendices

Appendix 1: The Interviews   239

Appendix 2: The Interviewers   246

Appendix 3: The Attitude Inventory   255

References   261
Index of Names   267
Subject Index   269

Note on References

Works to which reference is made are identified in the text
by author's name and publication date only.
Titles, and more detailed information, are given in the list
of References on pages 261–265.

Acknowledgements

The research for this report was made possible by a generous grant from the Nuffield Foundation and it has been carried out under the auspices of the Central Council for Health Education.

In the early days of the research I talked to many people who were in the youth service or concerned with adolescent problems. There are notes on our files of 53 of these people who gave freely of their time. Mr A. Chisnall, Mr Maurice Lee, Mr J. G. H. Newfield, Mr and Mrs E. Page-Symonds, and Mr H. A. Smith were particularly helpful during the pilot stage of the research. As the research moved from area to area much help was received from the Local Authorities, particularly from the staffs of the Education and Health Departments. I should like to thank all these people for their advice and assistance.

Dr A. J. Dalzell-Ward, Mr K. E. Watson and the staff of the CCHE made sure that the administrative side of the research ran smoothly. The seven interviewers especially recruited for this work were: Anne Bardsley, Conway Daly, John Dixon, Roger Farnworth, Naomi Honigsbaum, Laura Renouf and Gay Rice. The statistical consultant throughout the research was Miss Kathleen Gales. Most of the analysis was done by English Electric Leo Computers Ltd, under the guidance of Mr D. J. Flower, Miss R. Kerfoot and Miss R. Hoad. The factor analysis was carried out by Dr A. Hendrickson on an IBM Computer. Miss V. Evelyn and Miss R. Lang provided the secretarial assistance. Miss Lang also gave considerable help with the analysis. Mr B. Ellis gave valuable assistance in the preparation of the manuscript and the diagrams. I am grateful to all these people for the work they did.

I owe a special debt to the members of the Research Sub-Committee (listed on page 5) who gave encouragement and guidance throughout the three years of the research. Finally I should like to add my particular thanks to my three collaborators who are named on the title page.

MICHAEL SCHOFIELD

Foreword

Sir Herbert Broadley

This study of the sexual behaviour of young people had its origin in a discussion after a meeting of the International Union against Venereal Diseases and the Treponematoses. At the Conference papers were read on the incidence of promiscuity. These and other papers led to a more general discussion regarding sexual intercourse among young people and the probability that this might be a cause of the admitted increase in venereal diseases, particularly gonorrhoea.

The statistics presented referred to a very limited number of cases and were drawn from specialized sources, such as clinics attended by those apprehensive of venereal disease or by girls concerned with undesired pregnancies. Some of us who attended the meeting considered that the impression created was not representative of the young people of today and felt that an impartial survey should be undertaken covering all types and classes of young people. This was ultimately made possible as the result of the enthusiastic support of Dr A. J. Dalzell-Ward, the Medical Director of the Central Council for Health Education; the wise guidance of Dr J. D. Kershaw, who acted as Chairman of a specially created Steering Committee; the generosity of the Nuffield Foundation which gave a grant for the purpose of establishing facts in an area where there are too many ill-founded judgements, and, of course, Mr Michael Schofield who planned and carried out the research and prepared this report.

Considering the origin of the project as an attempt to determine how far the incidence of veneral disease might be due to increased teenage sexual intercourse it is reassuring to note the finding on page 231 of the report that 'These results suggest that promiscuity, although it exists, is not a prominent feature of teenage sexual behaviour. Consequently the risks of venereal disease are not very great.'

Promiscuity is not the same as indulgence in sexual intercourse.

It means sexual intercourse with several partners over a period of time. The report shows how small is the number of those young people indulging in promiscuity as thus defined. And it is promiscuity, not sexual intercourse limited to only two individuals, which can be the means of spreading the disease.

The research has gone far beyond the conception of those who originally proposed it and throws new light on many problems of great importance to social workers concerned with young people. On the main theme it is particularly significant to read on page 224, 'Our results have made it clear that premarital sexual relations are a long way from being universal among teenagers as over two-thirds of the boys and three-quarters of the girls in our sample have not engaged in sexual intercourse.' Notwithstanding all the influences to which the young people of today are exposed – greater independence; more money in their pockets and purses; the weakening of family bonds and religious influences; the development of earlier maturity, physically, emotionally and mentally; the impact of modern books, television, periodicals – it is clearly wrong to regard our young people as a bored, undisciplined, sex-obsessed generation.

It is impossible to say how the behaviour of today's younger generation compares with that of the past. Unfortunately no survey comparable with the present one has ever been undertaken before. This one is, indeed, an historic document. We can therefore only relate its findings to our individual recollections of perhaps nearly half a century ago – now dimmed by time and probably unrepresentative of the youth of those days. A survey undertaken in the twenties might not have reached results widely different from those of today.

Nevertheless the findings of this report do not justify complacency. They raise many problems to which attention must be paid. The sexual development of young people is a natural process, in the course of which wise guidance is needed. It is remarkable how few of those interviewed had learned 'the facts of life' from parents or school teachers. What they had picked up from various sources was often inadequate and frequently misleading. Widespread ignorance was found to exist regarding venereal disease, its symptoms and consequences. Far too little was known of, and less practised in, birth control methods. The whole question of the method and character of sex education must be reconsidered.

Sexual intercourse between young people before marriage exists and will continue. Whether we disapprove or consider it a perfectly natural and normal phenomenon must be for each of us a matter of personal judgement. What is needed is not moral denunciation or exhortation but the inculcation into members of the younger generation of a greater sense of responsibility, a recognition that whatever their actions or their behaviour they must fully understand and accept the consequences involved. Only so will a sane social system continue to evolve to meet the new challenges of this exciting and stimulating age.

Part One

The Design of the Research

I. Introduction

A. Aims and Scope

The object of the investigation was to obtain facts about the sexual attitudes and behaviour of young people aged fifteen to nineteen. In particular an attempt was made to measure the extent of sexual experience in this age group, and to identify some of the sociological and psychological factors associated with sexual experience.

Despite the welter of comment and opinion, there is a shortage of adequate knowledge about the sexual activities of young people. It was the object of this research to provide the basic information which is the essential first step before suitable educational measures can be developed.

In his series of Reith Lectures, Professor Carstairs broadcast the now famous passage (which has been widely quoted out of context) in which the relative importance of chastity and charity is questioned. This sparked off such a heated controversy that few people noticed in the same lecture his statement that 'if we turn to consider young people's sexual behaviour today, we encounter many vehement opinions, but little reliable data' (Carstairs, 1962). Dr Alex Comfort (1963), who has a rather more outspoken style, writes: 'In the absence of facts, poppycock of every kind flourishes in the public mind and much sheer moonshine in the medical textbooks.'

Like every other social research this one was limited by time and money. But a generous grant from the Nuffield Foundation made it possible to use techniques and methods which had been beyond the compass of previous investigations into sexual behaviour. Nevertheless our resources were not limitless, and it was necessary to put some restrictions on our objectives. Consequently it was decided that the scope of the research was to find out as much as possible about the sexual activities of teenagers within the following framework:

1. the information was obtained direct from the teenagers themselves;
2. the interviewers were especially recruited and trained for this
work;
3. the research was based on a series of random samples;
4. the questions on sexual behaviour were preceded by a large
number of questions on family background and leisure activities;
5. a sufficiently large sample was interviewed so as to be able to
describe certain norms of sexual behaviour;
6. care was taken to exclude all moral injunctions or value
judgements during the course of the interviews.

A large number of people connected with the youth service
were consulted before the interviews began. The research team
did not suffer from a shortage of advice from youth leaders and
others concerned with the care of youth. The striking thing about
the opinions of these youth workers is their complete lack of
uniformity. It is possible to put this down to a failure in observa-
tion, but youth leaders are not slow to supply considerable detail.
The real explanation seems to be that they are generalizing from
information acquired from a particular group.

Probation officers and others concerned with delinquents are
liable to forget about the thousands of boys who never get into
trouble. A social worker, who spends most of her time interviewing teenagers in a VD clinic is tempted to generalize about the
country's youth, although less than one in a thousand teenagers
ever get venereal disease. The Research Director attended discussion groups with parents who were slow to impart information
about their own children but became less inhibited when discussing the failings of other people's.

Although some useful advice was obtained from doctors,
teachers, probation officers and youth workers, much of the early
period which was spent on a study of the background of the
problem turned out to be a disappointment and produced only a
small amount of reliable information. On the question of today's
youth, it seems as if everyone has already taken up his position
and formed his attitudes and the small amount of available

factual data has not been weighty enough to persuade anyone to change his views.

For these reasons it was decided that the basic information to be used in this research should come from the young people themselves. There were obvious advantages in getting the facts direct from the teenagers, and some difficulties as well. The interviewers had to be sure that feelings of self-esteem did not distort the replies. There was a natural inclination to tell the interviewer rather less than the truth on some occasions. There was also the temptation to tell the interviewer what the teenager felt he wanted to hear, rather than give real opinions when questioned about attitudes.

This meant that special techniques had to be evolved to persuade each teenager to tell the truth. It was impossible to use the ordinary market research methods and a small corps of interviewers had to go through an intensive course of training so that they might learn how to win the confidence of the young people in a short time. Their task was made easier because boys and girls of this age and of this generation tend to be more frank about sex than is the case with older people.

Previous researches in this country and elsewhere into youth problems have used subjects recruited from youth clubs, university students or other restricted groups. But this leaves important segments of the population unrepresented. For example, 75 per cent of this sample were not members of youth clubs. It was decided that this research must be based on a random sample although it was known from the start that this was the most expensive sampling method. So far as we know this is the only research into sexual behaviour which has the advantage of being based on a sample of this kind. Even Kinsey (1948, 1953), who used very large numbers, did not use random sampling methods to find his subjects.

As one of the primary aims of this research was to determine the extent of sexual experience within the fifteen to nineteen age group, it was essential that the sample should be as representative as possible. Generalizations based on anything less representative than a random sample would be subject to the same type of criticisms which have been levelled at many other researches (Cochran,

Mosteller and Tukey, 1954; Himelhoche and Fava, 1955). All the teenagers who lived in each of the seven areas where this research was carried out had an equal chance of being interviewed.

It was obvious that intimate questions on sex behaviour could not be asked until the interviewer had built up a large measure of *rapport*. In any case we wanted to cover many other areas besides sex behaviour so that we could build up a general picture of contemporary youth culture and thus identify the non-sexual factors which seemed to be associated with certain kinds of sex behaviour. This meant that we also asked a large number of questions on leisure activities and on social behaviour in general.

Many of these sociological factors lend themselves to reasonably exact measurement (such as academic achievement, youth club membership, cinema attendance), but the fact that some of the answers to our questions were more difficult to quantify was not always a reason for excluding them. Thus some attempt was made to find out something about the extent of family discipline and the influence of the peer group. We also included questions to test the young people's knowledge of sexual matters and to estimate the extent of their sex education.

Our knowledge about the sexual norms of our society is very meagre and information about the sexual norms of the younger generation is almost non-existent. That is why it is not possible to make any comparisons between this generation of teenagers and previous ones because the information about past generations is missing. As a result of the 1,873 interviews carried out for this research on a representative sample of teenagers, it is now possible to make statements about the incidence of sexual behaviour in this age group. This will also mean that comparisons with future generations will be more meaningful.

At all times we tried to avoid any moral implications in the questions we asked. Our position was neutral. At no time did we attempt to change the teenagers' views or introduce any opinions of our own. It was not the role of this research to disseminate moral values nor did we assume a uniformity of moral standards in others. We hope the results of this research will assist those whose job is to help and advise young people, but we did not regard advice as part of our task. Our concern was to get the facts.

B. The Need for this Research

According to the BMA Report on Venereal Disease and Young People (1964): 'In spite of new drugs and improved methods of treatment, an increase in sexually transmitted diseases has taken place and this is most marked among young people.' The Registrar General's *Statistical Reviews* show that the percentage of illegitimate births among girls under twenty-one has also increased in recent years.

The BMA Report and others argue that this can best be explained by an increase in the amount of promiscuous behaviour among young people. Neither this research nor any other can show whether there has been an increase or not because the historical information is not available. But an increase in our knowledge of sexual behaviour as it is today should put us in a better position to tackle VD and illegitimacy as social problems.

The public disquiet about teenage sexual behaviour has increased the demand for more sex education. But there is considerable disagreement about the best method of presenting this information, by whom and at what age. There is a need for the concept of sex education to be based on a realistic assessment of adolescent sexual experience.

A rough measurement of the extent of this public disquiet is given by the amount of newspaper coverage. During the early stages of the research a press-cutting agency was employed to collect all the items which dealt with any aspect of teenage sexual behaviour. Over a period of four months 414 relevant cuttings were received. Of these, 55 per cent were critical of adolescent sexual activities, 15 per cent set out to defend these activities, and 30 per cent were neutral or expressed approval of some activities and disapproval of others.

It would be a mistake to make too much of these figures, for news coverage by the popular press can arouse and instigate as well as report public disquiet, and therefore a content analysis of press cuttings is measuring both cause and effect. However it is interesting to note that about half of those expressing concern were people who dealt with adolescents professionally. Even among these people there was no agreement as to the true state of affairs.

A rational discussion of the teenage problem has always been hindered by lack of information.

Some people have suggested that there is nothing new about the teenage problem. The development of adolescent into adult has always created difficulties. But there are some differences between this generation of adolescents and their predecessors, and these differences are discussed in detail in the next section of this chapter. Furthermore there seems to be a failure in the communication between parents and teenager. Parents have told our interviewers 'there's nothing she doesn't discuss with me', but within the next hour or so, our interviewers have learnt quite otherwise. Obviously there are some matters where communication between parents and adolescent can be very difficult and this is especially the case where problems of sex behaviour are concerned.

Indeed there are good reasons to suppose that there might be a change in the sexual behaviour of young people, because many of the circumstances have changed; the earlier onset of puberty; many girls are physically mature at thirteen and many young men reach maximum virility before the age of twenty; the emancipation of women and more general agreement that sexual fulfilment is desired by women as well as by men; the changed economic situation which allows young people more choice and more independence; the diminishing influence of the family and of religion; the growing recognition that lifelong monogamy preceded by absolute chastity is no longer the practice of many people; the publication of books in which Christian teaching on sexual questions is re-examined.* All these situational issues would lead one to expect a change in behaviour.

Eppel (1966) has shown that persistent criticism by adults is creating a gulf between the young people of today and adult generations. There is much justification in the claim of some of these young people to be left alone to lead their own lives, but no one generation is completely independent from the others, and the successes and failures of these young men and women will affect us all.

* In particular *A Quaker View of Sex* and *Sex and Morality*, both of which were read extensively.

If, as the Albemarle report (1960) suggests, 'adolescents are the litmus paper of a society', then for our sake as well as theirs it is necessary that we gain more knowledge about the sexual behaviour and attitudes of young people.

C. The Teenage Population

The power and influence of the teenage population is far greater today than in the years before the last war. Although there are signs that the importance of this group is sometimes exaggerated, not least among the teenagers themselves, it is still true that they have become a more salient section of the community.

Abrams (1961) has studied in detail the economic influence of this group, although it should be noted that his definition of teenager is much wider than ours, for he included everyone who is unmarried and under the age of twenty-five.

Although their total spending power is only 5 per cent of all consumer spending, they are the biggest purchasers of certain commodities. Thus they buy 42 per cent of all the records and record players that are sold, 37 per cent of all bicycles and motor-bicycles, 29 per cent of all cosmetics and toilet preparations, 28 per cent of all cinema admissions and 30 per cent of the money spent on other entertainments, 18 per cent of all recreational goods, 15 per cent of all cigarettes and tobacco, 15 per cent of all money spent on meals out and snacks, 13 per cent of all soft drinks, and 13 per cent of all the money spent on holidays. Their total spending is far higher than it used to be and tends to be concentrated on these commodities. 'Money at the disposal of Britain's average teenager is spent mainly on dress and on goods which form the nexus of teenage gregariousness outside the home' (Abrams, 1961).

People have become well aware of the increased spending power of the teenagers and the suggestion that 'they have too much money to throw about' is often used as an explanation for teenage misbehaviour. But their total spending power is not out of proportion to their numbers in the whole population. Their economic power has become noticeable because they spend their money on articles which are highly visible and audible, and because their spending tends to be concentrated on certain areas of the total market. They are also subjected to exploitation by many adults who have realized the commercial possibilities of the teenage market where a large part of the income is not committed to essential family expenditure like rents or mortgages, household goods, or children's food and clothes.

The visibility of this increased teenage economic power has led to its exaggeration. The teenage market is run by adults and all our social institutions are still dominated by older people. Youth has often been in revolt against the old-fashioned and out-worn ideas of the older generations and has challenged the traditional and conventional. The main difference now is that the balance has changed. In the past the adults had all the economic power. Now through the mechanics of supply and demand, the teenager has more money to spend and so his ideas and desires are treated with more respect by the commercial world.

The demands of teenagers which were once ignored have now become important, and their activities are reported in the mass media. In some areas, popular music for example, their demands completely dominate the market and the newspapers and periodicals give much of their space to stories about the latest recording stars, the new teenage fashions and the latest teenage craze.

But the newspapers are still run by adults and still reflect the views of the adults who respond to the new economic power of the teenagers with a strange mixture of bewilderment, scorn and envy. So teenagers are news, but only certain kinds of teenagers – those who are in trouble, those who are defying convention, those who are good copy.

The frequent articles in the press and the radio and TV programmes tend to create a teenage mythology. Just as a boy learns how to behave towards his family, or his schoolmaster, so by a similar social learning process he learns the role of a teenager. The press reports have created this image of the typical teenager and the young people who do not measure up to this archetype begin to feel that they are missing something, or else something is missing in them.

It has been shown that teenagers are better fed than in the past. They are taller and heavier. They are the healthiest section of the community and except for a very high rate of motor-cycle accidents (Lee, 1963), they have a very low mortality rate.

It is now well known that children mature at an earlier age than in the past. According to Tanner (1962): 'The age at menarche has been getting earlier by some four months per decade in Western Europe over the period 1830–1960.' It follows therefore that 'a girl today may expect to menstruate on average some ten months earlier than did her mother' (Tanner, 1961). Boys now complete their growth on average at about seventeen years of age; this compares with twenty-three years of age at the turn of the century. The average girl reaches menarche aged about thirteen-and-a-half; about a hundred years ago she reached it at about seventeen. This lowering of the physical age of maturity must mean that today's boys and girls are also sexually mature at an earlier age than their parents and grandparents. So they will feel sexual desire and be sexually at risk at an earlier age. Twenty years ago some activities between thirteen-year-olds would have been regarded as mere sexual play; today the same activities could have much more serious consequences. Physical development is of considerable importance in a study of sexual behaviour and we shall refer to this again in Chapter 13.

Not only have teenagers become more dominant, but also there are more of them. There are almost a million more teenagers now than there were ten years ago – an increase of 20 per cent. The number of young people aged fifteen to nineteen is expected to remain around three and a half million for the next ten years, then the expansion will continue and according to the Registrar General's *Statistical Review* there will be over four million teenagers in 1982.

Although the increase in the teenage population could have been foreseen, unfortunately the expansion of facilities for young people has not kept pace. Despite the warnings given in many reports (Crowther, Newsom, Albemarle, Robbins, the King George V Jubilee Trust), there is not enough room in the schools, colleges, universities and apprenticeship schemes. Consequently for many years to come there will be intense competition for the available places and inevitably there are going to be some young people who will be left disappointed and frustrated because the opportunities have not expanded at a rate proportionate to the increase in population. In addition there are several areas where there is a shortage of youth clubs and other recreational facilities.

One of the penalties of being young is that some youthful activities will be labelled deviant behaviour if only because young people are less inhibited than older generations and less inclined to be restricted by convention or the sour looks of neighbours. Therefore there will always be teenage problem groups and as the size of the teenage population grows, it is to be expected that the size of the problem groups will increase correspondingly. In addition it is well known that in the more serious problem areas, like juvenile delinquency, drug abuse and illegitimacy, the numbers are increasingly out of proportion to the increase in the population.

The young and unattached are the progenitors of change. They are more flexible in their attitudes and have no social status to safeguard. As long as they are unmarried the greater part of their income is uncommitted, and they will have power to pursue their particular ends without regard for adult society or its traditions. The rejection of adult values and standards is clearly illustrated in the dancing, dress and hair-styles of teenagers. A familiar jibe from adults is that nowadays they cannot tell the girls from the boys, but the teenagers themselves do not have any difficulty.

Many of the values of adult society are being challenged, sometimes unintentionally. Not only in appearance and clothes, but also in other more important things, such as sexual relations. This challenge will have most significance when the unintended consequences of teenage behaviour force adult society to take action as in the case of unmarried mothers or drug misuse. Inevitably the adult reaction will be restrictive and this will produce defiance in some of the young people.

Teenagers have become aware of their increased importance in the community. The commercial market panders to their demands and the mass media creates a teenage mythology. The most influential factors are their increased purchasing power and the younger age at the onset of puberty. These economic and physiological factors have so altered the situation that the sexual behaviour of teenagers is now more crucial than in the past. This presents a challenge which society has not yet been able to meet.

2. Research Plan

A. Other Researches into Sex Behaviour

Very few of the researches into sexual behaviour have sampled directly from the general teenage population. Most of them have been content to ask older people to try to remember the early sexual experience of their youth. The few that have dealt specifically with teenage sexual behaviour have always used captive or particular groups of the population, such as prisoners, hospital patients, soldiers and, most frequently, college students. No research has used a random sample of the general population of teenagers and very little attempt has been made to evolve new techniques for studying this area of human relations.

Nearly all these researches were carried out in America. The most important exception is Chesser's inquiry into the sexual, marital and family relationships of English women. The information in Dr Chesser's inquiry was collected by approaching general practitioners and inviting them to distribute a self-administered questionnaire to their patients. Only 23 per cent of the questionnaires distributed were returned. About 490 of those who replied were single women over eighteen and under twenty-one. Although useful information was obtained from the inquiry, it was not a study of teenage sex behaviour and the sample was over-represented in the higher educational and income groups.

The two books by Kinsey and his associates (1948, 1953) are by far the most extensive and best known of the American studies on human sexual behaviour. The broad purpose was 'to accumulate an objectively determined body of facts about sex which strictly avoids social or moral interpretation of the facts'. A total of 6,200 males and 5,800 females were interviewed. No statistically systematic method of selection was used, and it is difficult to ascertain from the first volume either the age or the educational level of the men interviewed. It is assumed that a very large proportion were students, but it is not known how many teenagers at lower educational levels were interviewed. 75 per cent of the women interviewed were college educated, whereas only 13 per cent of American women are college educated. In fact Kinsey and associates interviewed 297 non-college girls aged sixteen to twenty compared with the 920 non-college girls in our sample.

Kinsey did not use standardized questions; his interviewers simply had a checklist of questions to be asked at each interview; the different interviewers had a standard definition of the items but used different words to get the information. Once the subject had agreed to be interviewed Kinsey was relentless in his cross-examination; and used methods of persuasion which would not have been advisable to use with our sample of adolescents. He takes considerable care to show in his study of the male that these unstandardized interview techniques did not produce significantly different results between the three male interviewers. Unfortunately he did not repeat these tests in his study of the female. Our own results make it clear that it is far more difficult to get this kind of information from girls, and interviewing women about sex is more variable and uncertain than interviewing men; and Kinsey made it even more precarious by using men to interview women, whereas we found girls responded much more readily to female interviewers.

Nevertheless there is no doubt that the study by Kinsey, which is still being carried on by his associates, is by far the most important work of its kind. The usefulness of this work lies not only in the methods and results, but also in the frank critical assessment of their own work. These comments are very helpful to others undertaking similar studies and this research owes much to their pioneering work.

Many of the researches which were carried out over large segments of the population do not report age breakdowns, and therefore it is impossible to glean much information from them about the sex behaviour of young unmarried men and women. But the main disadvantage in all these researches is not the incompleteness of the analysis but the imperfections in the method of collecting the data. The overwhelming majority of previous researches have used subjects who are available and easy to interview, but not necessarily representative of young people in general; and the value of the results, in spite of the statistical sophistication of some, must remain very limited.

B. The Sample Design

Strictly speaking the young people in our random samples were not volunteers in the first place. They received a visit from one of the research team and then they had to be persuaded to cooperate. This was not always an easy task. The activities of some doorstep salesmen who pretend to be doing a research, but use this only as a sales gimmick, have made many people wary of all social surveys.

The difficulty is that if a person refuses, another cannot be brought in as a substitute. It is therefore important to try to get the actual person drawn for the sample to agree to an interview and this can only be done by being prepared to fit in with the time and place most convenient to the young person concerned. This method of obtaining interviews is expensive and takes far longer than the usual methods used by market researchers. Much of the work done on sexual behaviour in America suffers from the failing that the researchers have used students as subjects because they were available and likely to volunteer. But it can be shown that student sexual behaviour is not typical of the behaviour of all young people. The boys and girls interviewed for this research are much more representative of the whole teenager population and this has enabled us to present our results with more confidence.

In order to obtain a random sample of any section of the population, it is necessary to have a complete list from which to extract the names. The most usual method is to use the National Polling Register, but this list is of no value to a research studying people under the age of twenty-one. Various alternatives were considered, but the most complete list seemed to be the record of National Health patients kept by the local Executive Councils. This list covers 97·5 per cent of the population throughout the full age range (Gray and Cartwright, 1953), and it was thought that the percentage would be even higher for young people. The Clerk of the London Executive Council agreed to cooperate and a sample was drawn from a list of all the National Health patients aged fifteen to nineteen in the area designated London C, the first area to be sampled. Unfortunately the Ministry of Health did not allow the Executive Councils in other areas to supply us with lists from which to draw our samples, and so other sampling methods had to be used.

The next two areas were South A and South B where samples were drawn from the school attendance lists. Although the lists were almost a year out of date they proved to be satisfactory for drawing the samples of teenagers. But it was found that school attendance records had not been kept up to date in the other areas that we wished to visit, so a third method of sampling was devised. The remaining areas were visited in this order: North A, North B, London A, London B. In these four areas the sample was drawn from lists especially constructed for this research by a market research agency which was employed to locate all the teenagers living in selected districts in each area.

Despite the difference in sampling methods, the results from the seven areas are very similar, and where there is a difference, it is more reasonably explained by other factors than by the different methods of sampling. It is estimated that the total number of unmarried teenagers aged fifteen to nineteen in the seven areas was 24,093. In fact 1,873 interviews were completed and so one in every 13 teenagers was represented in the sample.

Table 2.1
The sample shown by age, sex and area groups

Age/Sex group	London A	London B	London C	South A	South B	North A	North B	Total
Younger boys	82	67	63	70	70	63	63	478
Older boys	65	62	61	64	72	65	67	456
Younger girls	74	68	60	70	72	64	67	475
Older girls	69	65	65	69	64	67	65	464
Total	290	262	249	273	278	259	262	1,873

These 934 single boys and 939 single girls were classified into two age groups according to their year of birth. The older boys and the older girls had an average age of eighteen and were not younger than seventeen, not older than nineteen at the time of the interview. The two younger groups had an average age of sixteen, and an age range of fifteen to seventeen.

The basic information on the size of the sample and sub-samples is given in Table 2.1. Between 249 and 290 were interviewed in each of the seven areas and no age/sex/area group is less than 60.

Areas marked A were particular wards of a town which were selected because they were expected to produce a relatively large proportion of young people from middle-class homes. Areas marked B were expected to produce mostly working-class teenagers. London C was an area chosen because we hoped to find young people from all types of homes, but in the event most of them were the children of artisans (Registrar General's Class III).

C. The Procedure

It cannot be assumed in any research that reliable information about sex behaviour can be easily obtained just for the asking. It does not require much skill or cost much money, first to make up a questionnaire on sex, and then to send it out to thousands of people in the hope that a few hundreds will reply. This has been done by newspapers, college magazines and agencies. The results are unlikely to be of much value. The number who do not answer the questions is often so large that they form a sizeable proportion of the population under consideration; nor is this a method that is likely to elicit the truth on such a personal matter.

This research was as much concerned with the method of getting the information as with analysing, interpreting and reporting the results. We realized that many people would be reluctant to co-operate once they knew the research was about sexual behaviour, and we felt others would prevaricate unless the whole exercise was made as easy and as pleasant as possible. We were allowed a long exploratory period to study the methodological problems, to seek advice from those concerned with youth work, and to try out different ideas and techniques.

Consequently it was with feelings of anticlimax that we came to the conclusion that the only satisfactory way of obtaining the data was by using good interviewers. Despite the progress and refinement of psychological tests, self-administered questionnaires and group discussion techniques, we came to believe that valid information about sex behaviour could only be obtained during the course of a lengthy face to face interview.

The questions were tried out in schools and youth clubs, and discussed with youth leaders and many others concerned with youth work, and groups of teenagers were invited to criticize and comment on the schedule of questions. Some of the questions did not reach their final form until they had been tried out on over 300 teenagers.

Ten young graduates were used as the interviewers in this research. After some experiments it was found that the best results were obtained when men interviewed boys and women interviewed girls. The five male interviewers and five female interviewers were selected for their ability to get on with young people and they were all required to undergo an extensive course of training before they started interviewing.

After the young person had been drawn for the sample he (or she) was sent an introductory letter telling him about the research and asking for his cooperation. The interviewer called at the teenager's home soon after he had received the letter and arranged with the boy and his parents a time and place for an interview. If he preferred to be interviewed at home the interviewer arranged to call back at a convenient time; sometimes it was possible to carry out the interview at the time of the first call. It was always stressed that privacy was essential if the interview was to be held at home. If he preferred to be interviewed away from home, the interviewer could arrange to meet him at a near-by office which had been hired especially for this research.

If the teenager failed to keep the appointment the interviewer was required to call back to try to arrange another interview. Sometimes this was not possible and of course there were some teenagers who would not agree to an interview in the first place. It was expected that there would be a high number of refusals and it was imperative that everything should be done to cut down this loss. In fact 328 would not agree to an interview and this represents a refusal rate of 14·9 per cent. The effect of these refusals is discussed in Chapter 14 when the important question of the validity of the results is considered.

The interviewers were instructed to continue to call on the teenager until it became clear that there was no chance of getting an interview. Interviewers were not allowed to give up before six call-backs had been made. When it was decided that a particular case would have to be classified as a refusal, the interviewer wrote up a detailed history and the reason for refusing, and the teenager was sent a letter and a form containing 16 questions about his background and leisure interests. About half those who refused an interview answered the questions on this form, so at least something is known about many of those who refused.

At the start of each interview the main task was to make the teenager feel at ease, so the interviewer concentrated upon establishing *rapport*. The schedule was so designed that only simple information was sought in the early part of the interview; this was followed by questions on leisure which the teenager usually found interesting; only then were questions on sex behaviour introduced, and this started with questions on dating and kissing, and gradually came to the more personal and intimate questions. The whole schedule consisted of 261 items of which 234 were direct questions. When all the questions had been asked the teenagers were given an attitude inventory. This consisted of 50 statements on controversial topics and they were asked to indicate whether they agreed or disagreed with these statements.

The record was checked by a supervisor soon after the interview had been completed, so that questions of validity and correct coding could be discussed with the interviewer while the answers were still fresh in his mind. When all the material had been collected, the information from the interview records was put on to 13,111 punch cards (seven cards for each individual), fed into a computer and analysed. This research plan is described in more detail in Appendices 1 and 2.

D. Presentation

In general the percentages given in Part Two of this report are based upon the four age/sex groups, i.e.:

    478 younger boys (aged 15–17)
    456 older boys (aged 17–19)
    475 younger girls (aged 15–17)
    464 older girls (aged 17–19)

However 42 of the 261 items were revised and modified after the first 249 interviews in London C. This means that the percentages calculated for these 42 items will be based on the results obtained in six instead of seven areas, i.e.:

    415 younger boys (aged 15–17)
    394 older boys (aged 17–19)
    416 younger girls (aged 15–17)
    399 older girls (aged 17–19)

For reasons explained in Chapter 8 the percentages given in Part Three (except Chapter 12) are based on the older age groups. On other occasions the percentages will be based on smaller segments of the sample; for example, in Chapter 4 there are percentages based upon only those girls who had experience of sexual intercourse, but these cases will be clearly identified when they occur in the relevant chapters.

In a few chapters the statistical information is supplemented by quoting from the actual words of the boys and girls at the interview. With so many answers to choose from and with so varied an assortment of responses, these quotations are bound to be selective. The quotations most likely to be chosen are those which make a point dramatically or where the answer gives a new slant to an old subject. But most teenagers are not as articulate as those quoted in this report. With some exceptions, a feel for words is not one of their attributes. Even so, with the help of a sympathetic interviewer, nearly all the young people were able to make their meaning clear.

The next five chapters (Part Two) give the basic results of the investigation into sex behaviour and attitudes; this is followed by six chapters (Part Three) on the association between sex behaviour and other factors; then the last chapters discuss the validity of the material and some questions of public concern.

Part Two

The Extent of Teenage Sexual Activities and Attitudes

3. Incidence

A. Dating

The first date is an important event in the life of an adolescent. Until this moment the social life of a boy has probably been restricted to an all-male group whose interests revolve around football, cycling or some other hobby where the presence of girls is not welcome. Even those boys who have grown up in a mixed group will reach the stage when there is a desire to pair off from the group and go out with a particular girl. As well as this inner desire which is a reawakening of sexual interest as the boy reaches puberty, there is also an outside pressure on each boy to find a girl and take her out. But not all boys feel this desire or give way to this social pressure and in this group 107 (22 per cent) younger boys (aged 15–17) and 34 (7 per cent) older boys (aged 17–19) had never gone out with a girl.

Adolescent girls are more likely to have been out on a date. Their earlier interests in family games, clothes and appearance lead naturally towards an interest in the opposite sex, and fantasies about boy friends are encouraged by comics, films and pop records before they ever go out with a boy. But the first date is still an important event, for it may be the first time the girl has been on her own with a boy, when she will experience her first physical contact as a reality rather than in fantasy. In this sample 43 (9 per cent) of the younger girls (aged 15–17) and 20 (4 per cent) of the older girls (aged 17–19) had never gone out with a boy.

Of the younger boys who had never been out with a girl, only a third said they would like to, whereas half the younger girls who had not been dated said they would like to go out with a boy. So many boys, and a few girls also, do not want to start dating before the age of seventeen.

As well as the 204 (11 per cent) teenagers who had never been out with members of the opposite sex, there were many others who had very little experience of dating. Over half (52 per cent) the younger boys and a third (33 per cent) of the younger girls had not been out with more than four of the opposite sex. But from the age of seventeen onwards many more went out on dates, and nearly a half (49 per cent) of the older boys and well over a half (58 per cent) of the older girls had been out with ten or more different people.

Dating is a useful activity that enables boys and girls to get to know each other, and eventually to find a wife or husband. The girls start younger than the boys and one in five boys do not start dating before seventeen. Thereafter the boys begin to catch up with the girls, but it is still a more important activity for a teenage girl than it is for a boy. Beyond the age of seventeen dating for teenagers is usual but not universal.

B. Kissing

The first specifically sexual contact experienced by most teenagers is a kiss. But children have experience of non-sexual kissing from parents and other adults, and during party games. An attempt was made to leave these out of the reckoning and to limit our definition of kissing to an activity which has some slight element of sexual arousal. After experimenting during the pilot stage of the research, it was found that the most satisfactory wording was: 'When was the first time you kissed a girl/boy on your own – and liked it?' This took the situation out of the context of 'kiss in the ring' and suggested an occasion which might have led on to further activities of greater intimacy.

The amount of kissing for both sexes is very similar to the incidence of dating. This suggests that a boy and girl often experience their first serious kiss on their first date. In the two younger groups all those who have been out on dates had experienced their first kiss at the same age. This was also true of the older girls, and among the older boys just 1 per cent more had been out on a date without experiencing a kiss. Perhaps these figures do no more than reflect the custom of giving the girl a good night kiss after taking her home.

Deep kissing, sometimes known as french kissing, where the tongue of one partner enters the mouth of the other, is an activity with a much more specific component in it. But it does not necessarily follow on from lip kissing and is shunned by some teenagers who take part in other forms of sexual activity. In fact over a third of the sample had never done this, and less than a half expressed any interest in deep kissing.

There are some signs that deep kissing is more acceptable to middle-class teenagers. Of the 91 middle-class older boys who had kissed a girl, 20 (22 per cent) had never tried deep kissing; but among the 85 working-class older boys who had kissed a girl, 31 (36 per cent) had not tried deep kissing. Of the 107 middle-class older girls who had been kissed, 15 (14 per cent) had not tried deep kissing; yet among the 76 working-class older girls who had been kissed, 21 (28 per cent) had not tried deep kissing.

More girls than boys had experienced this type of kissing; 72 per cent of all the girls compared with 54 per cent of all the boys. But many of the girls did not enjoy it. Only 10 per cent of the younger girls and 14 per cent of the older girls said they liked it very much, compared with 16 per cent of the younger boys and 27 per cent of the older boys who said they enjoyed it. Teenage boys appear to be less likely to have experienced deep kissing, but those that have tried it are more likely than the girls to enjoy the experience.

C. Petting

Kissing is a form of sexual contact accepted by most people even in semi-public places, but most other kinds of love-making usually take place in private. Furthermore they are subject to more restrictions, limitations and taboos, and can only take place when the circumstances are expedient. Those forms of sexual contact which fall short of sexual intercourse are often referred to as *petting*. This is an American expression used to cover a wide variety of activities from a simple caress to a situation closely resembling sexual intercourse. This is too wide a definition for this research as petting is not an entity in itself but a generic term applied to various acts which have many different social consequences. In this chapter it will be clearer and more useful if we define and specify eight forms of sexual behaviour that may precede intercourse. Dating, kissing and deep kissing have already been mentioned. The other five activities are described in the next four paragraphs.

Stimulating breasts over clothes. Boys were asked when they first felt a girl's breasts, and girls were asked when they first allowed a boy to do this. More than half the sample had experience of this activity. In the younger age group the incidence among the girls (60 per cent) was higher than it was among the boys (49 per cent); in the older age groups the difference between the sexes had narrowed, but it was still more common among the girls (79 per cent) than among the boys (74 per cent).

Stimulating breasts under clothes. Not many (1 per cent) people refused to answer questions once the interview had started, but it was at the point when a question on this activity was asked that a refusal was most likely. It seems to provide a strong dividing line between the sexually sophisticated and the others. It is also at this point that the incidence falls away by as much as 12 per cent or more in each of the four groups. About one-third (36 per cent) of the younger boys and about two-thirds (63 per cent) of the older boys had fondled the breasts of a girl under her clothes. This is also the point where as many boys as girls have the same experience for 38 per cent of the younger girls and 61 per cent of the older girls had allowed their breasts to be fondled by a boy.

Genital stimulation. This is really two kinds of activity. The boys were asked when they first touched a girl's sex organs, and then they were asked when they first let a girl touch* their sex organs. The girls were asked the same question but in reverse order. As expected more boys had stimulated a girl's genitals than girls had stimulated a boy's genitals. Among the boys 37 per cent had fondled a girl's genitals (active genital stimulation), compared with 28 per cent who had let a girl fondle their genitals (passive genital stimulation). Among the girls 33 per cent had let a boy touch their genitals but had reciprocated in only 20 per cent of the cases. It is at this stage where the incidence among the younger age groups falls away, and in this and the following activities the incidence is always twice as great among the older boys and girls. Over half (51 per cent) of the older boys had experience of active

* The word 'touch' was used in this context because in the vernacular 'touching up' means genital stimulation.

genital stimulation compared with 24 per cent of the younger boys; nearly half the older girls (44 per cent) had experience of passive genital stimulation compared with 22 per cent of the younger girls.

Genital apposition. This is the term used to describe the circumstances when the sex organs of the male are in close contact with those of the female, but where penetration does not occur. It may be a preliminary to full sexual intercourse, alternatively it may be a substitute for intercourse. In the sample 14 per cent of the younger boys and 38 per cent of the older boys had experienced genital apposition; in other words slightly more than a quarter (26 per cent) of the boys had experienced this activity. It was a rather less frequent activity for the girls: 13 per cent of the younger girls and 29 per cent of the older girls had experienced genital apposition; in total about one-fifth (21 per cent) of all the girls. In most cases where genital apposition is possible, the physical surroundings would also allow sexual intercourse with full penetration, and yet 43 boys (17 per cent of those with experience of this activity) and 72 girls (28 per cent of those with experience of this activity) said they would prefer genital apposition to sexual intercourse.

D. All Sexual Activities

The remaining form of sexual activity considered in this report is intercourse with full penetration. A few other activities, such as oral-genital contacts, were mentioned very occasionally in the interview, but these are more likely to occur after intercourse has been experienced. American researches sometimes report extensive oral-genital contacts, but it was very rare among the teenagers in this sample.

  ˙ The group who experienced intercourse in this sample of teenagers will be the subject of further detailed discussion. In this section only the straightforward incidence is reported and this is compared with the other activities.

  In the group of 478 younger boys (aged 15–17) a total of 55 (11 per cent) said they had experienced sexual intercourse at least once. A total of 138 (30 per cent) of the 456 older boys (aged 17–19) reported at least one experience of sexual intercourse. The figures for the girls are much smaller. Out of 475 younger girls, 29 (6 per cent) said they had experienced sexual intercourse at least once. Among the older girls 73 (16 per cent) out of 464 reported at least one experience of sexual intercourse. Thus 20 per cent of all the boys in the sample had experienced sexual intercourse and 12 per cent of all the girls.

When the nine forms of heterosexual activity described in this chapter are considered together, it becomes clear that there is a difference in development between boys and girls. In the early activities (dating, kissing and deep kissing), more girls than boys are involved. Thereafter the boys catch up with the girls and the gap gradually widens until there is a difference of 8 per cent.

The incidence of deep kissing is higher among girls than the incidence of breast stimulation, whereas for boys the opposite is the case. It seems that girls are more likely to permit this intimate type of kissing, though most of them do not like it; they are less likely to allow their breasts to be fondled. Kissing represents romance and is acceptable, but touching the breasts is thought of as a sexual act and therefore is less easily accepted.

The activity described as genital stimulation could take place in several situations when genital apposition would not be possible, for example in the cinema, in the front seat of a car or in a crowded room. This is shown by the fact that many more boys have touched a girl's genitals (24 per cent) than have experienced genital apposition (14 per cent). Yet there is very little difference between the number of girls who have fondled a boy's genitals (20 per cent) and the number who have experienced genital apposition (21 per cent). It is clear that very few girls are prepared to reciprocate in these situations, and even those girls who will permit genital apposition may not agree to fondle the boy's penis. This again demonstrates that most girls prefer a passive role and do not want to initiate a sexual activity.

The number of girls who had experience of genital apposition (21 per cent) is much greater than the number who have had sexual intercourse (12 per cent). It is not true to assume that a girl who agrees to genital apposition is on the threshold of sexual intercourse. It is significant that genital apposition is likely to occur in the same sort of place and in the same sort of circumstances where intercourse could have occurred. So there are a large number of cases when the teenagers chose to have genital apposition when they could have had intercourse.

In this sample 65 per cent of the boys who had experienced intercourse sometimes stopped short of it in favour of genital apposition, even though they could have had intercourse. As many as 73 per cent of the sexually experienced girls sometimes stopped short of intercourse in favour of genital apposition. Some of them deliberately use genital apposition as a form of birth control; the girl may encourage the boy to reach orgasm before full intercourse can occur.

About a quarter (17 per cent boys, 28 per cent girls) of all those with experience of genital apposition said they would prefer this to sexual intercourse. Some said they prefer it because it removes anxiety about pregnancy and venereal disease – although it is possible to catch VD during genital apposition, it is much less likely. Others agreed to genital apposition but disallowed sexual intercourse for moral reasons. According to their way of looking at things, intercourse troubled the conscience whereas genital apposition did not. These arbitrary lines between what is morally permissible vary quite a lot. One boy said that anything is allowed so long as it is above the belt.

A few teenagers may confuse genital apposition with sexual intercourse. It is just possible, although we have no direct evidence for this, that a boy may be under the impression that he has had sexual intercourse when he has not in fact penetrated the girl. It is still more possible that a boy who has experienced genital apposition will tell his friends (and perhaps our interviewers) that he has had full sexual intercourse. Thus there seem to be some situations where the teenagers had genital apposition in lieu of sexual intercourse.

This section has given the simple incidence figures for the various sexual activities. An evaluation of these rudimentary figures depends upon other standards and points of view. For those who denigrate all teenage sexual activity, the figures may seem high. But when contrasted with the recurring outcry about teenage immorality, these figures may seem low. Our task in the rest of this chapter is to examine these figures so that they become more meaningful.

E. Accumulative Incidence

It will be no surprise to anyone to find that the amount of sexual experience increases as the teenagers get older. Although later chapters will show that many other factors must be taken into account, there is no doubt that one of the most important influences upon the adolescent's sexual experience is chronological age. This is partly due to rapid changes in physical maturity during the years immediately following puberty, and also to the changes in the social circumstances which are closely tied to age at this time. Thus at the age of fourteen a boy may be discouraged by parents from taking a girl out even if he wanted to; but by the age of nineteen he is expected by adults and his own friends to be showing an interest in the opposite sex.

The ages of the boys and girls in this sample varied from fifteen to nineteen. Therefore percentages which indicate the extent of a particular activity are misleading because adolescents of fifteen who have not participated in a particular activity may well experience that activity before they reach the age of nineteen. This discrepancy is allowed for by dividing the sample into older and younger groups. But in this section a more detailed analysis by age will be carried out so that an estimate can be made of the number of adolescents who will have experienced a specific activity by a particular age.

This can be done by using the concept of *accumulative incidence* as devised by Kinsey (1948). This is defined as the percentage of all the people in the sample who have experienced an activity by a given age. This concept as used by Kinsey has been criticized because it relied upon accurate recall of adults about their early sexual experiences, and because it is assumed that there would be no variation in outside environmental circumstances between the generations (Cochran, Mosteller and Tukey, 1953). But neither of these criticisms are really applicable in this research. The teenagers are being asked to remember events which happened only a few years ago, and in some cases just a few months or weeks ago. Also as the age range of this sample only covers a span of five years, there is no question of a variation in conditions between generations.

Figure 3/1.
Accumulative incidence curves of eight activities for boys

The accumulative incidence of eight sexual activities is given in Figure 3/1 for boys and Figure 3/2 for girls. From these figures it can be seen (for example) that 15 per cent of all boys will have experienced deep kissing by the age of fourteen, and by the age of seventeen the figure is 61 per cent. Among the girls aged fifteen one in ten had allowed a boy to touch their genitals, but by eighteen nearly half (46 per cent) had experienced passive genital

Figure 3/2.
Accumulative incidence curves of eight activities for girls

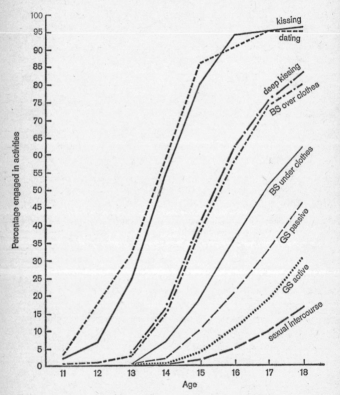

stimulation. By taking any point along the horizontal line, one can estimate the number of boys and girls who are expected to be experienced in a particular activity between the ages of eleven and eighteen.

The graphs show that kissing and dating are learnt at about the same time by both boys and girls; deep kissing and breast stimulation over clothes seem to go together for the girls, but the boys experience deep kissing at a later age.

The ascent of the lines indicates that between fifteen and seventeen the teenagers are learning fast; at fifteen less than a fifth of the boys have touched the genitals of a girl, but by seventeen nearly half have done this; at fifteen less than a fifth of the girls have experienced breast stimulation under clothes, but at seventeen over half have experienced this. If one were to make the assumption that the lines on these graphs would continue at the same angles, then by the age of twenty about half the boys and a third of the girls will have experienced sexual intercourse.

Despite the few unhappy cases reported in the newspapers from time to time, in fact less than one per cent of the boys or girls have experienced sexual intercourse before the age of fourteen. But two out of 100 fourteen-year-old schoolboys will be sexually experienced and so will one in about 200 schoolgirls of the same age if the results in our sample are typical. By the age of sixteen 14 per cent of the boys and 5 per cent of the girls will have had sexual intercourse. By eighteen a third of the boys and about one in six of the girls will have experienced heterosexual relations at least once.

F. Five Stages of Sex

The previous section of this chapter discussed the extent of particular sexual activities at various ages. This showed that sex experience during adolescence tends to follow a progression from no contact with the opposite sex, to dating and kissing, then through various degrees of physical intimacies, up to full sexual intercourse. At any one of these levels the specific sexual activity may be an end in itself, or it may be the stepping-stone to the next level of activity.

A consideration of these results now enables us to view this progression as five major stages of sex experience. Obviously the first stage must be that situation where the adolescent does not go out with others of the opposite sex.

The next two stages are an attempt to make a more meaningful division of the phenomenon often described as petting. One type of petting results in sexual arousal only. This will include kissing, deep kissing and the fondling of the girl's breasts over her clothes. These activities are differentiated from the other type of petting because no undressing takes place and kissing is the central activity. The other type of petting involves some disarrangement of clothing and close physical intimacy that is not usually acceptable in public. Thus this includes fondling the breasts under clothes, stimulating of the sex organs and genital apposition. These activities are more likely to lead to orgasm and often happen in the circumstances and surroundings in which sexual intercourse itself could take place.

The fourth and fifth stages are made up of those who have experienced intercourse. The fourth stage refers to those people who have had this experience with one person only; and the teenager reaches the fifth stage when he has sexual intercourse with more than one person. Thus we have a five-point scale as follows:

I. *Little or no contact with the opposite sex:* may have been out on a date but has never kissed.

II. *Limited experience of sexual activities:* has experience of kissing as defined in this research and may have experience of breast stimulation over clothes, but has never experienced this under clothes.

III. *Sexual intimacies which fall short of intercourse:* has experience of breast stimulation under clothes and may have experienced genital stimulation or genital apposition, but has no experience of sexual intercourse.

IV. *Sexual intercourse with only one partner.*

V. *Sexual intercourse with more than one partner.*

These five stages of sex experience are used throughout this report. In this chapter these stages are examined by age, area, social class and education; then the figures are weighted so that the intentional middle-class bias in our sample can be eliminated.

An analysis of these stages of sex experience by age emphasizes that this is the critical age period; for most boys the extent of their sex experience will increase considerably during the span of these five years. If this sample is typical, then about 45 of the 135 fifteen-year-old boys will have had sexual intercourse in the next four years (not including the six fifteen-year-old boys who have already had this experience). One third of the fifteen-year-old boys are in stage I, but only 7 per cent of the nineteen-year-olds are at this stage. Conversely 3 per cent of the fifteen-year-old boys are at stage V, but one third of the nineteen-year-olds are at this stage.

The same trend is apparent among the girls. Among the fifteen-year-old girls 16 per cent are at stage I and the number drops rapidly beyond that age until only 2 per cent of the oldest girls are at stage I. Most of the girls aged fifteen, sixteen and seventeen are in stage II, and the majority of eighteen- and nineteen-year-olds have reached stage III, although even at these ages over a third of the sample remain in stage II. As noted in Section D the number of girls with sexual experience is much lower than the boys, but it tends to increase with age in the same way. Only 2 per cent of the fifteen-year-olds are in stage V, whereas 13 per cent of the nineteen-year-olds have had intercourse with more than one person. These are also momentous years for girls and, like the boys, this is the age when they are learning new sexual experiences, and so moving from one end of the scale towards the other. About half the 100 fifteen-year-old girls at stages I and II will have moved on to stage III or higher before they are twenty. But for the girls, and not for the boys, there is a barrier between stages III and IV, and a large number remain at stage III.

Nevertheless a glance at the list below shows that too much emphasis should not be given to those with wide sex experience. Over half the boys (51 per cent) and girls (53 per cent) had got as far as stage II but no farther. Only 16 per cent of the whole sample (20 per cent boys, 12 per cent girls) had experience of sexual intercourse.

Stages of sex experience	Boys %	Girls %
I	16	7
II	35	46
III	29	35
IV	5	7
V	15	5

The percentage at each stage of sex experience varied only a small amount in the seven areas visited by the research team. The boys in London are more sexually active than elsewhere; but the difference between the London girls and the others is not so marked. In the three B areas more teenagers are in stages IV and V than in the A areas; on the other hand there are more teenagers from the A areas in stage III. London C seemed to have provided an unusually large number of stage II older girls; this was the first area visited and it is possible that the inexperienced interviewers missed several girls who should have been in stage III. But all these differences are small and overall there is a remarkable similarity in the figures for the seven areas.

When stages of sex experience were analysed by social class, it was found that there were more middle-class girls in stage III. Among the younger girls there were a few more working-class girls in stages IV and V, but in the older group there is practically no difference in the number of girls who have experienced sexual intercourse. Among the boys there are signs that the working class are more likely to have intercourse before the others and there were more middle-class younger boys in stage I. There are more middle-class older boys in stage III and more working-class boys in stages IV and V. The association between social class and sexual experience is considered in more detail in Chapter 8.

The influence of education is shown by relating the stages of sex experience to the various types of school attended by the teenagers. Among the younger boys the percentages at each stage hardly varied from school to school with the exception of grammar school boys who had far less experience than the others. The percentage of sexually experienced boys at independent or private schools is only 1 per cent less than for the secondary modern schools; most of the latter group had started work at the time they were interviewed, whereas nearly all the younger boys were still attending their private schools when they were interviewed by our research workers.

Among the older boys the difference between schools is more pronounced. The boys who went to secondary modern or comprehensive schools had the most sexual experience, and the grammar and private schoolboys had the least. It is surprising to find that 24 per cent of the older boys educated at private schools were still at stage I, as middle-class boys reach physical maturity earlier than working-class boys (Tanner, 1962). This suggests that social pressures are stronger than physical growth. But this generalization should not be emphasized too much because 34 per cent of the private school boys are at stage III and 22 per cent have experienced sexual intercourse.

There is some indication that secondary modern and comprehensive school girls pass more quickly from stage II to stage IV or V than grammar or private school girls of this age who seem more likely to remain at stage III for a longer period. Even among the girls who have left school, the ex-secondary modern and ex-comprehensive girls are more likely to be at stage II or stage IV, whereas the grammar and private school girls are more often at stage III. This suggests that the better-educated girls are prepared to allow more sexual intimacies as long as these stop short of sexual intercourse.

An overall comparison of the four types of schools suggests that boys at grammar and private schools start their sexual experience later than the boys at secondary modern or comprehensive schools, perhaps because they have less free time and less money to take girls out. This also applied to the grammar school girls but not, surprisingly, to the private school girls.

G. Weighted Incidence Figures

In order to get adequate numbers of middle-class teenagers in our sample, three of the seven areas were chosen particularly because we expected to find a large proportion of middle-class girls and boys in them. As the middle-class adolescents were over-represented in our sample, the incidence figures given in this chapter may not be exactly like those one would expect to find in a sample which was strictly representative of the whole teenage population.

In this section we shall attempt to redress the balance by removing the middle-class bias that we deliberately introduced. This can be done by comparing one of the basic characteristics in our sample with the same characteristics in the total population as given in tables of national statistics. Then the incidence figures obtained in our research can be 'weighted' so that the characteristic has the same distribution in our sample as it has in the total population.

Ideally the characteristic to be used would be social class as classified by the Registrar-General. Unfortunately the national figures of the distribution of social class were not available when this research was in progress. However there is another characteristic which has been shown to be highly associated with social class (Douglas, 1964) and this is the type of secondary school attended. The distribution of fourteen-year-old children attending various types of secondary schools is published each year by the Ministry of Education.

When we compared these figures with the proportions in our research, we found that the teenagers at comprehensive, grammar and private schools were over-represented in our sample and the secondary modern teenagers were under-represented. This difference gave us a weighting ratio which we applied to each person in our sample according to the type of school attended; this statistical exercise changed the proportions of social class in our sample, so that it was the same as in the total teenage population of England and Wales.

In fact this complicated weighting procedure made very little difference to the results. In only two cases do the sample percentages vary by more than 1 per cent, and in the other cases it has had practically no effect at all. Therefore we feel justified in concluding that the results we obtained in our sample would not have been much different if we had been able to obtain a much larger sample from a much wider area. We believe our results provide a good indication of the sexual behaviour of all teenagers in this country.

4. Early Experiences

A. The First Contacts

Less than 5 per cent of the teenagers had been out on their first date before they were twelve, but by the age of thirteen a quarter of the boys and almost a third of the girls had already had their first date. Before they reached sixteen, over 70 per cent of the boys and over 85 per cent of the girls had experienced dating. Therefore most teenagers make their first serious contact with the opposite sex between twelve and thirteen.

The first date was usually a visit to the cinema. Just over half (51 per cent) of the adolescents went to the cinema; the next popular place, but a long way behind, was outdoors – altogether 15 per cent went for a walk or met their first date outdoors. People also went to a dance (6 per cent) or a party (4 per cent) on their first date. About 3 per cent went to a club and 2 per cent stayed at home; the rest (19 per cent) did something else, or could not remember, or had never been out on a date.

Though a few have been kissed but have not been out on a date, and still fewer have dated but not kissed, by and large the two activities seem to start at the same age. Less than 3 per cent can remember kissing before the age of twelve. Almost a quarter (23 per cent boys, 25 per cent girls) had their first kiss before they were fourteen. By sixteen 70 per cent of the boys and 80 per cent of the girls had experienced a kiss (as defined in Section B of Chapter 3). As in dating the boys were slower than the girls to start this activity.

It seems possible that the first time a teenager experiences a kiss with any kind of sexual component in it is at the end of the first date when, in some social circles, the good night kiss is obligatory. In this sample 20 per cent said they had their first kiss on the doorstep, 18 per cent in the cinema, 17 per cent outdoors and 10 per cent at parties. Neither school nor youth clubs are likely places, as some people have feared; in the whole sample only 2 per cent had their first kiss at school, and 1 per cent at a youth club.

The similarity of the figures has shown that kissing and dating is likely to occur at the same age, perhaps on the same day. This association was further explored when the teenagers were asked if they usually kissed a girl (boy) the first time they went out with her (him). Nearly 40 per cent said they did; a quarter (22 per cent boys, 27 per cent girls) replied fairly definitely, sometimes indignantly, that they did not; one in ten (12 per cent boys, 8 per cent girls) implied that it depended on the circumstances, and 5 per cent of the boys said they did if they got the chance. So for over half the teenagers a kiss on the first date with a new friend is a possibility, and for most of these it is a probability.

Deep kissing is a much less common activity and both boys and girls start this much later. Less than 16 per cent had experienced this before the age of fifteen (compared with 51 per cent who had kissed). The girls were quicker to learn this activity; by the age of eighteen 77 per cent of the older girls had experienced deep kissing compared with 61 per cent of the older boys.

Breast stimulation over clothes is an activity that the boys learnt before deep kissing; 6 per cent had done this before the age of fourteen, whereas only 3 per cent had experienced deep kissing. There is no difference between the two activities as far as the girls are concerned; 3 per cent had experienced breast stimulation over clothes before the age of fourteen, compared with the 4 per cent who had experienced deep kissing. Over a third (36 per cent) of the fifteen-year-old boys claimed to have fondled a girl's breasts over her clothes, and more than a third (38 per cent) of the fifteen-year-old girls admitted that this had been done to them. Thenceforward the girls and boys continue to have their first experience of breast stimulation at about the same age.

This section has shown that these stage II activities tend to be learnt earlier by the girls than the boys. Over a quarter of the boys and a third of the girls will have experienced kissing, deep kissing and breast stimulation over clothes before they are sixteen. Nearly half the boys and over half the girls will have participated in all these stage II activities before the age of seventeen.

B. Early Inceptive Behaviour

The American expression *petting* is used to describe a wide variety of activities from a simple caress to a situation closely resembling sexual intercourse. This was too imprecise for the purpose of this research and so we introduce the word *inceptive* to cover all the behaviour previously described as being at stage III of sex experience, namely, breast stimulation under clothes, active and passive genital stimulation, and genital apposition.

As expected these inceptive activities tend to start later as they require privacy and involve a certain amount of undressing. Less than 4 per cent of the boys and under 1 per cent of the girls had started breast stimulation under clothes before they were fourteen; 12 per cent of the boys and 8 per cent of the girls had started by fifteen. The girls continued to be behind the boys and at seventeen 60 per cent of the boys and 51 per cent of the girls had experienced it.

No girl admitted genital stimulation before the age of thirteen; 2 per cent of the boys had experienced both active and passive forms of this activity by fourteen. Thereafter there is a big sex difference with boys first learning the active part and girls first experiencing the passive part. In fact over three-quarters of the girls had never touched the genitals of a boy. It is clear that many of the girls who allow a boy to touch their genitals do not reciprocate.

Almost one half (49 per cent) of the sample of 2,000 teenagers had inceptive experience, but these activities appear to be less acceptable to working-class boys and girls. There was practically no class difference between those who had sexual intercourse and those who did not; but middle-class teenagers were much more likely to get satisfaction from inceptive activities.

The boys and girls were asked where they were when these activities took place for the first time. As noted earlier the first kiss is most likely to be on the doorstep, outdoors or at the cinema. But the place where an inceptive activity occurs on the first occasion is more important because this type of behaviour leads to a greater intensity of sexual arousal, and is likely to take place in the kind of circumstances where intercourse also could take place.

Inceptive activities are most likely to happen for the first time at the girl's home – according to the boys, and is equally likely to take place at the boy's or their own home – according to the girls. It also took place outdoors sometimes, and very occasionally at parties. It hardly ever happened on the doorstep, at the cinema, at a youth club or at school. The girls report more activity in cars for both breast stimulation and passive genital stimulation. In fact only 10 per cent of the boys had the use of a car and more than a third of these were not in stage III–V. This suggests that some of the girls who experienced these activities in cars were going out with boys older than themselves, and in some cases with adults.

An overall look at the location of these inceptive activities makes it clear that they most often occur for the first time in a private home. Even when it happens at a party, this is nearly always at one of the teenagers' homes. So places supervised by other adults, like school, club or cinema, figure low in the list, but the place where the parent is in charge is high on the list. It must be assumed that this sexual experimentation does not go on with the parents in the room, but it is clear that they cannot evade some of the responsibility.

C. Homosexuality

Kinsey (1948), Westwood (1960) and others have shown that homosexuality is far from rare among young males, and so we could expect to find evidence of homosexual activities in this sample. But a research designed to get information about the homosexual histories of teenage boys would require a rather different approach than the one used in this survey which was designed primarily to find out about heterosexual experience.

Despite the widespread readiness of teenage boys to talk about most sexual matters, questions about homosexual activities often cause embarrassment, particularly if the boy is still involved in some way. Consequently we decided not to press these questions. We wanted to avoid the situation where one boy told other boys in our sample that they would be persuaded to talk about homosexuality if they agreed to an interview; this might put up the rate of refusals which would prejudice our chances of collecting representative information about heterosexual experiences.

About a fifth (21 per cent) of all the boys said they knew of homosexual activities among their school friends, and 5 per cent admitted they took part themselves. These figures are probably underestimates. Westwood (1960) found that sexual play between boys aged thirteen to fifteen was usually a form of curiosity, and was not recognized or acknowledged as homosexuality by the boys themselves. After a phase of experimentation there was usually a latent period even for the boys who would eventually become adult homosexuals. Between sixteen and nineteen those with homosexual tendencies went through a period of shame and guilt combined with a strong determination to combat these inclinations. Only at a later age, usually in the early twenties, can the homosexual begin to accept himself and find his way to the homosexual coteries.

Therefore it can be seen that boys aged fifteen to nineteen will not readily answer questions about homosexuality, and information about these activities is more easily obtained by asking older people to look back to the time when they were teenagers.

Just under 2 per cent of the boys admitted to homosexual experience with adults, although 35 per cent said that at least one man had made sexual advances to them. In the attitude inventory 47 per cent of the boys agreed that homosexuals should be severely punished and 35 per cent disagreed with this statement, so many of the men who were alleged to have made sexual advances to these boys risked being severely repulsed. However it is not unknown for manifestations of friendship towards a boy to be mistaken for signs of homosexuality (Schofield, 1965).

Among the boys who had homosexual experience with other boys there is little difference between the social classes. Homosexuality was slightly more prevalent at segregated schools, and much more prevalent at boarding schools. Among the boys 23 per cent said they knew of homosexual activities which had occurred at their segregated school (4 per cent admitted taking part themselves), compared with 17 per cent who said homosexual activities occurred at their coeducational school (5 per cent admitted taking part). At the boarding schools 44 per cent said homosexual activities between the boys were not unknown (28 per cent admitted taking part), whereas at the day schools 18 per cent said homosexual activities went on between the boys (only 3 per cent admitted taking part).

A similar trend was found in the girls' schools although the figures are smaller; homosexual activities occurred in 13 per cent of the segregated schools, 10 per cent of the coeducational schools; it was also reported in 39 per cent of the boarding schools and 11 per cent of the day schools. Kinsey (1953) found less homosexuality among the females he interviewed. We found 12 per cent who said there were homosexual activities at school and 2 per cent who admitted taking part.

Slightly less than 1 per cent of the girls admitted homosexual activities with an adult, and 9 per cent said that a woman had made sexual advances to them. If these figures are credible, then it seems as if about one in ten girls to whom homosexual advances are made is likely to succumb, and about one in seven boys to whom homosexual advances are made may submit. But for the reasons given at the start of this section, and also because some of these percentages are based on small totals, it would be a mistake to attach much importance to any of these figures about homosexual activities.

D. The First Experience of Sexual Intercourse

Very few (0·9 per cent) boys have sexual intercourse before the age of fourteen and even fewer (0·1 per cent) girls have this experience. Even before fifteen the figure is still less than 3 per cent for boys and less than 1 per cent for girls. Although some young teenagers appear to be sexually precocious and although the newspapers occasionally report cases where the age of a mother is fourteen and the putative father is the same age, our figures indicate that very early experience of sexual intercourse is rare. Among fifteen-year-olds 6 per cent of the boys and 2 per cent of the girls had experienced sexual intercourse. This suggests that the fears often expressed about the extensive sexual activities between schoolboys and schoolgirls may be exaggerated. Although every secondary school probably contains a few boys and girls who are sexually

experienced, it is unlikely that they are more than a very smal
minority.

Information was obtained about the age of the other person at
the time of the first experience of sexual intercourse. It was found
that over half (46 per cent) of the sexually experienced boys had
intercourse with a girl of about the same age, 31 per cent with an
older girl and 12 per cent with a younger girl. Among the experienced girls, a third (33 per cent) had intercourse with a boy of
about the same age, 66 per cent with someone who was older and
1 per cent with a younger boy.

Girls who first had intercourse before they were seventeen
almost always had an older partner; of the 19 per cent who started
at fifteen, all but 3 per cent were with older people; of the 26 per
cent who started at sixteen, all but 3 per cent were with older partners. The fourteen-year-old boys always started with older girls;
the fifteen-year-old boys were as likely to start with older girls
as with those of the same age (9 per cent out of 20 per cent
were with older, 11 per cent with the same age); the sixteen-year-
old boys were more likely to start with girls of the same age (17 per
cent of the 32 per cent were about the same age, 10 per cent older
and 5 per cent younger).

Therefore a third of the boys and two-thirds of the girls are
introduced to sexual intercourse by an older partner. In general
the girls start later, but their partners are still older than they are.
Furthermore the number of male adults who have introduced girls
to sexual intercourse is quite large (38 per cent of all those with
this experience); the number of female adults who have introduced
boys to intercourse is very small (2 per cent) – the proselytizing
older woman in search of virgin boys is either a myth, or very
unsuccessful.

The teenagers were asked if they thought it was also the first
time for their partner. Only 29 per cent of the boys and 21 per cent
of the girls thought it was the first experience of sexual intercourse
for both of them. Altogether 64 per cent of the boys thought their
first girl was already experienced, and 70 per cent of the girls
thought their first boy had previous experience of sexual intercourse; 7 per cent of the boys and 9 per cent of the girls were uncertain or unable to answer this question. Allowing for the fact

that an experienced boy might be tempted to tell the girl that this was also the first time for him, and an experienced girl would be unlikely to volunteer the information that she was not a virgin, these results show a remarkably high number of cases where the partner was more experienced at the time of the teenager's first experience of intercourse.

Several other questions were asked about the first experience of sexual intercourse. For example, nearly all the girls (82 per cent) maintained that the boy on this first occasion was a steady; 16 per cent described the first partner as an acquaintance and only 3 per cent said the boy was a pick-up, i.e. someone they had met on the same day as intercourse took place. The figures for the boys are more equally spread over these three categories, probably because their idea of a 'steady' is quite different from the definition the girls would give. In fact 45 per cent of the boys described their first partner as a steady, 34 per cent as an acquaintance and 16 per cent as a pick-up; very few boys had their first experience with a prostitute. Even allowing that the girls may have been over-defensive when answering this question, it seems likely that the first experience of intercourse for boys as well as girls was usually with a friend, and often with someone they knew very well.

When those who had experienced sexual intercourse were asked where they had met their first partner, all sorts of places were mentioned. Some met at a dance, others at a party, club, cinema, school or outdoors, while others said they had grown up together. Boys occasionally go out in groups to look for girls and this seems to be the way some of them met their first sexual partner. But in general there seems to be no particular place where teenagers go to find sexual partners, and in the vast majority of cases they met their future sexual partners during the ordinary intercommunication among young people.

But the answers to the question on where the first experience actually took place are much more revealing. In most cases it seems to have happened in the parental home of the partner; among the boys the first experience was in the girl's home in 50 per cent of the occasions, and among the girls the first experience was in the boy's home in 43 per cent of the occasions; in addition to this a further 12 per cent of the girls had their first experience in digs or a flat occupied by the boy. This is in accordance with the finding that the first sexual partner is often older and, for both sexes, the initiation is more likely to take place in the home of the more experienced partner.

Occasionally it took place in the home of the girl or boy experiencing intercourse for the first time. In fact the first experience of sexual intercourse took place in the parental home of one or other of the young people concerned in more than half of all the cases. So parents who worry about their sons and daughters coming home late at night should, perhaps, start wondering what is happening in their own front room when they go out in the evening.

No other place occurs as often as the parental homes of the teenagers; even in those cases where the first experience was at a party, this was usually at the home of one of the teenagers (but usually when his parents were out or away). The first experience which was outside was more likely to be in an urban park or the rural countryside for a boy, and more likely to be in a car for the girl; this reflects the much larger number of girls whose first experience was with an adult who was more likely than the teenagers to have a car.

The first sexual intercourse was often unpremeditated. Only 14 per cent of the boys and 15 per cent of the girls said it was planned, compared with 84 per cent of the boys and 82 per cent of the girls who said it was unpremeditated. The replies of the teenagers showed that very few of them had set out with the intention of having intercourse on that particular evening.

It just seemed to follow on naturally. (boy, aged 17)
We were just sort of mucking about and it just sort of happened. (boy, aged 16)
It was there for the taking; you know – just followed naturally. (boy, aged 17)
We went for a drink, back to his flat. It just seemed to happen. I don't know why. I think he was the first boy I'd met that made me feel I really wanted to. (girl, aged 18)
It wasn't planned, no. Mind you I was always ready for it. I dare say she expected it, too. (boy, aged 17)

The point was pursued still farther when the experienced teenagers were asked: 'Have you any idea why it happened?' This

T – c

would be a difficult question for anyone to answer, especially as the interviewers were forbidden to prompt at this moment or help the teenagers to find the appropriate words. Naturally many of the replies were vague and inarticulate, but it was a good question because it forced the teenager to look back on this first episode.

Their replies reveal the big difference in attitude between the two sexes. The boys were most likely to reply that they were impelled by sexual desire (46 per cent) whereas the girls were more likely to say they were in love (42 per cent). This would confirm the suspicions of those who see the male as essentially a predatory animal whereas the female is amative and romantic.

He wanted to. It wasn't rape or anything. Just that I was in love with him. I still am. It wasn't animal savagery on his part. (girl, aged 17)
He kept on telling me that this sort of thing is all right for two people who are in love and plan to get married. I thought about it and agreed. I just sort of thought, 'well he does love me and he wants to marry me, so why not?' Just like that. (girl, aged 18)
I went on holiday to have fun. I wasn't in love with her, or anything. That's why I felt bad afterwards. (boy, aged 18)
Because I felt I had to prove to myself once and for all that I could, and perhaps also because I wanted to. (boy, aged 19)
I felt like it. I felt I was entitled to it after four months. (boy, aged 16)
You just get tired of kissing and that. (boy, aged 19)

A large number of boys (25 per cent) and quite a few girls (13 per cent) were driven towards their first experience for reasons that can best be summed up by the word *curiosity*. Admonitory articles in the press and hand-wringing by important people have given some adolescents the impression that the average teenager is sexually experienced, and some of these boys and girls must have wondered why they were exceptional and whether they were missing something.

A few boys (3 per cent) and more girls (9 per cent) said they were under the influence of drink at the time when they first had sexual intercourse. Two girls said they had their first experience because they were bored. No one gave drugs as a reason and indeed the drugs usually associated with teenagers (cannabis and amphetamines) have no aphrodisiac effect and are more likely to decrease sexual performance (Finestone, 1957).

Although it has been shown that for both boys and girls the partner is often older and more experienced at the time of first intercourse, yet there is little evidence that the teenagers were pushed into this against their will. Not surprisingly more girls (34 per cent) than boys (5 per cent) said they were persuaded to participate, but only one girl said she was forced into it. None of the girls were paid for their first experience and most (65 per cent) of the girls and nearly all the boys (95 per cent) stated that they were quite willing.

But this first experience was not always an unqualified success and did not always result in sexual gratification. Less than half the boys (48 per cent) and less than a third of the girls (30 per cent) said they liked it when they were asked for their reaction to this first experience of sexual intercourse. On the other hand some of them said they actively disliked it (7 per cent of both boys and girls), while others said they were disappointed (14 per cent boys and 7 per cent girls). More girls were ashamed (25 per cent) than afraid (15 per cent) and even some of the boys felt ashamed (10 per cent) or afraid (5 per cent).

The boys were more likely to express their feelings in terms of pleasure and enjoyment, or the lack of it. The girls were more inclined to describe their later reactions after the sexual excitement was over.

Rather pleased with myself. Swaggering, in fact. It's only natural, isn't it? (boy, aged 17)

I didn't know what had happened actually. I was quite enthralled by it all. (boy, aged 18)

I felt a bit older, that was about all. Everybody had been talking about it and now I'd done it. Something to tell my mates. You don't feel much of a person yourself afterwards; at least I didn't. (boy, aged 17)

Well, I wouldn't say it was anything fantastic. (boy, aged 19)

Tears. Up until then I'd thought of it as something I'd wanted to save until marriage. It seemed so silly that I'd lost it all in one night. (girl, aged 16)

I wasn't actually disappointed. I didn't feel it was wrong, but it just didn't seem to have worked out right. I must have been worried about having a baby. (girl, aged 18)

Hell, what's all the fuss about. (girl, aged 18)

Leaving aside those who did not express a strong opinion either way, it still leaves over a third of the boys (36 per cent) for whom the first experience of sexual intercourse was not a success – that is, nearly half of all those boys who expressed an opinion. The equivalent figures for girls show that 54 per cent – that is, two thirds of all those who expressed an opinion – were disenchanted with their first experience. These are unexpectedly high figures, especially for the boys who might have been reluctant to admit to the interviewer that they did not immediately take to sexual intercourse like a duck to water.

More specifically the teenagers were asked if they came to a climax during their first experience of sexual intercourse. Not everyone understood the word *climax* and in some cases it might have been inappropriate to go into detailed explanations, but the interviewers managed to make themselves understood in all but 14 (5 per cent) cases.

Not surprisingly the boys were much more likely than the girls to have an orgasm. Indeed it is possible that boys often reach a climax too soon at the first experience of sexual intercourse. Of the 193 experienced boys, 81 per cent said they reached a climax, 17 per cent said they did not and 2 per cent were uncertain. Only 28 per cent of the 102 experienced girls reached a climax, while 62 per cent said they did not and 10 per cent were either unsure or did not understand the question. It seems probable that complete sexual satisfaction for both boy and girl is not a likely outcome of the first premarital sexual experience.

When they were asked if their partners had come to a climax, it is not surprising that some (21 per cent) of the boys did not know; even 13 per cent of the girls were uncertain. Three-quarters of the girls knew that their partners had reached a climax, whereas 31 per cent of the boys were aware that their partners had not. It seems likely, however, that some of the boys have been over-confident in their claim that their first girl reached a climax; on the other hand it has been noted that the boy's first sexual intercourse has usually been with an experienced girl.

As so many of them did not enjoy their first sexual intercourse, one is prompted to ask why they should continue to repeat the experience if it was not a success the first time. A few of them (6 per cent boys, 11 per cent girls) did not try again, and there was an interval of over six months for another 7 per cent of the boys and 6 per cent of the girls before they had their second experience. Moreover 7 per cent of the boys and 30 per cent of the girls said they were not interested when they were asked: 'How did you feel about having sex another time?'

But the disillusioned ones were in a minority. Most of them, girls as well as boys, were ready to try again, and within a month 54 per cent of the boys and 63 per cent of the girls had experienced sexual intercourse more than once; 7 per cent of the boys and 2 per cent of the girls had their second experience within twenty-four hours of the first.

More girls (34 per cent) than boys (26 per cent) had sexual intercourse again within a week of their first experience. The girls may start later than the boys, and be more reluctant at first, but these figures and the next chapter on frequencies show that once they have crossed this barrier, they are not more inhibited than the boys.

The teenagers were asked if they had intercourse with their first partner on more than one occasion. We found that over half the boys (54 per cent) and three-quarters of the girls (76 per cent) repeated the experience with the same person. The relationship continued for quite a long time in many cases, for a fifth of the boys and more than a third of the girls had sexual intercourse with their first partner on more than five occasions.

The boys, who in general were more likely to enjoy their first experience, were also more likely to move on to fresh fields and new conquests. Although the girls often felt unhappy about the first experience, they were prepared to try again with the same boy, sometimes for a considerable period. It is clear that, in some circumstances at least, the first sexual intercourse did not weaken or strain the relationship between the girl and the boy, and it may even have deepened and strengthened their association.

This first experience of sexual intercourse was sometimes a fortuitous adventure. It took place, sometimes in their own homes, more likely in their partners' who were often older and usually more experienced. Nearly all of them, however, agreed that they were willing participants to the initiation, although the introduction, when it came, was unexpected for many of the younger ones. This first experience was not often a great success, but most of them went on to their second experience after a fairly short interval, often with the same person.

E. Early Starters

Is the adolescent who starts dating or kissing at an early age more likely to have premarital intercourse? Some connexion between physical maturity and sexual behaviour is to be expected; for example, some teenagers develop physically much later than others and these boys and girls would tend to be older before they experienced sexual arousal. Although the physical facts do not, in themselves, mean that premarital intercourse is necessarily associated with early physical development, the following paragraphs of this section will make clear that early sexual behaviour and premarital intercourse are linked in some way.

Dating. Boys who started dating before the age of fourteen were more likely to have had experience of sexual intercourse. Girls who started dating before the age of fourteen were also more likely to be sexually experienced. In both cases those who started dating early are significantly different from the others.

Kissing. Boys and girls who started kissing before the age of fourteen were more likely to have had premarital sexual intercourse than the others in our sample.

Breast stimulation. Boys who started breast stimulation under clothes before the age of sixteen were more likely to be sexually experienced, and so were girls who permitted this.

Genital stimulation. Boys who had active genital stimulation and girls who had passive genital stimulation before the age of seventeen were more likely to have had premarital intercourse.

For the purposes of this research, a boy who has had sexual intercourse at fifteen or earlier is said to be an 'early starter'. Only 2·3 per cent of the girls have had sexual intercourse by the age of fifteen, so for our definition of an early starter among the girls, we will advance the qualifying age by one year; therefore we define an early starter as a girl who has had sexual intercourse at sixteen or younger. In the whole sample 6·4 per cent of the boys and 5·4 per cent of the girls are early starters according to this definition. Taking into account only those who have had sexual intercourse, 33 per cent of the boys and 47 per cent of the girls are early starters. It can be shown that boys and girls who start intercourse early will also start other sexual activities at an early age. For example, among the boys:

56 per cent of the early starters had their first date at thirteen or younger compared with 31 per cent of the other boys with experience of sexual intercourse.

52 per cent of the early starters had their first kiss at thirteen or younger compared with 25 per cent of the other boys with sexual experience.

93 per cent of the early starters had experienced breast stimulation at fifteen or younger compared with 41 per cent of the other boys with experience of sexual intercourse.

44 per cent of the early starters had experienced active genital stimulation at fourteen or younger compared with 11 per cent of the other boys with experience of sexual intercourse.

Among the girls the same tendency is apparent. Those who have early experience of sexual intercourse are much more likely to start inceptive behaviour at an early age. For example:

52 per cent of the early starters dated at thirteen or younger compared with 40 per cent of the other girls with experience of sexual intercourse.

41 per cent of the early starters had their first kiss at thirteen or younger compared with 28 per cent of the others with experience of sexual intercourse.

55 per cent of the early starters had experienced breast stimulation at fifteen or younger compared with 26 per cent of other girls with experience of sexual intercourse.

48 per cent of the early starters had experienced passive genital stimulation at fifteen or younger compared with 12 per cent of other girls with experience of sexual intercourse.

Thus we can say with some assurance that those who start minor sexual activities at an early age are more likely to have sexual intercourse before marriage. Furthermore those who have started premarital intercourse at an early age are more likely to have started other sexual activities earlier than their peers; and this is true not only of inceptive behaviour, but also of socially acceptable behaviour like dating and kissing.

F. Characteristics of the Early Starters

This last section will attempt to see if there are any other differences between those who have sexual intercourse at an early age and the other experienced teenagers. We will use the same definition of early starters as before (i.e. boys whose first experience of sexual intercourse is at fifteen or younger; girls whose first experience of sexual intercourse is at sixteen or younger). It is important to remember that these comparisons are with the other sexually experienced teenagers – not with all the boys and girls in the sample. (The sexually experienced are compared with the others in Part Three, Chapters 8–12.)

We found that 4 per cent of the early starters and 11 per cent of the other experienced boys were still at school. Apart from these, 69 per cent of the early starters left school at the age of fifteen compared with 58 per cent of the other experienced boys. Therefore the early starters were more likely to leave school at the statutory minimum age; indeed the age of fifteen seems to be the critical age for these early starters as most of them have their first experience of intercourse during their last year at school or soon after leaving school.

The early starters were also more likely to come from working-class homes; 85 per cent compared with 77 per cent of the other experienced boys. Although there was little difference in religious affiliation, fewer early starters came from religious homes; 14 per cent of the early starters came from homes where one or both of the parents went to church compared with 22 per cent of the other experienced boys. The early starters were also more promiscuous; 86 per cent of them had more than one partner, compared with 73 per cent of the other experienced boys.

The early starters among the girls reflect the results found among the boys. For example, 70 per cent of the early starters left school at fifteen compared with 54 per cent of the girls who had sexual experience at seventeen or later; 89 per cent compared with 72 per cent came from working-class homes; 11 per cent compared with 16 per cent came from religious homes; and 45 per cent of the early starters compared with 28 per cent of the others had more than one sexual partner.

The first experience was less likely to be in a home (his own or his partner's), and more likely to be outside. This suggests that the first experience of sexual intercourse is more likely to be on the spur of the moment for early starters. When the boys were asked to suggest a reason why this first intercourse happened, a quarter of the early starters found it difficult to give any reason at all. This seems to reinforce the suggestion that this first experience was improvisatory. The most frequent reasons given by the early starters were sexual desire and curiosity, and these are also the reasons most often given by the boys who started later. But only 4 per cent of the early starters gave love as the reason whereas 14 per cent of the other boys gave this reason. Among the girls love was given as the reason by 30 per cent of the early starters compared with 48 per cent of the others. All the girls were less interested in sex and more interested in love than the boys, but the girls who were early starters were not so romantic as the others.

We found that only a few enjoyed their first experience of sexual intercourse, but the early starters, among both boys and girls, more often said they had enjoyed it. It seems as if age and maturity do not guarantee the success of the first experience.

Not unexpectedly the early starters were more likely to have people older than themselves as their first sexual partners. Among the boys the partners of the early starters were older in 39 per cent of the cases compared with 18 per cent of the others; among the girls 84 per cent of the early starters had older partners compared with 50 per cent of the others.

When the boys were asked to describe their first partners, it was found that 23 per cent of the early starters had a fiancée or a steady as their first partner, compared with 50 per cent of the others. In 44 per cent of the cases the partner of the early starters was classified as an acquaintance, compared with 27 per cent of the others. The partner was a pick-up for 27 per cent of the early starters compared with 15 per cent of the others. So the partners of the early starters are likely to be girls they have not known for long, usually about the same age or a bit older. All the experienced girls were likely to claim that their first partner was a fiancé or a steady, but the early starters were less likely to make this claim. In fact 68 per cent of the partners of the early starters were steadies compared with 88 per cent among the others. While 23 per cent were acquaintances of the early starters compared with 12 per cent of the others; none of the others said their first partner was a pick-up, but one (2 per cent) of the early starters admitted this. So the girls who are early starters are less likely than the others to have their first sexual experience with a regular boy friend, and are more likely to have a casual acquaintance as their first partner, and it is usually someone older than they are.

*

This chapter has shown that dating and kissing usually starts between the age of thirteen and fifteen; the boy is most likely to take the girl to the cinema on this first date, and most adolescents of that age assume that a kiss is an integral part of the date. Deep kissing is a much less common activity and seems to start at about the same time as breast stimulation over clothes. All these are activities that the girls learn before the boys; by the age of seventeen nearly half the boys and over half the girls will have experience of these activities.

Inceptive behaviour consists of more intimate, less socially acceptable activities which require privacy. Now the boys are no longer lagging behind the girls, but tend to learn these activities at the same time as the girls, and sometimes earlier. The dominance of the boy in the sexual situation is more apparent, and he now plays the active part while the girl is passive. Among boys of fifteen, less than one in five (17 per cent) have reached the inceptive stage; among the boys of seventeen over half (54 per cent) are at this stage, and at nineteen the majority (70 per cent) have inceptive experience. The percentages among the girls is higher among the younger ones, lower among the older; 29 per cent of the fifteen-year-olds had reached the inceptive stage, 48 per cent of the seventeen-year-olds, and 63 per cent of the girls who were nineteen were at stage III or beyond.

Very early experience of sexual intercourse is relatively rare. Some teenage girls are introduced to sexual intercourse by adults; this hardly ever happens to boys, but their first partners were often older and usually more experienced. So the first experience was usually an indoctrination by someone else for boys as well as girls.

The first experience of sexual intercourse usually took place in a parental home, often with someone they had known for a long time. Although rarely planned beforehand, there is very little sign of force or excessive persuasion. The boys were impelled by sexual desire, but most girls gave love as the reason; a few decided to try it because they were under the impression that most teenagers had premarital intercourse. Alcohol was hardly ever an influencing factor.

The majority did not get much enjoyment from their first experience; shame and fear were a common reaction among the girls, and disappointment was a common reaction among the boys. Boys nearly always reached a climax, but only a quarter of the girls did. Nevertheless most of them repeated the experience before long, often with the same person, and in some cases the association continued for a long time.

Finally it has been found that those who start dating, kissing and inceptive behaviour at an early age are also more likely to have early sexual intercourse, and there are a number of differences between these early starters and others who have later sexual experience.

5. Frequency

A. The Intensity of Dating

The extent of teenage sexual experience can be measured in several ways. In the previous chapter we were concerned with those who started their sexual experiences at an age earlier than the average. In Chapter 3 we reported on the incidence – the number of people who had experienced a particular activity. In this chapter we shall concentrate upon frequency – the extent to which a particular activity is practised. In particular we shall consider the frequency of three activities – dating, inceptive behaviour and sexual intercourse.

The first date a boy or girl arranges may be looked upon as the first serious socio-sexual activity and the more mature development of the activity is when the boy and girl decide to go steady, or become engaged. In between the extremes dating is recognized as a convenient social arrangement that gives a boy or girl a chance to know each other in the light of their different sexual outlooks.

In our sample girls began their dating at the average age of 13·8 years, and boys began at the average age of 14 years. Girls are also ahead in the number of dates they have, and in the number of enduring relationships. Most teenagers go through an experimental period where they have a series of very short relationships before they start to date the same person with any regularity; the younger boys and girls want to try out several different types of partners, whereas the older ones are passing through this period and in time they come to prefer a longer association. Thus 78 per cent of the older boys have been out with the same girl more than six times compared with only 58 per cent of the younger boys; and 25 per cent of the younger girls have not been out with anyone more than six times, but this applies to only 8 per cent of the older girls.

As well as the difference between older and younger age groups, there is a difference between boys and girls; twice as many boys as girls have experienced only very short dating relationships, whereas 784 (83 per cent) girls have experienced long term relationships compared with 625 (68 per cent) boys. The difference between the sexes is shown even more clearly when only the longer relationships are considered (i.e. those who have taken out the same person more than six times). This confirms that girls are more likely than boys to have a series of enduring relationships. Even the younger girls have more long relationships than the older boys, and the older girls are far ahead of the other three groups. For example, 44 per cent of the older girls have had at least five enduring relationships, whereas only 29 per cent of the younger girls, 26 per cent of the older boys and 22 per cent of the younger boys have had as many enduring relationships. This suggests that a girl seeks a longer, possibly more mature, relationship in her dating behaviour, while a boy prefers to be more diverse and less committed.

This difference between the sexes will not be news to those who have to work with young people, but it is rare for the boys and girls to be warned about this. Consequently a boy may unwittingly hurt a girl because he expects her to react in the same way as a boy would in a similar situation; and at other times a girl may expect an allegiance from a boy which he is not ready to give.

B. Frequency of Inceptive Activities

In Section C of Chapter 3 the number of young people with inceptive experience was reported. But a few of these people have had this experience only once in their lives, while others engaged in this activity many times in the last year with several different people. Therefore besides knowing the incidence, it is useful to have information on the frequency, and this is best shown by the number of times the activity occurs over a specific period, and by the number of different people with whom it occurs. This information gives some indication of the depth of the experience, and the overall extent of inceptive behaviour among teenagers.

All the teenagers with inceptive experience were asked how often it had happened in the last year, and they were also encouraged to talk about their partners on these occasions. Although boys are often the initiators, and more of them had inceptive experience, those girls who had this experience were likely to take part in these activities more often than the boys.

On the other hand boys had more partners than girls, even though they had fewer experiences altogether. Only 18 per cent of the girls compared with 37 per cent of the boys have had more than three partners. There was a pronounced difference in the type of relationship that existed between partners who had inceptive experience. The girls were more likely to carry on inceptive activities with their fiancé or steady, whereas the boy was more likely to have casual partners such as slight acquaintances or girls they had picked up on that particular day.

The difference in frequency and number of partners between girls and boys shows that girls tend to have more experiences with fewer partners, whereas the boys do not have inceptive experiences so often, but have more partners. The figures on incidence (Chapter 3) may have given the impression that the boys are far more sexually active than the girls, but when the frequency figures are considered, they suggest that the total sexual outlet of girls is similar to that of boys.

C. Sexual Intercourse Frequencies

At each level of sexual activity so far considered in this chapter, it has been noted that the girls tend to seek a more permanent relationship. This tendency is even more pronounced at the level of sexual intercourse. In actual incidence the boys are almost twice as active as the girls, but when teenagers were asked how many times they had intercourse in the last year, the answers revealed that the girls were more active than the boys. For example, 30 per cent of the boys were having intercourse about seventeen times in the last year, whereas 30 per cent of the girls were having intercourse about forty times in the last year. Although about half of all the experienced teenagers have less than ten experiences in a year, as the frequencies of the other half get higher, the difference between boys and girls becomes more marked.

The girls have sexual intercourse more often than the boys, but they have fewer partners. There seems to be an inverse relationship between the number of partners these teenagers have and the number of times they have intercourse with any one partner. As in other levels of sex experience girls are much less likely to commit themselves than boys, but when committed they are more sexually active.

These observations are reinforced when we look at the type of relationship the boys and girls had with their partners. As in the case of other levels of activity those with experience of sexual intercourse were asked about their partners and their replies show that over half the boys have intercourse with their steady girl friends. But they also have intercourse with others, particularly acquaintances and girls whom they do not know at all. Hardly any have had intercourse with a prostitute.

Although boys only rarely mentioned their fiancées as their sexual partners, nearly a quarter of the girls had intercourse with their fiancés and a very large number with their steady boy friends. Only two boys and one girl mentioned both a steady and a fiancé(e) in answer to this question, therefore we can add these two categories together and this shows that 86 per cent of the girls' liaisons were with steady boy friends whereas the boys show only 56 per cent of this type of relationship.

When the frequency rates were divided into under and over 25 experiences of intercourse in the last year, it was found that many girls were having extensive experience with one partner, whereas the boys were having fewer experiences with more partners. Thus 58 per cent of the girls with more than 25 experiences had restricted themselves to one partner, but the equivalent figure among the boys was only 4 per cent. An approximate calculation shows that the sexually experienced girl had an average of 2·3 partners, and the experienced boy had an average of 6·2 partners.

D. Reactions to Sexual Intercourse

In Chapter 4 it was noted that the majority did not like their very first experience of sexual intercourse, but three-quarters of the boys and half the girls stated unequivocally that they now enjoyed it. Other girls said that they did not enjoy the act itself, but enjoyed giving pleasure to their boy friend.

This still leaves 28 per cent of the boys and 39 per cent of the girls who did not always enjoy it, and some of these did not appear to enjoy it at all. So sexual intercourse among experienced teenagers is not always a success. Even among the boys only about half invariably have an orgasm, and over a quarter of the girls hardly ever or never reach a climax.

Adults who criticize teenage morality always seem to assume that sexual intercourse is irresistible unless some form of restraint is put in the way. These results show that other factors may be at work. Group pressures or a desire to be thought of as experienced and worldly may persuade some teenagers to take part in sexual intercourse although they do not really enjoy it; there may be strong pressures upon a boy to prove his masculinity, and upon a girl from the fear that she will lose the boy if she does not agree to intercourse. One can imagine a situation where neither the boy nor the girl really wants it, but both of them feel impelled to participate.

E. Boys Compared with Girls

Two types of frequency have been examined:

1. The number of experiences over a measured period.
2. The number of partners.

This has revealed differences between girls and boys. Girls are much more likely than boys to sustain a relationship at each level of sex activity. In their dating behaviour girls begin at an earlier age than boys, they have more boy friends and their relationships last longer. At the more advanced levels of intimacy the boys have more partners than the girls, but the girls are sexually more active. Girls prefer a more permanent type of relationship in their sexual behaviour. Boys seem to want the opposite; they prefer diversity and so have more casual partners. It might be said that the girls adopt a more rational approach considering the risk of pregnancy or venereal disease, but a more likely explanation is the emotional difference between boys and girls. The boy seeks adventure while the girl looks for security.

There is a hint, however, of a small pocket of less cautious girls who engage in more casual relationships. Although 86 per cent of all the girls who have had sexual intercourse claim that their partners are close friends, there remain 14 per cent who admit to intercourse with casual partners. Indeed 5 per cent of all the older girls (about a third of all those with experience) have had more than one partner, and a few of them have had a large number of partners.

The most important fact to emerge from this chapter is that the experienced girls are just as sexually active as the experienced boys, but there is a direct association between the type of relationship a girl has achieved and the degree of intimacy she will permit. If her date with a boy is on a fairly superficial level, then she is unlikely to be persuaded. But if she sees her boy friend as her future husband (whether they are officially engaged or not), she is more likely to agree to intercourse, and in some cases she is eager to anticipate marital relations. Ehrmann (1959) also found that the sexually most active girls were those who were going steady. But this is not necessarily the case for boys, who have more partners and shorter less binding relationships. In this research it has been shown (Chapter 3) that more boys have sexual intercourse, but this chapter reveals that those girls who do have sex, tend to have it more often than the boys.

6. Knowledge about Sexual Matters

A. Conception

All the teenagers were asked how old they were when they first found out about 'the facts of life'. After testing several other phrases, it was found that a knowledge of conception was best described in this way. The average age at which a boy learnt about the facts of life was 12·5 years and for a girl it was 12·2 years. Four boys said they did not understand conception and another eleven boys and two girls could not remember when they first found out about this. Apart from this, about a quarter of the boys and a third of the girls said they knew about the facts of life at the age of eleven or earlier. By thirteen two-thirds of the boys and three-quarters of the girls knew about conception. Whether or not their information was accurate is not relevant in this context; the important point is that most adolescents have heard at least one version of how babies are born soon after entering secondary school, if not before.

Most boys (62 per cent) and many of the girls (44 per cent) learnt about conception from their friends, usually through jokes which were quite often smutty and obscene. In over a quarter (27 per cent) of the cases the girls obtained this information from their mothers, but boys rarely learnt this from their mothers. Fathers seem to have no role at all at this stage of their daughters' education and sons do not fare much better. Only 7 per cent of the boys learnt about conception from their fathers and the same number obtained this information from books. Girls are still less likely to learn from books and it appears that the many thousands of books published on this subject for adolescents (Dalzell-Ward, 1960) are read after they have heard about conception from other sources, if they are read at all. Teachers appear to fulfil a more important role for both sexes and are the second most frequent source for boys – but a long way behind school friends; 12 per cent of the boys and 18 per cent of the girls first heard about conception from teachers. For both sexes they are probably the most important source of accurate information.

But the significance of the part teachers play can be better understood when we combine the source of information with the age when they first learnt about the facts of life. Those who learn from friends or from parents tend to get the information early, while those who learn from teachers are more likely to get the information at fourteen or later.

The younger the boy learns the facts of life, the more likely he is to learn from friends. As he gets older the influence of the teacher increases and the influence of the parent decreases. Those who feel that the parents are the right people to give sex instruction should note that there seems to be a maximum age when parents will do this. If the parents have not instructed the child by twelve or thirteen, it becomes more and more unlikely that they will ever do so.

As other studies (Spinley, 1953; Newson, 1963) have shown, there are differences in upbringing between the social classes. The middle-class adolescents learn about conception before the working-class children. Some commentators have suggested that sex is talked about more simply and naturally in working-class homes, and it is the middle-class parents who are reluctant to discuss sexual matters with their children. But this is not what we found. The average age of learning the facts of life for middle-class boys was 12·3 compared with 12·7 for working-class boys. Among the girls the middle class average age was 11·9, and the working class average age was 12·5. So the middle-class girls were in advance of the boys of their own class and well in advance of either sex in the working class.

This class difference between girls may be related to age of first menarche, as Tanner (1962) has shown that middle-class girls tend to reach puberty before working-class girls. It is possible that some middle-class mothers feel that it is necessary to warn their daughters before their first menstruation and this in turn leads to an explanation of conception. It is possible, of course, that working-class mothers are equally anxious to forewarn their daughters, but find it more difficult to put this into words. Bernstein's (1961) work on the use of language has shown that there are wide social class differences in the way parents are able to make use of abstract terms and generic notions in order to instruct their children. It also seems to be true that middle-class parents are more affected by the new ideas in health education (Schofield, 1964) and are more likely to be aware of the importance of sex education.

When the source of knowledge is analysed by social class, it is found that the middle-class mother is much more likely to have talked to her daughter about the facts of life; indeed middle-class girls are the only group who are more likely to have heard about conception from parents than from friends.

The school teacher is more likely to be the source of information for working-class girls, but not for the boys. Only 13 per cent of working-class boys learnt the facts of life from a teacher, and this compares with 12 per cent middle-class boys. But 24 per cent of working-class girls learnt from a teacher, and this compares with 13 per cent of the middle-class girls. So for a quarter of the working class girls, the teacher is an important influence.

By far the most important source amongst working-class boys is their friends; about two thirds of the boys learn the facts of life from people of their own age. It is clear that the working-class boy is the one who most needs sex education at school, and as will be shown in Section C of this chapter, he is the one who is the least likely to get it.

B. Parental Advice about Sex

It has been shown that parents are only rarely the initiators of sex knowledge. But parents can play a continuing role as sex educators, and many people have suggested that this is the best method: the parents should avoid a lecture on sex, but should continue to inform the child as the need arises. We tried to find out how far this worked out in practice. In fact, we found that 67 per cent of the boys and 29 per cent of the girls said that they never at any time had any advice about sex from their parents.

We've never discussed it. My mother always says it's filthy. (girl, aged 19)
I can't ask my mother anything. She just looks at me dubiously and says, 'What do you want to know for?' She thinks I'm learning too fast. (girl, aged 16)
The only advice I got was from my dad when he said, 'keep your legs crossed and say no'. (girl, aged 17)

No, they never told me anything. There's no need for it, really. (boy, aged 15)

It is possible that some of these adolescents were advised by their parents, but they did not listen, or perhaps found the advice so unacceptable that they dismissed it from their minds. Even so it is remarkable that over two thirds of the boys and a quarter of the girls felt that neither of their parents had helped them to deal with the problem of sex.

The remaining 33 per cent of the boys and 71 per cent of the girls were questioned about the kind of advice they received from their parents and their answers were classified into four categories. These were operationally defined in the following way:

Biological – where reproduction was explained without reference to human physiology.

Physiological – where the differences between the male and female were explained without a discussion of sexual intercourse.

Technical – where reproduction was explained with a description of sexual intercourse.

Moral – where any reference to sex was accompanied by a parent or teacher saying some behaviour was right or wrong.

Quite a large number of girls (34 per cent) received physiological advice, compared with only a few boys (10 per cent). The number who received technical information was about the same for both sexes – 13 per cent of all the boys in the total sample and 12 per cent of the girls. But 53 per cent of the girls received moral advice compared with 12 per cent of the boys. It is difficult to escape the conclusion that although the girls received far more advice than the boys, it was vague and unspecific in most cases.

Of course there were some cases when a boy or girl received advice that covered more than one of the categories which have been listed. Most of the parents who gave moral advice did not give technical advice as well, but parents who gave technical advice also gave moral advice to their daughters in many cases, but less often to their sons. These categories give some indication of the kind of advice, but the quality and extent of the advice also varied considerably; to take two examples of this kind of advice, one parent merely told her daughter, 'no one wants soiled goods', while another mother instructed her daughter on the use of contraceptives.

In some countries sex education in the schools is not allowed because it is believed that parents are the proper people to instruct the child. But our results suggest that this is unlikely to work out very well.

She's given me some do's and dont's. In her opinion I shouldn't go very far at all; no further than necking; you can get too easily carried away. I think she is right, but I haven't kept to it. (girl, aged 18)
My mum left a book lying around. She expects me to find out for myself. (girl, aged 17)
I think my mother should have explained about periods and intercourse and everything, because I still don't really understand it. (girl, aged 16)
I don't think I'd have liked to have learnt about sex from my parents. (boy, aged 19)

C. Sex Education at School

When the teenagers were asked if they had ever received any sex education at school, over half (53 per cent) of the boys replied in the negative. Schools seem to be more concerned with giving sex education to girls than to boys. Altogether 86 per cent of the girls compared with 47 per cent of the boys had received some kind of formal sex education while they were at school.

Whether they go to private or state schools, eight out of ten girls will receive sex education. Seven out of ten boys going to private school are likely to receive sex education; but less than half the boys going to state schools receive sex education, and this was just as true of those at grammar schools as for those at secondary modern, technical or comprehensive.

The lack of sex education is exactly where it is most needed; it is the working-class boys who are least likely to learn about sex from their parents, and are least likely to receive sex education at school.

The type of sex education has been classified into categories using the four definitions that were used in the previous section on parental advice. This shows that one in three private school boys received technical information, but state-educated boys rarely received anything more than biological and physiological instruction. There was less difference between the schools as far as the girls were concerned; most of them received biological and physiological instruction, but few of them received technical information.

These categories are only rough indicators of the type of sex education and they do not always convey the quality of the instruction. One girl reported that 'a teacher tried once; he started on about frogs, but after he said about three lines on tadpoles and the fellows all laughed, he packed it in'. Another girl told our interviewer that there was only one lesson 'with a young mistress where we asked questions like was it right to have it before marriage'. There must be some doubt as to whether these situations can be classified at all as sex education.

It was all rather vague. I thought it embarrassed him as much as it embarrassed us. (boy, aged 15)
There was a film in the fifth year, but I never went up to the fifth year. (girl, aged 15)
We always used to have a little snigger about it. She used to draw the diagram but she never mentioned the word 'sex' or 'babies'. It was always little rabbits. (girl, aged 18)
We had the lot – even the sex life of the broad bean. (girl, aged 16)
Before we left the reverend told us not to do it, the doctor told us how not to do it, and the head told us where not to do it. (boy, aged 18)

Doubtless there were other occasions when the instruction was clear, sensible and well planned. But we were left with the overall impression that there was a lack of frankness in the teaching. Sex education, when it occurred, seemed to concentrate on biological and physiological matters and seemed to be unrelated to human affairs, except when it was wholly concerned with putting across a particular moral point of view.

D. Birth Control

Everyone in the sample was asked if they knew anything about the sort of precautions people took to avoid pregnancy. Most of the teenagers (84 per cent boys, 82 per cent girls) claimed to have some knowledge of birth control. All those who made this claim were questioned further. Those without experience of sexual intercourse were asked what birth-control methods they knew about, and the sexually experienced were asked what methods of birth control they had used.

In many cases the teenagers were not aware of the precise technical term of a method they were attempting to describe; the sheath, for example, was nearly always known by a commercial brand name. Some boys did not mention withdrawal as a form of birth control because they felt it was too obvious to mention. The contraceptive pill has received a lot of publicity, but in fact it was not a contraceptive method that was available to most of the teenagers at the time they were interviewed. All these influences make it difficult to estimate the extent of knowledge about birth-control methods among teenagers, although there is not much doubt that their understanding was sketchy, even among those who claimed to be knowledgeable on the subject.

I've heard the term, but I don't really know what it means. (boy, aged 15)
Even when I read about it, I couldn't seem to take it in. (boy, aged 17)
Mum says if I'm going to sleep with a boy, I'm to ask her and she'll tell me. (girl, aged 18)
There's the Greek method. Apparently one can temporarily sterilize oneself by heating one's sex organs in boiling water. (Interviewer: Boiling?). Well, warm. I don't think it's much good. (boy, aged 16)
I use the British Railways system – just pull out on time. (boy, aged 18)

All the teenagers with experience of sexual intercourse were asked if they always took precautions. Less than half (43 per cent) the boys always used some form of birth control; about two-thirds (68 per cent) had used contraceptives more than once or twice; and a quarter (25 per cent) of the boys having sexual intercourse had never used any kind of birth-control method.

Not unexpectedly far fewer girls used any birth-control methods. A fifth (20 per cent) said they always did, but it was not always clear whether this referred to precautions taken by the girl herself, or by her boy friend. Well over half (61 per cent) said they never took precautions and if this is added to those who occasionally use birth-control methods, it is found that eight out of ten girls having sexual intercourse were at risk.

Many girls feel that birth control is the man's business, so all the experienced girls were asked if they insisted that their sexual partners took precautions. About a third (35 per cent) always insisted, out nearly half (45 per cent) did not insist. The other girls had insisted sometimes (15 per cent), or once or twice (5 per cent). Although the girls must bear nearly all the consequences of an unwanted pregnancy, the majority neither took precautions themselves, nor insisted upon their partners using any contraceptive method.

When the teenagers who used birth control methods were asked what kind of precautions they used, their replies made it clear that nearly all the girls depended upon the man to take the precautions; 78 per cent mentioned the sheath and 40 per cent mentioned withdrawal, but only 14 per cent had used diaphragms and 9 per cent had used chemical methods.

Eight out of ten of the boys who took any kind of precautions relied upon the sheath. About a quarter said they also used withdrawal as a birth-control method, but this may be an underestimate; it was always difficult to get accurate answers on this category because teenagers are not always familiar with the word withdrawal' and many do not consider it to be a form of birth control. Very few boys relied upon the girl to provide any method of birth control.

I must say it didn't occur to me to use anything like that. (boy, aged 17)
Oh no, I won't use them. It destroys the whole thing. (boy, aged 18)
He don't bother. (girl, aged 18)
Well, I suppose I'm too shy to bring the subject up. (girl, aged 19)
He says if it were natural to use them, we'd have been born with them on us. (girl, aged 17)

It is often assumed that one of the strongest deterrents to permissive behaviour is the fear of pregnancy, and many people allege that young people are now more permissive precisely because contraceptives are easier to obtain. The sexually experienced girls were asked if they were ever afraid that they might become pregnant, and the experienced boys were asked if they feared that their girl friends might become pregnant. This possibility had never been considered by 8 per cent of the boys and 12 per cent of the girls. A further 41 per cent of the boys and 18 per cent of the girls said that the possibility of pregnancy had not worried them. But this is a real fear for 51 per cent of the experienced boys and 70 per cent of the experienced girls.

It is not of course surprising that a far larger number of gir. fear the consequences of pregnancy, for they are the ones who hav to deal with the problem and have to face the embarrassment an difficulties of conception before marriage, an illegitimate birth c an abortion. Not only does the girl have to endure the physica strain, but also the social hostility towards unmarried mothers c illegal abortion is directed against the girl rather than the putativ father. Only in the case of a forced marriage does the father shar some of the consequences of an unwanted pregnancy.

Although only a very few boys were putative fathers and sti fewer girls had been pregnant, an attempt was made to get th reactions of the teenagers to this situation. Altogether 165 younge boys and 274 older boys were asked what they would do if the: girl friend was going to have a baby; this represents 35 per cent c the total sample of younger boys and 60 per cent of the older boys the more inexperienced boys were not asked this question becaus the possibility was too hypothetical to produce useful answer: The replies of those who were asked the question reveal that i many cases (40 per cent) the possibility had not been entertainec and others (19 per cent) said they would go to their parents fo advice. However over a quarter (28 per cent) said they would offe to marry the pregnant girl. This shows a willingness to shoulde some of the responsibility. Unfortunately it is by no means certai that the shotgun marriage is always the right solution to thi problem.

The old fashioned attitude towards the fallen woman and th unmarried father provided for only two possible solutions honourable and dishonourable. Under this dichotomy the boy come out quite well, for about half (47 per cent) offered to marr the girl or at least talk to their parents about it, while only abou one in eight (13 per cent) suggested any of the 'dishonourable solutions such as denial of responsibility, offer of financial help attempts to arrange abortion or adoption, or said they would d nothing about it.

Many (40 per cent) of the boys had no clear idea what the would do in these circumstances, but when the girls were aske what they would do if they found they were going to have a baby only a very few (6 per cent) were unable to answer the question *pregnancy is a much more relevant contingency to a girl than to a boy.*

I'd try to persuade her to get rid of it, and if that didn't work, I'd marry her. (boy, aged 16)
I don't know what I'd do . . . I mean it's what girls are for isn't it. (boy, aged 19)
I'd kill myself. (girl, aged 17)
I'd be left holding the baby, I suppose. (girl, aged 18)

As with the boys, some of the girls were thought to be too inexperienced to give meaningful replies to this question, but the answers of the 399 girls showed that by far the largest number (38 per cent) would take the problem of their pregnancy to their parents. This represents more than one out of three of the girls who were asked this question, even so some people may find it surprising that more girls did not first think of their parents when faced with this problem. Over a third indicated that they would like to keep the child, either by marrying the father (20 per cent), or by making other arrangements (18 per cent). Less than one in ten (9 per cent) would want the baby to be adopted, and still fewer (7 per cent) would try to get rid of it. In view of the reported number of abortions, these last figures may be underestimates, and indeed it must be expected that the replies to this hypothetical question might be quite different from the dismayed action a girl would take in reality if she discovered she was pregnant. Nevertheless these figures do show that abortion and adoption are not a solution for many girls.

The results in this section suggest that the girls have a very real fear of pregnancy and yet they do almost nothing to take precautions. In the whole sample 82 per cent said they knew something about the sort of precautions people take to avoid pregnancy, and yet only three (less than 0·5 per cent) girls had ever bought a contraceptive and nearly all the experienced girls left it to the boy to decide what form of birth control he would use, if any.

The consequences of making their partner pregnant was not such a dominant fear for the boys. Less than half the sexually experienced boys always used a contraceptive, although 84 per cent replied that they knew about the sort of precautions people took to avoid pregnancies.

Of the 190 boys who had ever possessed a contraceptive, 139 ha experienced sexual intercourse; the other 51 either felt the need t be prepared or, more likely, were carrying around a sheath as kind of status symbol. Most (40 per cent) of them bought the contraceptives from chemists and others (18 per cent) from barber 32 of the boys who obtained their contraceptives from chemists barbers were in the younger age group and so were aged fifteen t seventeen. No one in the sample got their contraceptives from slot machine. A very few obtained them from surgical stores (4 p cent) or agents (5 per cent). But a large number (33 per cen obtained them from friends, and individual cases suggest tha sometimes a sheath is sold and resold many times between schoo boys.

The occasional newspaper report about the discovery of a nun ber of contraceptives as a result of a search of the pockets lockers of schoolboys by a zealous master is not usually of muc significance. Some people would feel more concerned by the fac that 54 of the 193 sexually experienced boys (i.e. 28 per cent) hav never owned a contraceptive.

It has been noted that 57 per cent of the sexually experience boys did not always use a contraceptive, and 65 per cent of th experienced girls did not always insist that their boy friend use one These teenagers were asked if they had any particular reason fo not using contraceptives. A few (6 per cent) boys and a large number (15 per cent) of the girls found it impossible to answer thi question; many of the girls implied that it was up to the man to tak this decision. Furthermore, this kind of question is bound t produce some answers that are rationalizations, and some whic are vague or inarticulate. Some of the teenagers who were answer ing this question had only limited experience of sexual intercours and it is therefore not altogether surprising that they did not hav contraceptives at the isolated moments when intercourse occurred

But some of the answers reveal fairly strong attitudes among th teenagers. A fifth (21 per cent) of the boys and a quarter (25 per cent of the girls did not like the idea of using any contraceptive method it is not always clear whether the girl's dislike refers to femal contraceptives or whether she is echoing the opinions of her bo friend. A large number (29 per cent) of boys gave replies that ar est classified under the category of 'don't care'; these replies usually showed a lack of concern and a disinclination to think about birth control; rather surprisingly 12 per cent of the girls held similar attitudes. Another group held that contraceptives were not necessary for a variety of reasons. Taking these three groups together, it suggests that 56 per cent of the boys and 49 per cent of the girls have very little interest in birth control and will e slow to profit from instruction in the use of contraceptives.

A few boys (5 per cent) and girls (7 per cent) did not know enough to be able to make use of birth-control methods. Religious reasons for not taking precautions were given only rarely (6 per cent) by the girls and hardly ever (1 per cent) by the boys.

It is clear from the results reported in this section that many of the girls who are having premarital sexual intercourse are running the risk of becoming pregnant. Likewise many of the boys are not making use of birth control. Some would be more likely to take precautions if contraceptives were more readily available, but the majority are either not aware of the risks, or at the moment of sexual excitement are not disposed to consider the consequences of an unwanted pregnancy. As sexual intercourse within marriage is socially accepted, it is not too difficult to make preparations and have contraceptives available. But premarital intercourse is discouraged, and therefore when it does take place, it is unpremeditated and clandestine; in these circumstances birth control is less likely to be practised. Unfortunately the consequences of an unwanted pregnancy are far more serious for the unmarried than for the married.

E. Venereal Disease

Until 1963 the incidence figures for the venereal diseases indicated cases and not patients; individual patients who contracted syphilis or gonorrhoea on more than one occasion during the year under review added to the total. In that year the form (V.D.(R).) on which information is supplied by all clinics was revised to provide more detailed information, including this distinction between 'cases' and 'patients'. In 1964 there were 36,574 cases of postpubertal gonorrhoea among 31,306 individuals. So in previous years the totals have been inflated considerably by individuals who have been infected more than once during the year. Since 1963 there has not been a significant change in the total number of people who have been infected.

The new method of recording also indicated the age groups of infected patients for the first time. In 1965 a total of 190 boys and girls under the age of sixteen were infected; this represents less than one per cent of all those who caught VD. Of the 1,707 who had primary or secondary syphilis, 8·6 per cent were nineteen or younger. Of the 31,118 who had gonorrhoea, 13·1 per cent were nineteen or less.

A study of venereal disease among unmarried people aged fifteen to fifty found that single males over the age of twenty are ten times more likely than teenagers to get VD, and single girls over the age of twenty are three times more likely to be infected (Hitchens and James, 1965). The chief medical officer of the Ministry of Health noted in his annual report for 1965 that most cases of venereal disease occurred in people aged twenty-five and over.

This report also showed that 1,917 boys aged nineteen or under had gonorrhoea. The contribution which immigrants* make to the incidence of the venereal diseases has been studied by the Co-operative Clinical Group of the Medical Society for the Study of Venereal Diseases (1965). Of the men 52·8 per cent were born in the United Kingdom. Using these figures and the total number of boys aged fifteen to nineteen in the country, it can be estimated that 0·055 per cent of the boys were infected; in other words one in over 1,600 British-born boys caught VD.

In the same year 2,015 girls aged nineteen and under had gonorrhoea. According to the British Co-operative Clinical Groups 82·8 per cent of all women with gonorrhoea were born in the United Kingdom. Thus it can be estimated that 0·095 per cent of the girls aged fifteen to nineteen were infected; and so about one in a thousand British-born teenage girls get VD.

Perhaps it is not altogether surprising that young people's knowledge about venereal diseases is limited. Many sex educators find it a distasteful subject and fear that the children might be alarmed

* Many of these are foreign seamen treated at British ports, thus giving a false impression of the number of true immigrants who get VD.

time is spent on this disease when other information about sex is being given. Nevertheless it has been the subject of a fairly widespread propaganda campaign and several people have commented on the rise in the VD rates among young people in the last few years. This research attempted to find out how much the teenagers knew about the venereal diseases, and where they obtained this information.

First they were asked if they knew anything about VD, and 16 per cent of the boys and 13 per cent of the girls replied that they did not. Those who replied in the affirmative were asked to describe the symptoms. Now this is a difficult question to answer, particularly for girls, and it is possible that some of the young people knew, or partially knew, the symptoms but could not bring themselves to name the affected part of the body. On the other hand this question came late in the interview after a long period had been spent discussing sexual matters.

In fact about a third of the sample was unable to describe any symptoms although they had heard of VD. The other replies were extremely varied and indicate that a large amount of misinformation is spread about this disease. Less than one in ten mentioned discharge as a symptom, and less than one in twenty mentioned a spot or chancre. Over half of the teenagers did not know anything about the symptoms of either gonorrhoea or syphilis, and would not be able to recognize either disease if they were infected. There was no difference in this respect between the girls and the boys, and the older age groups appeared to be no better informed than the younger.

VD? What does it stand for? (boy, aged 17)
It's caused by women not washing themselves right. (boy, aged 15)
It's a disease caught from men. (girl, aged 16)
Our history teacher told us Louis the something had it; his toes were falling to pieces. (girl, aged 18)
It starts on your stomach and grows to your face and more or less eats you away. (girl, aged 17)
I'm told Sylvia B— gets it ever so bad every winter. (girl, aged 16)

Most people (33 per cent of the boys and 30 per cent of the girls) learnt about VD from their friends; the other important sources were TV (16 per cent boys, 17 per cent girls) and books (15 per cent boys, 11 per cent girls); girls were more likely than boys to learn from their parents (3 per cent boys, 10 per cent girls) or at school (7 per cent boys, 13 per cent girls); posters were only rarely the source of knowledge (4 per cent for both boys and girls).

In order to check the effectiveness of these sources, the replies describing the symptoms were arbitrarily divided into correct and incorrect responses, giving the teenagers the benefit of the doubt in many cases; then these two classifications were compared with the sources of information. This analysis revealed that books and friends appear to be the best source of accurate information, but friends are also the biggest source of misinformation. In the few programmes on television devoted to this subject the description of the symptoms has been correct, albeit a little vague, but the response is equally divided between correct and incorrect. Posters do not usually give much information on symptoms, but emphasize the dangers and indicate where help may be obtained. This analysis makes it appear as if parents and school teachers give equal amounts of reliable and unreliable information. Of course it is not the accuracy of the actual source which is being measured here, but the effect it has on the teenagers which is, after all, the important aspect.

In our sample ten boys thought they might have got VD at one period of their lives. Four went to a clinic – two of these were infected and two were not; one went to his own doctor (result not reported); the other five did nothing about it and the symptoms disappeared.

Five of the girls thought they had VD at one time or another. Three went to a clinic – one was infected and two were not; the other two said the symptoms disappeared. Of course it is quite possible that the seven boys and girls who did not go to a clinic were misinformed and were not infected; but one cannot be sure about this.

Most of the teenagers had heard about the venereal diseases, but we found that there was still much ignorance about VD and some of the misapprehensions and old wives' tales still persisted. About half the young people in our sample would not be able to recognize the symptoms if they were infected. Television programmes utter dire warnings about VD but they do not describe the symptoms so that a teenager could tell if he is infected or not. Some of the books on sex education do not mention the venereal diseases at all. There is still some doubt whether a person who suspected that he had got VD would really go to a clinic.

They say they've got to stick a red hot needle right up you to cure it. (boy, aged 16)
It gives you spots on your face. (boy, aged 18)
Don't tell me anything about it. I don't want to know. (girl, aged 16)
I've never worried about it. I'm very careful myself. (boy, aged 19)
It can't be all that bad or they wouldn't put it on the telly. (girl, aged 15)

It is quite possible (although statistically improbable) that some of the teenagers we questioned had VD and were quite unaware that they were infected (and, of course, there was no way our interviewers could know). Perhaps it is a slight consolation that both boys and girls with experience of sexual intercourse were more likely to be better informed about the symptoms (see Section D of Chapter 10). Venereal disease can always be completely cured providing it is detected and properly treated in the early stages. Therefore it is imperative that those who may be exposed to this risk should be able to recognize the disease. The results of this research indicate that many of them would not know if they were infected.

7. Attitudes

A. The Attitude Inventory

A new social attitude inventory was designed especially for this research. Although it was decided that the information about sexual behaviour could only be obtained by direct questions at a face-to-face interview, it was found that answers to most of the simpler attitude questions could be obtained more efficiently by using the inventory, thus making it possible to shorten the already long interview. In other cases the questions on the interview schedule were complementary to the attitude inventory.

The various drafts of the social attitude inventory were tested in the first area visited by the research team. At the end of each interview the teenager was asked to give his opinions about these statements. He was encouraged to ask questions and make comments, and the interviewer made a note of all cases where there was some doubt about the meaning of the statement. Analyses were made of the responses throughout this period and a study was made of inventories which contained responses which were inconsistent to see if this was because the statements had not been understood. As the statements were being continually modified during the interviews in this area, none of the inventories filled in by adolescents from London C are included in the results. The final draft of the inventory was not completed until the research team had moved on to the second area (South A).

Several other sources were used before the final draft of the inventory was completed. The aim was to produce a list of statements covering the important areas in a teenager's life, such as attitudes to the family and its restraints, other teenagers, marriage, the moral code, sex, crime, etc. For some months the research unit had employed a press-cutting agency to send them all the newspaper clippings about teenagers, including the oft-expressed opinions of adults about young people. In a short time a large number of press cuttings was collected. This included quotations from adults of varying sympathies and outlooks about teenagers and their behaviour. There were also other quotations from teenagers themselves, about each other and how they behave or should behave. Other press cuttings were from parents about their teenage children. Still others were statements from the representatives of official bodies. A content analysis was made of this large collection and the most frequent items were rewritten as a series of attitude statements.

In addition other statements were listed from the questionnaire circulated by the BMA Committee on the problem of venereal disease, from Eysenck's Social Attitude Inventory (Eysenck, 1954), and from an earlier personality test (Terman and Miles, 1936) which contained a number of statements about teenagers.

After further testing and discussion this list was eventually reduced to fifty statements. Items were rejected because they were too topical for a research extending over three years, because the idea or vocabulary would have been clear only to middle-class teenagers, or because the statements might have caused embarrassment or resentment.

This attitude inventory was used in six of the seven areas. The time it took the adolescent to complete the inventory varied considerably, but the average time was less than ten minutes. Most of the teenagers found it interesting and only a very few regarded it as an imposition. In all 780 boys and 761 girls completed the inventory. All of the fifty opinion statements were about things in which most teenagers had strong interests and they were asked to indicate their agreement or disagreement with each statement. The full results are given in Appendix 3. The next section summarizes the main attitudes revealed in these results; the remaining five sections of this chapter discuss some of the opinions and beliefs which emerged during the interview and compares these with the relevant responses in the attitude inventory.

B. Opinions and Beliefs

Despite many varied remarks to the contrary, the influence of the family appears to be strong for most young people. A large majority of boys and girls felt that *the family should spend an evening at* *home together at least once a week* (7)*. Three out of four of them agreed that *people should realize their greatest loyalty is to their family* (16). Over half the boys and nearly half the girls felt that *most parents ought to be stricter with their children* (2), while a third of the boys and half the girls disagreed with the statement that *teenagers should be able to go out in the evening without having to tell their parents where they are going* (39). This is a surprising result considering that these young people were at just the age when they are seeking independence from parental controls.

Most of the teenagers felt that *the advantages of living at home with the family outweigh the disadvantages* (31) and disagreed with the idea that *young people can only really be free if they live away from home* (24), although about half of them had to admit *I'm usually a bit bored when I stay at home in the evenings* (33).

Nor is there much evidence of anti-authority attitudes. In their careful study of the moral values of adolescents the Eppels (1966) found that only a minority had a generalized hostility to authority although many were disinclined to accept it without question. In this research the young people do not think that *the police are unfair in their treatment of teenagers* (25), but they were equally divided in their opinions about the statement that *most adults say one thing and do another* (8).

Hemmings (1960) found that 65 per cent of the women students he questioned said that their views on 'general moral principles' were the same as their parents, though only about 29 per cent said they were the same on sex. Most of the teenagers in our sample confirmed this view; over half agreed with the statement *I would rather go to my parents for advice than to my friends* (37), although few of them sought advice from their parents about specifically sexual matters. Nor were all of them inclined to take advice about work from their parents; opinions were evenly divided on the statement that *parents should advise their children about the sort of work they should do* (14).

Most of the boys agreed with the statement *I think I'll have a better job than my father has when I am his age* (35) and a majority

* In this chapter the words in italics are the actual statements used in the attitude inventory. The numbers after the statements refer to their position in Appendix 3 where the percentage results are given.

of both sexes disagreed with the idea that *the average teenager expects to live much the same kind of life as his parents do* (42). Seven out of ten agreed that *I'd rather work for someone strict and fair, than for someone who is easy going* (30), whereas there was considerable uncertainty about the suggestion that *most teenagers are bored with their jobs* (5). The young people left the impression that they wanted to be interested and involved in their work, but sometimes the employers failed to take advantage of this.

But commercial and other pressures towards the development of a teenage culture have created a kind of artificial barrier between the generations, and there is no doubt that some teenagers feel that they do not always receive the understanding and tolerance they merit. Only one in three of the young people disagreed with the two statements *I learn more from friends of my own age than I can learn from my parents* (10) and *very few adults really understand teenagers* (40). More than half of them agreed that *today's teenagers are very different from teenagers in the past* (12), and did not agree that *teenage boys spend too much time thinking about their clothes and hair styles* (15).

A large majority agreed that *it always pays to be honest* (3). On the other hand almost a half felt that *there is no harm in travelling without a ticket occasionally if you can get away with it* (28). This is probably because standards are less rigorous about stealing, but young people have a high standard for truthfulness especially in personal relations.

Most of these young people were not interested in religion. The majority felt that *the average man can live a good life without religion* (18) and only a quarter agreed that *the Church is the best authority to decide on matters of right and wrong* (34). But this does not mean that their attitude to life was entirely permissive. Less than half agreed that *life is so short that having a good time is more important than anything else* (1). Morris (1958) saw signs of the emergence of a relatively undemanding common-sense ethic among adolescents as they got older. A large number agree that *each person should decide for himself what is right and wrong* (6). But this sense of right and wrong is closely identified with Christian principles of morality even if they have rejected the dogma of the Church. In some cases their views are more restrictive than many of their parents. A majority do not agree that *it should be made easier for married people to get divorced if they want to* (22) and most of them felt that *teenagers have sex thrown at them all the time from advertisements, films and T V* (36). Opinions were divided about the statement that *all homosexuals should be severely punished* (44). About a quarter of the boys and girls agree that *foreigners should stay in their own country* (30) and that *it would be best to keep coloured people in their own districts in order to prevent too much contact with whites* (46).

Eppel (1966) found:

evidence of a change in some aspects of their moral codes and sentiments but it involves a shift in emphasis and focus and a re-evaluation of the sanctions for moral conduct rather than an adoption of a completely new set of principles or the approbation of radically different forms of conduct.

The results obtained from our attitude inventory would agree with this view as far as the non-sexual topics were concerned. They wish to be better than their elders, but not so very different.

In some ways this outline of teenage attitudes is a story of lost opportunities. They value a high degree of permissiveness among their own equals, but they are less likely to show the same tolerance to other groups. They look forward to going to work, but there is a danger that this enthusiasm will get deflated by disappointing working conditions. Most noticeable of all is the desire to show loyalty and respect for their family. In fact the influence of parents on children continues to be very great. Quarrels in the family are not usually caused by the teenage children rejecting everything the parents care about, but because the young people do not accept all the parental standards.

C. Attitudes to Marriage

Very few of our sample rejected the prospect of marriage; 6 per cent of the younger boys and 3 per cent of the older boys said at the interview that they did not want to marry; hardly any of the girls (1 per cent in each age group) said they did not want to marry. Another 7 per cent of the boys and 1 per cent of the girls felt unable to answer the question. But although most of the boys and nearly all the girls wanted to get married, over a quarter of both boys (28 per cent) and girls (27 per cent) agreed with the statement that *it is best to have a good time before you are married because after that life is pretty dreary* (9).

A big difference between the sexes about the ideal age of marriage was revealed at the interview. Among the boys 35 per cent of the younger and 43 per cent of the older said they did not want to marry before the age of twenty-five; the corresponding figure for girls is 9 per cent in both age groups.

The majority of boys and girls would prefer to marry after the age of twenty-one, but the proportion is much bigger for boys than for girls and is also bigger for older girls than for younger girls. Over a third (38 per cent) of younger girls would like to marry before they are twenty-one. This shows the tremendous prominence of marriage as an immediate goal in the lives of many teenage girls. More than one in four of the boys and girls agreed with the statement *girls believe today that if they are not married before they are twenty-one they are on the shelf* (17).

The boys would prefer to marry later. Less than 10 per cent wanted to marry before they were twenty-one. Only a half of them actually disagreed with the statement about life being dreary after marriage, and about one in every five agreed that *girls should not get married before they are twenty-one* (47).

But most of the boys, and still more girls, were not against early marriage and indeed a very large number do marry when they are young. Although marriage under the age of twenty-one still requires the consent of parents or of a magistrate's court, the number of minors getting married has increased considerably in recent years. The total number of bridegrooms under twenty-one was 65,146 in 1966 (15 per cent of all the men who were married in that year), while 171,695 girls were married (40 per cent of all the women married in 1966).

One of the most frequent reasons for early marriage is that a child has been conceived. But even without the duress of pregnancy young people get married in order to get away from parental restrictions, or as a sign of independence, or to demonstrate their maturity to others. In fact teenage girls who marry early to assert their liberty are quite mistaken; they are actually denying themselves many of the freedoms and benefits of female emancipation.

Not unexpectedly most of them (62 per cent boys, 89 per cent girls) said they expect to remain faithful after marriage. However 9 per cent of the boys and 1 per cent of the girls said they thought they would have sex with others besides their spouse after marriage. Perhaps more surprising are the 17 per cent boys and 6 per cent girls who said they were not sure when they were asked this question: Do you think you will have sex with anyone else after you are married?

For most boys and nearly all girls marriage is an expected, almost inevitable, part of a person's life. But in spite of its inevitability about a quarter of the teenagers see marital life in an unfavourable light and seem to suggest that enjoyment ends when marriage begins.

D. Attitudes to Sex Education

In Figure 7/1 we bring together the responses of three interview questions and one of the attitude statements on the subject of knowledge about sex. A quarter of the boys and a third of the girls felt they should have been taught more about sex by their parents. So the boys did not get much advice from their parents, and there was not much demand for it. It is clear that more boys would rather learn about sex from their teachers than from their parents. A third of the girls had also hoped to learn more from their teachers although many more girls (86 per cent) had already received some kind of sex education at school.

The third item in Figure 7/1 shows that many boys and girls want help with their sex problems from their school teachers. There are also some signs that the teenagers have not been altogether content with what little sex education they have been getting. In fact 77 per cent of the boys and even 66 per cent of the girls agreed with the statement that *it is important for a person who gives sex education to have had some first-hand experience of sex* (32). In Section B of this chapter it was noted that the teenagers had only a limited amount of respect for adult advice. Most teenagers agreed with the statements *I learn more from friends of my own age than I can learn from adults* (10) and *very few adults really understand teenagers* (40).

Figure 7/1.
Attitudes to Sex Education

Do you feel you should have been taught more about sex by your parents?

YES

25%

37%

Do you feel you should have been taught more about sex at school?

YES

43%

35%

There is no need to teach about sex in schools, because you can find out all you need to know for yourself.

DISAGREE

70%

78%

AGREE

21%

13%

Do you feel you know all there is to know about sex?

NO

50%

56%

BOYS   GIRLS

The last item of Figure 7/1 emphasizes what a difficult task the teacher has to face, for nearly half the boys and girls think they know all there is to know about sex. Our later questions, particularly on birth control and venereal disease, showed that much of this confidence was misplaced and that their knowledge on sexual matters was very often limited. It was the younger adolescents who were sure that they did not have anything more to learn about sex and this over-confidence decreased as they got older.

Although it is clear that a large part of the teacher's task is to correct misinformation, this research has shown that there is a lively demand for information about sex, and there are indications that this demand is not being fulfilled.

E. Inhibiting Factors

All the boys who had experienced sexual intercourse were asked if they were ever afraid that the girls might become pregnant, and the experienced girls were asked if they feared pregnancy. Nearly half the boys did not worry about it; 8 per cent said they had never thought about it and 41 per cent said they did not think it would happen to their girl friend; 51 per cent of the boys said that they had been afraid of a possible pregnancy on one or more occasions. The attitude of the girls is quite different. Only 12 per cent said they had not thought about it and another 18 per cent said they did not worry about it. This leaves 70 per cent of the experienced girls who have feared pregnancy.

Most of the boys (66 per cent) agreed with the statement that *if a boy gets a girl pregnant he should be willing to marry her*. The same number (66 per cent) of girls agreed, but it is interesting to note that very slightly more girls (19 per cent) than boys (18 per cent) actually disagreed with this statement.

There is little doubt that fear of pregnancy is still an inhibiting factor for some people; nearly a third (30 per cent) of the experienced boys and nearly a half (44 per cent) of the experienced girls said they sometimes stopped short of complete intercourse because of the risks of pregnancy. Furthermore over half (54 per cent) the boys who had experience of genital apposition said they had refrained from sexual intercourse because of the risks of pregnancy and this applied to almost a third (31 per cent) of the girls with experience of genital apposition but not of sexual intercourse. Thus 9 per cent of the boys and 7 per cent of the girls in the whole sample were using genital apposition as a form of birth control and a substitute for sexual intercourse.

A general attempt was made to find out what had stopped those who had not had sexual intercourse. Apart from those who had very little contact with the opposite sex (i.e. those in stage I), all the others who had not had experience of sexual intercourse (i.e. all those in stages II and III), were questioned about this. When they had revealed the full extent of their sexual experience, they were asked: Is there any reason why you don't go farther than this?

This was a very demanding question and required the sort of response which was difficult to put into words for many of the teenagers, and beyond the capabilities of others. The possibility had not occurred to many of them, while others took it for granted that their first experience of sexual intercourse would occur after they had married. Care had to be taken not to disturb these young people or leave the impression that the interviewer was disappointed with their reply, so in 24 per cent of the cases we did not press for an answer. Another 14 per cent of the boys and 2 per cent of the girls said there was no reason why they should not go farther, implying that they would take the chance when it occurred.

An important inhibiting influence was fear of pregnancy, just as it was the most usual reason for restraint given by the experienced teenagers (stage IV and V); rather surprisingly this applied to more boys (42 per cent) than girls (17 per cent). The most usual restraint for girls (45 per cent) and an important restraint for boys (22 per cent) were moral reasons, although only a few (3 per cent boys, 5 per cent girls) specifically mentioned religious reasons. The girls' reputation was also an important factor about as often for the boys (11 per cent) as for the girls (9 per cent); this reinforces the suggestion made later (Section G) that girls who permit premarital intercourse are disparaged by some boys, even by the boys who are seeking to have intercourse with them. This is similar to the idea that it is important for the girl to keep her virginity which was mentioned by some girls (4 per cent), but only a very few boys (1 per cent) were concerned for their own virginity. Fear of venereal disease appears to be the least important of the reasons; only 1 per cent of the boys and 2 per cent of the girls gave this as a reason for not having sexual intercourse.

F. Attitudes to Sex before Marriage

The responses to the question and the first statement shown in Figure 7/2 are very similar. Boys are more in favour of intercourse with their fiancées than girls, and also disagree more strongly that *sexual intercourse before marriage is wrong.* The older age groups are more permissive than the younger boys and girls. More teenagers reject premarital intercourse for themselves in the question, than as a general principle in the statement. Among the older boys less than a third (29 per cent) believe that sex before marriage is definitely wrong but nearly half (46 per cent) said they did not want sex with their fiancée.

Nearly half the boys appear to be in favour of premarital intercourse whereas less than a quarter of the girls hold this view. It is interesting to compare these attitudes with those expressed on sex education. Girls are more interested in learning about sex than boys, but boys are far more permissive than girls in their attitude towards sexual experience itself.

Furthermore many girls expect boys to be more experienced. Many more girls than boys believed that *sexual intercourse before marriage is all right for boys but not for girls.* Although only a minority in any group supported this double standard of sexual morality as many as 45 per cent of the younger girls and 39 per cent of the older girls agreed with this statement, compared with only 25 per cent younger boys and 21 per cent older boys. The other statement on this idea confirms that girls are prepared to endure sexual behaviour in boys which they would not tolerate in themselves; 45 per cent of the girls compared with 31 per cent of the boys agreed that *when it comes to sex there is one standard for men and another for women* (26).

G. Attitudes to Virginity

Figure 7/3 reveals the basic moral dilemma that teenagers are faced with and the confusion that exists among them on moral questions.

Figure 7/2.
Attitudes to Sex before Marriage

Would you like to have sex with your fiancé(e) before you marry?

YES 40% 22%
NO 46% 67%

Sexual intercourse before marriage is wrong

DISAGREE 45% 24%
AGREE 35% 61%

Sexual intercourse before marriage is all right for boys but not for girls

AGREE 23% 42%
DISAGREE 56% 44%

BOYS GIRLS

Many (45 per cent) boys are not against premarital intercourse but a majority (64 per cent) wish to marry virgins. Only a quarter of the boys said they did not mind either way and one in ten said they definitely did not want to marry a virgin. It seemed a little tactless to ask this question of girls who had already experienced sexual intercourse, but a very large number (58 per cent) of the others (stages I–III) wanted to be a virgin when they married. This conflicts slightly with the previous figure (7/2) where 22 per cent of the girls said they would like to have sex with their fiancé, but this includes people who already have had this experience; the others probably mean they wish the first experience to be with the man they are going to marry whether this be before they are married or after.

Over half (51 per cent) the boys would like to have sex experience but two thirds (64 per cent) want to marry virgins. Some of the boys drew a sharp distinction between girls to have sex with and girls to marry.

Most girls do not want to have sex before they marry, and they believe that their boy friends want to marry a virgin. They also believe, more often than the boys, that a girl who has sex before marriage gets a bad reputation. But many of them do not mind if their boy friend has sex elsewhere before they are married. A third (36 per cent) stated definitely that they wanted their boy friend to have sexual experience, and another quarter (26 per cent) were undecided; only 38 per cent were against their boy friend having sexual experience.

It is clear that all teenagers expect the girls to be much more circumspect than the boys. Girls are slightly more consistent and realistic in the attitudes they express on these issues. They are more likely to realize that there is a double standard for men and women, and a majority accept the view that girls who have sex before marriage get a bad reputation. They also want to be virgins when they marry and realize that this is what the boys expect; more girls than boys believe that most boys want to marry virgins. The number of girls who want to be virgins when they marry is higher than the number of boys who expect their wives to be virgins. Indeed over a third of the boys either preferred their wife not to be a virgin or were not concerned either way. It is possible that the girls have

Figure 7/3. *Attitudes to Virginity*

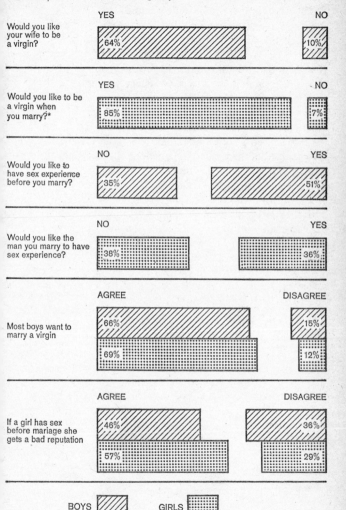

Would you like your wife to be a virgin?
YES 64%
NO 10%

Would you like to be a virgin when you marry?*
YES 85%
NO 7%

Would you like to have sex experience before you marry?
NO 35%
YES 51%

Would you like the man you marry to have sex experience?
NO 38%
YES 36%

Most boys want to marry a virgin
AGREE 66% / 69%
DISAGREE 15% / 12%

If a girl has sex before mariage she gets a bad reputation
AGREE 46% / 57%
DISAGREE 36% / 29%

BOYS   GIRLS

*Excludes girls who have had sexual intercourse

been overestimating the desirability – from the boys' point of view – of being a virgin on their wedding day.

A final aspect of this question is revealed by considering the sexual experience of the two older groups in relation to their views on virginity. We found that the percentage of girls wanting to be virgins on their wedding day is large among non-experienced and inceptive girls, but the inceptives (stage III) are slightly less in favour of virginity than those in stages I and II. The number of boys wanting virgins as marriage partners drops for the sexually experienced although it still remains over half. But 41 per cent of the experienced boys are not concerned about the girl's virginity. To 4 per cent of the sexually experienced boys marriage to any girl is not an attractive proposition.

From this section there emerges the impression that there is a group of boys who are keen to lose their own virginity but are critical of girls who provide them with this opportunity. If they wish to marry at all they are intent on marrying girls who are virgins and thus preclude marriage from their premarital sexual relationships. Girls, aware of the dangers, play a defensive role. They wish to protect their own virginity but expect boys to gain sexual experience, and find it acceptable that the boys should be able to do what they rule out for themselves.

Part Three

The Difference Between Sexually Experienced Teenagers and Others

8. Family Background

A. Associated Factors

The next five chapters will be devoted to investigating the association between sexual experience and other factors. In previous chapters we have noted that inceptive activities form an important part of the sexual behaviour of young people. It would be misleading to limit our definition of sexual experience only to those who have had intercourse, because this would leave out a large number of people who have experienced extensive sexual arousal during the course of inceptive activities. Accordingly we have compared other non-sexual factors with three levels of sexual activity, formed by reducing our previous scale of sexual experience as follows:

Stage I
Stage II } the non-experienced (N)

Stage III the inceptives (I)

Stage IV
Stage V } the experienced (E)

The *experienced* are those who have had intercourse with one or more partners; these will be designated E-boys and E-girls in the following chapters.

The *inceptives* are those who have not had sexual intercourse, but have experience of breast stimulation under clothes, genital stimulation and/or genital apposition; these will be designated I-boys and I-girls.

The *non-experienced* are all those who do not fall into one of the other two groups; they will be designated N-boys or N-girls in the following chapters.

We have tested the relationship between these three levels of sexual activity and many other variables by using the χ^2 test. When the test has revealed a significant association between the level of sex activity and one of these variables, we have shown this by giving the value of p. When $p = 0.001$ it signifies that the probability of this association occurring by chance is one in a thousand; if $p = 0.01$ the chances are one in a hundred. Levels above $p = 0.05$ (20:1) are usually considered not significant. In some cases we have also reported the fact that there is no statistical relationship between sex experience and another factor because in the past other people have suggested that there might be an association. When the letters NSS in brackets are found, this indicates that the association has been subjected to a statistical test and it has been found that it is not significant.

The χ^2 test applied here assumes that this is a simple random sample whereas in fact this is a series of random samples with different sampling fractions and this would require a less rigorous test. Therefore when it is found that the difference is significant when calculated on this basis, it is reasonably certain that this difference is due to something other than chance.

These statistical tests and all the figures given in Chapters 8–11 refer to the older age groups only (456 boys and 464 girls) because sexual experience is correlated with age and therefore we can partially eliminate this influence by reporting on boys and girls of about the same age, i.e. between seventeen and nineteen.

B. Early Background

It has been shown (Glueck, 1952) that juvenile delinquents tend to come from broken homes and it might have been expected that precocious sexual behaviour was more likely to be found in children from homes where one of the parents is dead or absent. But this research shows that adolescents who come from broken homes are not more likely to be sexually experienced (NSS).

In this sample 9 per cent of the older boys and 12 per cent of the older girls came from homes where one parent had been absent ever since the child was very young. In another 9 per cent of the cases one of the parents died or moved away when the child was ten years old or over. Accordingly a comparison was also made between those living with two parents at the time of the interview, and all those living with only one parent; but there was no association between the level of sex activity and those living with one parent or two (NSS). A similar test compared those living with two parents, and those living with stepmothers, aunts, stepfathers and foster parents; this indicated that those living with substitute parents are not more likely to have more sexual experience (NSS).

It was found that about a third (32 per cent) of the sample were living in the house where they were born; about a quarter (26 per cent) had moved home once, 17 per cent have moved twice, 13 per cent three times and 12 per cent more than three times. It has been suggested that these movements have an unsettling effect upon children as they have to get used to new surroundings, adjust to new schools and teachers, and make new friends. But this does not appear to make any difference to their subsequent sexual behaviour. A χ^2 test on the 920 older boys and girls revealed no association between the level of sex activity and the number of times they moved home (NSS).

As a measurement of social class we used the Registrar-General's five classes, adding together in the first instance classes I and II (the children of professional men, managers and supervisors) and classes IV and V (the children of semi-skilled and unskilled manual workers). When we compared the three major social groups with the three levels of sex activity, we found no association between social class and sex activity among the boys, but it does appear that the higher up a girl is on the social scale, the more sexual experience she is likely to have ($p = 0.02$); although the proportion of E-girls does not vary much from class to class, the proportion of I-girls in classes I and II is much greater than in classes III, IV and V.

Class III consists of non-manual workers and skilled manual workers; these were divided so that the non-manual were added to classes I and II and the manual to classes IV and V. Once again it was found that there was no association between the level of sex activity and manual or non-manual workers for the boys (NSS), but that girls from the homes of manual workers were likely to have had less experience of inceptive behaviour ($p = 0.01$).

Another analysis was made comparing middle-class teenagers (classes I and II) with all the other classes. The results were similar; there was no difference between the middle-class boys and the others (NSS), but middle-class girls are more likely to have had inceptive experience than the girls from other classes ($p = 0.01$).

The difference is accounted for solely by the large number (53 per cent) of middle-class girls with inceptive experience compared with 35 per cent in the rest of the sample. If the more straightforward, but less meaningful, comparison is made and the sample is divided between those girls who have experienced sexual intercourse and those who have not, then there is very little difference between the classes; 15 per cent of the middle-class girls have had premarital intercourse, and so have 16 per cent of the girls from other classes.

Some writers (Myrdal and Klein, 1956; Bott, 1957) have suggested that the social class of the mother (assessed by her occupation before marriage) has more influence on the child than the father's social class. But in this research no association was found between sexual experience and the occupation of the mother before marriage for either boys or girls (NSS). Of course this is not a very good test because some (8 per cent) mothers did not have a job before marriage, a number of teenagers (10 per cent) did not know what work their mother did before marriage and an unknown number of middle-class mothers may have taken unskilled jobs before they got married. Even so these results seem to show that the mother's social class is not an overriding influence on sexual behaviour.

Jephcott (1962), Kerr (1964) and others have been very concerned about the effects upon the child when the mother is out at work all day. In this sample 21 per cent of the mothers went out to work full time and 32 per cent went out part time; this refers to the situation at the time of the interview when the boys and girls were already teenagers; no doubt less mothers went out to work when their children were younger.

A comparison was made between those mothers who were working full time and those who were not working, leaving out of account those mothers who worked part time. It was found that there was no association between the level of sex activity and those boys whose mothers did not work (NSS); similarly the working situation of the girls' mothers appeared to have no effect upon the extent of their sex experience (NSS).

A detailed analysis was made of the position of each teenager in the family. In fact there seemed to be no relationship between birth order and sexual experience. The oldest child was not likely to be either more or less sexually experienced (NSS); nor was the youngest child (NSS); nor was the only child in the family (NSS).

This section has reported a whole series of tests where no significant association has been found between sexual experience and home background; the only exception is the social class of the girls but not the boys. These negative results seem to us to be important because they are unexpected. An absence of family life and a disturbed childhood is given as the reason for a number of social problems, including lax morality and sexual promiscuity. Furthermore there are grounds for believing that there is a connexion between a disturbed family situation and juvenile delinquency (Whyte, 1943; Cohen, 1955), adult crime (Reckless, 1961; West, 1963), mental disorder (Hollingshead and Redlich, 1958; Myers and Roberts, 1959), alcoholism (Lolli, 1961), and most forms of deviant behaviour (Clinard, 1958). But the results reported in this section suggest that teenage sexual behaviour is not associated with early background.

C. Relations with Parents

The previous section reported on the circumstances surrounding the home life of the teenagers. The actual atmosphere and feeling in the home are more difficult to measure, but because they are important some attempt will be made in this section to report on the adolescents' relations with their parents and relate this to their sexual behaviour.

All the teenagers were asked: How do you get on with your father? Such a question is apt to get a non-committal reply, so the interviewers were instructed to use two standardized supplementary questions. First they asked: What do you like least about your father? Then they asked: What do you like best about your father? Then similar questions were asked about the relationship with the mother. This procedure encouraged the teenagers to be much more communicative, and from their replies the interviewers rated them on a five-point scale. This scale appears to have some reliability as there was very little difference between the areas, or between the two age groups.

These results were analysed into non-experienced, inceptive and experienced and it was found that there was no association between the three levels of sex activity and the boys' relations with their fathers (NSS). Among the girls, however, there was a clear relationship between these two factors; girls who got on very well with their fathers were far less likely to be sexually experienced ($p = 0.001$).

The association between the level of sex activity and the relations with their mothers was significant for both boys and girls; boys who did not get on well with their mothers were more likely to be sexually experienced ($p = 0.05$); girls who got on well with their mothers were less likely to be sexually experienced ($p = 0.001$).

The teenagers were also asked if they thought their parents were happily married. Only about 5 per cent of the sample said their parents were unhappy together, while the other replies were put into three sequent categories – very happy, happy, average. Once again no relationship was found between the level of sex activity and the marital happiness of the boys' parents (NSS); but among the girls a strong association exists ($p = 0.001$).

D. Home Influence

The background circumstances and the relationships within the home would obviously have an important effect upon the upbringing of a child. Beside these factors several other questions were asked about the home and in particular we tried to detect the amount of parental influence on the children and to ascertain parental attempts to enforce discipline.

When they were asked if their parents insisted upon knowing where they went, 43 per cent of the boys and 42 per cent of the girls implied that the situation never arose because they always volunteered the necessary information; for the others the parents of boys were rather less insistent than the girls' parents; among the boys 13 per cent of the parents always wanted to know where they were going and 24 per cent did not insist upon knowing; among the girls 32 per cent always wanted to know where they were going and 8 per cent did not insist.

This parental concern with their children's whereabouts is

slightly correlated with the level of sex activity. A boy whose parents always want to know where he is going is likely to have had less sexual experience ($p = 0.02$); similarly a girl whose parents insist on knowing where she is going is likely to have had less sexual experience ($p = 0.05$).

The parents of the teenagers had met all their friends in 62 per cent of the cases among the boys, and 85 per cent of the cases among the girls. For 10 per cent of the boys and 6 per cent of the girls the parents had met hardly any of their friends. But those who introduced all or some of their friends to their parents are neither more nor less sexually experienced than those who never let their parents meet their friends (NSS).

One form of discipline that a parent is reluctant to relinquish is the time the children have to be in at night. When the teenagers were asked what time their parents expected them to be in at weekends 35 per cent of the boys and 17 per cent of the girls said their parents did not mind when they came in; but 31 per cent of the boys and 46 per cent of the girls were expected to be in before midnight, except on special occasions.

It was found that there was a very strong association between this factor and sexual experience for the boys ($p = 0.001$) and a less strong but significant association for the girls ($p = 0.01$). The N-boys were much more strictly controlled than the E-boys; one in five (19 per cent) of the N-boys had to be in before eleven whereas hardly any E-boys were required to be in at this time. Among the girls over half (56 per cent) of the N-girls had to be in before midnight compared with about one in three (38 per cent) of the E-girls.

Also on the subject of getting home at a specified time, it was found that there was an association between sex experience and the time a teenager was required to leave a party. Not surprisingly many of the parents made a special exemption when their children were going to a party; for 63 per cent of the boys and 43 per cent of the girls no particular time was specified and the teenager was allowed to stay at the party as long as he liked. In fact it was found that those whose parents expected them to leave a party at a particular time had less sexual experience than the others, and this was true for boys ($p = 0.02$) as it was for girls ($p = 0.01$). Other questions were asked about parties and these will be reported in Chapter 11.

The amount of discipline the parents attempted to impart, and the extent to which this discipline is accepted or rejected by the teenagers, are both important factors in the upbringing of a child, but this is by no means the only influence. One of the most pervasive and powerful influences is simply the amount of time the teenagers spend with their parents. There are marked differences in the ages at which adolescents cease to be constantly under the supervision of their parents. It is now recognized that the peer group has an important role in the socialization process and, of course, the values transmitted by the peer group differ from those to be found in the parent–child interaction. It would not be surprising, therefore, if teenagers who spend only a little time with their parents have different attitudes to sex.

Girls tend to spend more time at home than boys; a third (35 per cent) of the girls said they spent more time with their family than outside the home compared with one in five (19 per cent) of the boys. Even so, over half (53 per cent) of the girls and two-thirds (67 per cent) of the boys said they spent more time outside home; the remainder are accounted for by those who spend most of their time at home but not with their families, and those not living at home. There is a strong association between sexual experience and boys who spend most of their free time outside the home ($p = 0.001$); girls who spend most of their time away from their home are also likely to have had more sexual experience ($p = 0.02$). In terms of the three levels of sex activity, 52 per cent of the N-boys, 70 per cent of the I-boys and 82 per cent of the E-boys spent more of their time outside the home; 51 per cent of the N-girls, 38 per cent of the I-girls and 34 per cent of the E-girls spent more of their time at home.

Only 25 per cent of the boys and 30 per cent of the girls went on summer holidays with their parents; 43 per cent of the boys and 44 per cent of the girls went on holidays without their parents; the remainder did not go on holiday in the summer before the interview. When those who did not go away plus those who went away with their family are compared with those who were away from parental influence during their holidays, it is found that there is a strong association between the level of sex activity and holidays without parents among the boys ($p = 0.001$), but not among the girls (NSS). It was found that 36 per cent N-boys, 55 per cent I-boys and 64 per cent E-boys went on holidays without their parents; but 41 per cent N-girls, 53 per cent I-girls and 49 per cent E-girls went on holidays without parents.

In a few cases (5 per cent) the teenagers were without parental supervision as the parents went away and they stayed at home. It would be inadvisable to make any judgements on this situation because although some had the house to themselves and took the opportunity to throw a teenage party, others were restrained by the presence in the home of elder siblings or other relations. But we did attempt to discover if they ever got the chance to entertain their friends away from the presence of their parents.

Nearly half (45 per cent boys, 44 per cent girls) said they never had the house to themselves so that they could entertain their friends, but several (17 per cent) boys and a few (9 per cent) girls were able to do this while their parents were away, and many more (35 per cent boys, 43 per cent girls) were able to do this when their parents went out for the day or the evening; 3 per cent of the boys and 4 per cent of the girls did not live at home and so the question did not arise.

Many of the results of this research show that the behaviour of teenagers depends upon the facilities available and this factor is no exception for there is a strong association between the level of sex activity and the opportunity to entertain friends at home without parents for both boys ($p = 0.001$) and for girls ($p = 0.01$). Boys, and to a lesser extent girls, who occasionally have the house to themselves are likely to have more sexual experience. Many more E-boys had the opportunity to bring back their friends to their home when their parents were not there. The I-girls had this opportunity more often than the E-girls, but both of these groups entertained without their parents far more often than the N-girls. This suggests that facilities in the home are an important factor and the suggestion that teenagers will find a way to express their sexual desires whatever parental restrictions are imposed cannot be confirmed by the results of this research.

E. Parental Circumstances and Attitudes

Two-thirds of the teenagers did not go to church or chapel or any form of religious meeting. About one in every ten went less than once a month. This leaves about a quarter who attended church with any kind of regularity; only 14 per cent of the boys and 19 per cent of the girls said they went every week.

Church attendance was strongly associated with the levels of sex activity both for the boys ($p = 0.001$) and for the girls ($p = 0.001$). We found that 44 per cent of the N-boys went to church at least once a month compared with 22 per cent I-boys and 11 per cent E-boys; 32 per cent of the N-girls went to church at least once a month compared with 31 per cent of the I-girls and 9 per cent of the E-girls. So those who did go to church were far less likely to be sexually experienced. Only one in ten of the experienced boys and girls went to church at least once a month compared with one in three of the other teenagers.

But there was very little difference between the level of sex activities and the various denominations. Neither boys nor girls from the Church of England, the Nonconformist churches, the Roman Catholic Church or the Jewish faith were more or less likely to be non-experienced, inceptive or experienced (NSS). The only exception to this general conclusion is between Roman Catholic boys and girls. The Catholic boys are likely to be neither more nor less experienced than the average, but the level of sex activity among Catholic girls is less than for other denominations. But many of these young people were not interested in religion and their answer to this question merely reflected the religious affiliations of their parents.

The teenagers were also asked if their parents went to church. In 10 per cent of the homes both parents went to church; in 11 per cent, only the mother regularly went to church, and in 2 per cent, only the father attended church.

Rather unexpectedly there was no association between parental church-going and the levels of sex activity. So although their own church-going was very relevant to their sex behaviour, whether or not they came from a religious home did not appear to be pertinent.

This is in line with the overall impression created by comparing the level of sex activity with the home situation. The circumstances in the home do not appear to be an important influence on the young people's sexual behaviour, but the attitude and actions taken by the parents are much more important. So we find that teenagers are not much affected in this respect by the number of times they moved home, by an absent parent or a broken home, by their social class (except for girls) or their mother's job before marriage, by their position in the family, by their religious affiliation or by the church-going of their parents.

On the other hand we have seen that the relations with the parents and their marital happiness, the discipline in the home and the opportunities and facilities provided, and in particular the interest and concern of the parents for their teenage children and the amount of time they spend together, all seem to be important influences on the sexual development of the adolescent.

9. Education and Work

A. School Record

In Section F of Chapter 3 we found only slight variations in the sexual behaviour of adolescents from different types of schools. The largest difference was between secondary modern and grammar schools. Boys who attended grammar schools were likely to be less experienced ($p = 0.01$), and so were girls ($p = 0.001$). Boys who went to private school were neither more nor less experienced, but the proportion of I-girls from private schools was greater than chance ($p = 0.02$). Teenagers who were not N-girls or N-boys tended to be inceptive if they went to grammar or private schools, but tended to be experienced if they went to secondary modern or comprehensive schools.

There is absolutely no difference as regards the level of sex activity between girls who went to a co-educational school and those who went to a segregated school (NSS). There was a very slight tendency for the E-boys to come from a co-educational school and the N-boys and I-boys to come from a segregated school (NSS). There was no sign of an association between the level of sex activity and teenagers who went to a boarding or day school. Although there were only a few (5 per cent) boarders among the teenagers, they appeared to be neither more nor less experienced than the school children who lived at home.

In our sample 45 per cent of the older boys and 40 per cent of the older girls had taken the 'O' level GCE examination. Those who had taken this exam tended to be less experienced than the others ($p = 0.001$ for boys; $p = 0.01$ for girls). Among the boys 45 per cent of the non-experienced, 52 per cent of the inceptive and 25 per cent of the experienced had taken GCE; 31 per cent of the N-girls, 45 per cent of the I-girls and 29 per cent of the E-girls had taken the exam. There is no difference in the level of sex activity between those who passed in five or more subjects and those who passed in four or less (NSS).

On the other hand boys who passed 'A' level GCE tended to

have less experience than other boys ($p = 0.01$), but this was not true of girls (NSS). There is probably some slight correlation between academic attainment and the level of sex activity, but a more important influence is the age they leave school.

At the time of the interview 14 per cent of the older boys and 7 per cent of the older girls were still at school. Among the others it was found that there is an association between the level of sex activity and the age they left school for boys ($p = 0.05$) and for girls ($p = 0.01$). E-boys and E-girls were more likely to leave school at fifteen but those who stayed on were as likely to be inceptive as non-experienced.

It is interesting to note that those who have attained higher academic standards and those who stay on at school tend to be inceptive but not experienced. A similar tendency was found among middle-class teenagers (Chapter 8). For some reason working-class teenagers who leave school at the statutory minimum age do not remain at the inceptive stage for long; but middle-class teenagers and those who stay on at school appear to get more satisfaction from inceptive behaviour.

All the teenagers, whether they had left school or not, were asked if they liked school. Their replies were classified into three categories. About a half (57 per cent boys, 48 per cent girls) said they liked being at school; another third (30 per cent boys, 29 per cent girls) said they had mixed feelings; fewer boys (13 per cent) than girls (23 per cent) said they disliked school.

Teenagers who disliked being at school were much more likely to be E-boys ($p = 0.01$) or E-girls ($p = 0.001$). Only 11 per cent of the N-boys said they disliked school compared with 22 per cent of the E-boys; 17 per cent of the N-girls said they disliked school compared with 38 per cent of the E-girls.

Two-thirds (63 per cent) of the boys and nearly half (45 per cent) of the girls said they had no special problems at school. Others mentioned such things as the teachers (12 per cent), the work (10 per cent), the discipline (7 per cent) and many other things. There is an association between the level of sex activity and those who had problems at school. Among the boys 30 per cent of the non-experienced, 36 per cent of the inceptives and 46 per cent of the experienced had school problems of one kind or another ($p = 0.02$).

A similar tendency was found among the girls ($p = 0\cdot01$); 48 per cent of the N-girls, 56 per cent of the I-girls and 70 per cent of the E-girls had special problems at school. Thus many of the teenagers were pleased to leave school as soon as possible, and these were often the ones who would have the most sexual experience.

Some of the teenagers continued with their formal education after they had left school; 23 per cent of the boys were attending evening classes at the time of the interview; most (18 per cent) were taking vocational subjects that were directly related to their work, but a few (3 per cent) were going to evening classes in general education, and a few (2 per cent) were going to classes to get further information about hobbies or leisure pursuits. Not so many girls went to evening classes; altogether 12 per cent attended, made up of 7 per cent going to classes on vocational subjects, 1 per cent on general education and 4 per cent on leisure pursuits. There appears to be no relationship between the level of sex activity and attendance at evening class (NSS).

A comparison was made between those who went to evening class twice a week or more often, and those who went once a week or less. But it was found that there was no association between the level of sex activity and the number of times a teenager attended evening class (NSS). It has been suggested that those who continue with their education have less sex experience because they have less free time, and this may be the case for those still at school; but it does not seem to apply to those who go to evening classes who have the same amount of sex experience however many classes they attend.

Although there are small signs of difference in intelligence (as shown by the type of school and exam results) between the sexually experienced and the others, the main differences seem to be personality factors; E-boys and E-girls had more problems at school, had lost interest, and wanted to leave as soon as possible.

B. Occupational Record

In our sample 80 per cent of the boys and 82 per cent of the girls were in full-time employment; 2 per cent and 5 per cent respectively were unemployed. This left 14 per cent of the boys who were at school, 4 per cent at university; 7 per cent of the girls were still at school with 6 per cent at university or technical college.

Boys who were working were more likely to be sexually experienced ($p = 0\cdot01$). Only 8 per cent of the E-boys were at school or college. Among the girls those with experience seemed more likely to be unemployed, but the numbers are small (NSS); 5 per cent of the N-girls, 3 per cent of the I-girls and 10 per cent of the E-girls had left school but were out of work at the time when they were interviewed. The number of girls at work did not differ (82 per cent at all three levels), but 14 per cent of the N-girls, 16 per cent of the I-girls and 8 per cent of the E-girls were at school or college, which shows a trend similar to that found among the boys although the numbers are too small for it to be statistically significant (NSS).

A quarter (29 per cent) of the boys were in non-manual jobs and half (51 per cent) were in manual jobs. With the girls it was the other way round; half (57 per cent) were doing non-manual work and a quarter (24 per cent) were doing manual work. Although it was possible to detect a slight tendency for non-manual workers to be inceptive and manual workers to be experienced, in fact the association between the levels of sex activity and manual or non-manual jobs was only just significant for girls ($p = 0\cdot05$), and not significant for boys (NSS).

When the teenagers were asked if they liked their job, a large number (52 per cent boys, 44 per cent girls) said they were very content, others (22 per cent boys, 26 per cent girls) were fairly content but had some reservations, and only a few (7 per cent boys, 10 per cent girls) said they did not like their job. It has often been said that one of the causes of teenage misbehaviour is boredom; if this is the case, then it would appear that the boys and girls are bored during their leisure, for the vast majority seem to be happy in their work.

Among the girls there was a slight tendency for the least contented to be the most experienced ($p = 0\cdot05$), but this tendency was not apparent among the boys (NSS); indeed as many as 57 per cent of the E-boys said they were very content with their job compared with 54 per cent of the N-boys and 45 per cent of the I-boys who said they were very content; among the girls who were very content with their work, 48 per cent were N-girls, 44 per cent were I-girls and 32 per cent were E-girls.

T – E

Job contentment notwithstanding, one in five (20 per cent) boys and over a quarter (28 per cent) of the girls had been in three or more jobs during the short time in which they had been in employment. The more experienced a boy is, the more jobs he is likely to have had ($p = 0.01$), and there is a similar association between sex experience and the number of jobs for girls ($p = 0.001$). Half the E-girls and nearly a third (31 per cent) of the E-boys had been in more than two jobs; only 7 per cent of the N-boys have had four or more jobs, compared with 19 per cent of the E-boys; only 6 per cent of the N-girls have had four or more jobs compared with 25 per cent of the E-girls.

There is an association between the level of sex activity and their weekly wage for boys ($p = 0.01$) and for girls ($p = 0.02$). Those who are paid high wages are more likely to be sexually experienced. The difference between the N-boys and the E-boys would be even more striking were it not for the I-boys who, in this case, are not in a midway position; in general they seem to make rather less than the N-boys. Thus it can be seen that the difference in wages between boys who have experienced sexual intercourse (E-boys), and those who have not (N- and I-boys), is very great indeed.

The trend is very similar for the girls. Although the girls are paid less than the boys overall, the dividing line is still between the E-girls and the others. As with the boys, the I-girls do not make more money than the N-girls; the experienced girls usually get much higher wages than the inceptive or non-experienced girls.

A special effort was made during the interview to get an estimate of the amount of money each individual had left to spend. Starting from the amount received in wages, we found out and deducted the amount paid in rent or given to the parents to pay for their keep; we further deducted any other unavoidable or regular outgoings such as fares and other commitments, but not money paid for hire purchase or into a clothing or Christmas club. This was worked out between the teenager and the interviewer until they arrived at an agreed sum that was left to spend in an average week. For teenagers still at school the sum was calculated after deductions had been made from the pocket money allowed by parents or the grant in the case of students at college.

The amount of spending money available to these teenagers

aged seventeen to nineteen spread over a wide range. For 5 per cent of the boys and 4 per cent of the girls there was less than ten shillings a week; at the other end of the scale 7 per cent of the boys and 2 per cent of the girls had more than seven pounds a week to spend. But the majority had between one and four pounds each week; 39 per cent of the boys and 39 per cent of the girls had under two pounds; 37 per cent of the boys and 43 per cent of the girls had between two and four pounds; 24 per cent of the boys and 18 per cent of the girls had over four pounds to spend each week.

There is a very strong association between spending money and the level of sex activity. Boys who have a lot of money to spend are much more likely to be experienced ($p = 0.001$); and this is also true of girls ($p = 0.02$). Only 5 per cent of the N-boys and 3 per cent of the I-boys have over six pounds a week to spend, but 24 per cent of the E-boys have this amount. Only 16 per cent of the N-girls and 18 per cent of the I-girls have over four pounds to spend, but 30 per cent of the E-girls have this amount to spend.

It is possible that many of the factors noted in this chapter are interconnected. It might be argued that teenagers who left school at fifteen had more sexual experience because there were more opportunities and facilities for sex after they had started work. But we believe it is a kind of restlessness that impels the E-boys and E-girls to leave school.

Perhaps one might expect the E-boys and E-girls to be earning more because they have had a longer working career. In fact it is the blind alley jobs that pay the highest wages in youth employment. It might also be said that the sexually experienced teenagers had more jobs because they were in employment over a longer period; if they left school at fifteen, they would have been at work for about three years by the time we interviewed them, whereas others who left school at seventeen or sixteen would have been at work for only one or two years, and so would have had less time to change jobs as often. But even allowing for this there is a large difference between the number of times the experienced teenagers changed their jobs, and the relatively few times the others changed; and this seems to indicate that a kind of vocational restlessness is associated with sex activity among teenagers.

10. Groups

A. Group Membership

As the child grows up he becomes less dependent on his family and mixes with friends outside the home. In our sample the amount of time spent at home depended upon the age of the teenager. Among the younger age groups a third (33 per cent) of the boys and almost half (45 per cent) of the girls spent more time with their families than outside the home; but among the older teenagers, only a fifth (19 per cent) of the boys and a third of the girls (35 per cent) spent more time at home.

There was an association between the level of sex activity and the amount of time spent away from their families; E-boys were much more likely to spend more of their free time outside the home ($p = 0.001$) and so were E-girls ($p = 0.02$). This association is independent of the age influence because it will be remembered that in this part of the report (Chapters 8–11) only the older age groups are being used to test the relationship of sex activities with other factors.

Questions about groups are not always successful because the interviewee is not always clear what is meant. The boundaries of such groups tend to be nebulous and their membership is constantly changing. First of all we asked about their leisure activities (reported in the next chapter) and then we asked about the people with whom they spent most of their time after work or school and at week-ends. Assuming that a group comprised three or more people including the person being interviewed, we found that about three-quarters (74 per cent) of the older boys and about two-thirds (64 per cent) of the older girls went round with a particular group of friends.

There is an association between the level of sex activity and group membership both for boys ($p = 0.01$) and for girls ($p = 0.05$). Those who were in mixed groups were most likely to be sexually experienced; furthermore many of the boys who went round in single sex groups were also sexually experienced, but this was not often the case with the girls.

The influence of the group varied considerably from one person to another. Among the boys nearly half (49 per cent) met the group at least three times a week, and a fifth (19 per cent) met daily. The girls tended to meet less frequently; a quarter (26 per cent) met three or more times a week, but only 7 per cent said they met every day. The association between the level of sex activity and the time spent with the group is strong for boys ($p = 0.02$), but not so strong for girls (NSS).

Most teenage groups have a recognized meeting-place where they foregather at least at the start of an evening. Often it was in one of their homes (18 per cent), at a youth club (7 per cent) or at school (2 per cent). Other groups met in commercial premises such as bars (12 per cent), dance halls (8 per cent) or coffee bars (6 per cent). A few (4 per cent) said they met outside, another 12 per cent mentioned other meeting-places and the remaining 31 per cent were not members of a group.

We found there was a difference in the level of sex activity between those who met in their homes or youth clubs, and those who met in dance halls, coffee bars or licensed premises for both boys ($p = 0.02$) and girls ($p = 0.01$). Both N-boys and N-girls were more likely to meet at home or in youth clubs, and E-boys and E-girls were more likely to meet in commercial premises.

B. The Influence of the Group

As the adolescent spends more and more time in a teenage group, he begins to adopt opinions and beliefs obtained from his friends, and sometimes these attitudes are in conflict with the opinions and beliefs of his parents.

All the teenagers were asked if they would prefer to talk over a personal problem with their parents or with someone else. Over half (54 per cent) said they would go to their parents for advice, but 20 per cent of the boys and 30 per cent of the girls said they would go to someone of their own age. It was found that N-boys are much more likely to go to their parents for advice ($p = 0.01$) and this was also true of N-girls ($p = 0.05$).

Some of the teenagers said they would seek advice from their brothers or sisters, or adults other than their parents, but 11 per cent of the boys and 3 per cent of the girls said that if they had a personal problem they would keep it to themselves and not tell anyone. There seemed to be no association between these self-sufficient or lonely people, and their level of sex activity.

Later in the interview a similar question was asked, except that this time the problem was specified as something to do with sex. In these circumstances the E-girls were even less likely to go to their parents for advice ($p = 0.001$). The E-boys were also less likely to seek advice from their parents ($p = 0.01$).

An indirect attempt was made to see if their standards of sexual behaviour were influenced by other teenagers. Everyone was asked: Do you think your friends have more or less sex experience than you? Not surprisingly 34 per cent of the boys and 29 per cent of the girls answered that the behaviour of their friends varied – some had more, some less. But the others gave fairly definite replies.

I'm in the middle – a few more, a few less. Some of them go out looking for tarts. (boy, aged 18)

Most of them exaggerate, but some are quite a bit more experienced than me. (boy, aged 16)

Far more. They seem to revel in it. (girl, aged 18)

My friend said, 'Digger's only this size', and we all said, 'o-oh, she should know'. (girl, aged 17)

I have less, I should think. I've heard boys talking about me, say: 'She's a cold fish'. (girl, aged 19)

I don't think anyone could have less than me. (girl, aged 16)

I suppose boys don't like me because I look small and childish. (girl, aged 17)

Most of them have less sex than me. I think I'm better looking really. (boy, aged 18)

About a third (30 per cent boys, 31 per cent girls) thought their friends had about the same amount of experience, and about the same number (27 per cent boys, 35 per cent girls) thought their friends had more sex experience; only 7 per cent of the boys and 5 per cent of the girls thought their friends were less experienced. Most teenagers, whatever their level of sex activity, felt their friends were having as much sex as they were, if not more.

C. Close Friends

In Section E of Chapter 4 we noted that teenagers who start dating at an early age were more likely to have sexual intercourse. In fact there is a strong association between the age of the first date and the level of sex activity for boys ($p = 0.001$) and for girls ($p = 0.001$). There is a similar association between the age of the first kiss and sex activity for boys ($p = 0.001$) and girls ($p = 0.001$). But the age when they start dating is not the only significant association; there also appears to be an association between the duration, and so the strength, of the relationship. The E-boys were much more likely to date a girl over a long period ($p = 0.001$) and so were the E-girls ($p = 0.01$).

Over a third of the boys (38 per cent) said they had a steady girl friend at the time of the interview, and still more (58 per cent) girls said they had a steady boy friend. We did not attempt to define what was meant by steady when we asked this question, but we did ask them how long they had been going out with their steady girl or boy friend. In fact 2 per cent of both boys and girls had been going out with their steady for less than a month, while 7 per cent had been going out less than three months. On the other hand there were some long relationships, for 15 per cent of the boys and 27 per cent of the girls had been going out for over a year.

We felt that any relationship which had been going on for more than three months could reasonably be called steady. On this definition 30 per cent of the boys and 52 per cent of the girls were going steady. Not altogether surprisingly there is a strong association between the boys with steady girl friends and their level of sex activity ($p = 0.001$). There is a similar association between girls with boy friends and the level of sex activity ($p = 0.01$).

More specifically the teenagers were asked if they were in love. Over a quarter (29 per cent) of the boys and exactly half (50 per cent) of the girls said they were in love at the time the interview took place; a further 21 per cent of the boys and 15 per cent of the girls had been in love in the past, leaving half (50 per cent) the boys and a third (35 per cent) of the girls who said they had never been in love. There is a strong association between those who have been in love and the level of sex activity ($p = 0.001$ for both boys and girls).

The girls were much more likely to say they were engaged; 16 per cent of the girls compared with 4 per cent of the boys said they were engaged. This suggests there is a misunderstanding between many courting couples; the girl feels sure that they are going to get married, but the boy thinks that he has not yet committed himself. But another reason for the difference is that many teenage girls marry boys who would be too old to qualify as teenagers for this research. In 1966, 21 per cent of all the girls aged nineteen in England and Wales were married, but only 4 per cent of the nineteen-year-old boys were married.* Over a quarter (27 per cent) of the older girls said they hoped to be married before they were twenty-one compared with only 8 per cent of the older boys. Even more (38 per cent) of the younger girls hoped to marry before they were twenty-one compared with 9 per cent of the younger boys. Marriage is a much more immediate prospect for a teenage girl than it is for a teenage boy.

Among the girls who said they had steady boy friends, 15 per cent were having sexual intercourse with them; among the girls who were engaged, 37 per cent were having sexual intercourse with their fiancés. Among the boys with steadies, 41 per cent were having sexual intercourse with their girl friends; among the few boys who were engaged, 39 per cent were having sexual intercourse with their fiancées. This suggests that a large number of the sexually experienced teenagers have premarital intercourse with very close friends, and often with the person they will eventually marry. This is confirmed by the fact that a third of the E-boys and three-quarters of the E-girls had sexual intercourse with one partner only in the last year, and 25 per cent of the E-boys and 65 per cent of the E-girls have never had intercourse with more than one partner.

In addition to the engaged couples who decide to have sexual intercourse before their wedding day, there are also courting couples who decide to get married when it is found that the girl is pregnant. This further increases the number of experienced teenagers who only have premarital intercourse with the person they

* From the Registrar-General's *Review* of 1966.

will marry. It seems likely that much of the premarital sexual activity of teenagers is not promiscuous behaviour.

Some people seem to use the word promiscuity as if it means the same thing as premarital intercourse. But promiscuity is usually taken to mean sexual intercourse with several partners over a period of time. We found that those who were most active sexually had intercourse with only one person, while those who had many sexual partners had intercourse less often. People often equate promiscuity with debauchery, but it is our impression that the boys who wish to be promiscuous spend a lot of time looking for girls, but are not often successful in finding willing partners.

D. Friends as a Source of Information

Precocious boys who learn about sex at an early age are more likely to be sexually experienced by the time they are eighteen ($p = 0.001$); only 14 per cent of the N-boys knew the facts of life before the age of twelve compared with 34 per cent of the E-boys; and 48 per cent of the N-boys were over fourteen before they found out compared with 31 per cent of the E-boys. This association between the levels of sex activity and early knowledge about sex does not seem to apply to girls (NSS).

But the source of this information is more important for girls than for boys. Girls who first heard about the facts of life from their parents are likely to be N-girls or I-girls ($p = 0.05$); there appears to be a similar tendency for the N-boys but the figures are smaller (NSS). Those who get their first information about sex from their teachers are also more likely to be N-girls ($p = 0.01$), but this is not true for boys (NSS). By far the largest number of people learnt the facts of life from their school friends and this was strongly associated with the level of sex activity for both girls ($p = 0.001$) and boys ($p = 0.001$).

Girls who had never received any advice about sex from their parents at any time were more likely to be E-girls ($p = 0.05$); 26 per cent of the N-girls, 30 per cent of the I-girls and 41 per cent of the E-girls had never received any advice about sex from their parents. This did not apply to the boys (NSS); two-thirds (67 per cent) of the boys, whatever their level of sex activity, had never received any advice about sex from their parents.

In Section B of this chapter it was found that the more experience a girl had, the less likely she was to go to her parents for advice about sex ($p = 0.001$); 59 per cent of the N-girls, 42 per cent of the I-girls, but only 22 per cent of the E-girls would go to their parents. The experienced boys were also less likely to seek advice from their parents ($p = 0.01$); 58 per cent of the N-boys, 46 per cent of the I-boys and 36 per cent of the E-boys said they would go to their parents. So the teenagers who are most likely to have a serious sex problem are also those who are least likely to go to their parents for help.

Sex education seems to have had remarkably little effect on the subsequent sex behaviour of the teenagers. Rather less than half the boys received sex education at school. Those who were given some form of sex education were neither more nor less experienced in their sexual activities (NSS). More girls received sex education, but there is no association between those who received it and the level of sex activity (NSS). Nearly half the older boys (47 per cent) and girls (43 per cent) thought they should have been told more about sex at school, but this desire for more information was equally prevalent in all three levels of sex activity (NSS).

About half the boys felt they knew all there was to know about sex; just as many of these were N-boys, I-boys or E-boys (NSS). Among the girls the percentage who felt they knew all about sex was about the same for N-girls (47 per cent) or E-girls (52 per cent); it was the I-girls who were the least confident for only 36 per cent of those felt they knew all there was to know ($p = 0.05$).

In Chapter 6 it was reported that only a few teenagers would be able to identify venereal disease. It was found that boys with good knowledge about VD were much more likely to be experienced ($p = 0.001$), and this was also true of the experienced girls ($p = 0.01$). We found good knowledge about VD in 8 per cent of the N-boys, 11 per cent of the I-boys and 27 per cent of the E-boys; 9 per cent of the N-girls, 12 per cent of the I-girls and 20 per cent of the E-girls appeared to be correctly informed about VD. Among the boys with experience of sexual intercourse 35 per cent revealed only slight knowledge of VD and 38 per cent appeared to have no knowledge at all. Among the experienced girls 52 per cent revealed slight knowledge and 28 per cent had no knowledge. It appears, therefore, that three-quarters of the boys at risk and four out of five girls at risk would not know if they had been infected.

It has already been reported (Section D, Chapter 6) that the majority of teenagers with experience of sexual intercourse do not use contraceptives; 25 per cent of the E-boys and 61 per cent of the E-girls never used any method of birth control. It is difficult to know if this is due to lack of knowledge or lack of concern. But this section has shown that knowledge on sexual matters is not a pre-requisite of premarital intercourse.

The sexually active teenagers tended to find out about sex from their friends and to eschew information or advice from their parents. Sex education given in the schools does not seem to have inhibited sex activities nor does it seem to have encouraged it 'by putting ideas into their heads' as some have feared. Many teenagers think they know all about sex whether they have had practical experience or not. In fact those with sexual experience are slightly more informed, but good knowledge about sexual matters is far from widespread.

The results reported in this chapter have shown that teenage groups are an influence on sexual behaviour. The sexually experienced girl is likely to be in a mixed group and the experienced boy is likely to spend a lot of time with his group. Those who meet in commercial premises are more often sexually experienced than those who meet in youth clubs or in their own homes. Boys who are non-experienced tend to think that their friends have more sex than they do ($p = 0.05$); this, combined with the strong pressures towards conformity in teenage groups, must be one of the influences that leads a boy on to sexual experimentation.

Boys and girls who are courting have more sex experience. Many of the teenagers marry the only person with whom they have had sexual intercourse, either because they feel premarital intercourse is only permissible between couples about to be married, or because an unexpected pregnancy leads to marriage.

11. Leisure

A. Youth Clubs

The type and number of youth clubs varied considerably in the seven areas where the research was carried out. In one of the London boroughs there were hardly any facilities, but in the area we designated South A, there was one of the largest and best equipped youth clubs in the country. In the whole sample a third of the younger boys and younger girls were members of youth clubs. In the older groups 23 per cent of the boys were still members, but only 11 per cent of the girls. The girls seemed more inclined to drift away from youth clubs as they got older.

Although most of the older boys were not in a youth club, many of them were members of some kind of club or association such as a sports club (13 per cent), jazz club (4 per cent), political club (1 per cent), pre-service unit (1 per cent) or the scouts (1 per cent). The girls were less likely to join these kinds of associations although 5 per cent were in jazz clubs and 4 per cent in sports clubs.

There was no association between youth club membership and the level of sex activity (NSS). E-boys and E-girls were just as likely to be club members as not. Nor was there any difference between the boys who went to segregated clubs and those who went to mixed youth clubs (NSS). There were not enough girls in segregated clubs to be able to make this comparison.

Club members were asked when they last went to their club and this revealed a difference between the girls and boys. Although as many E-girls were still members, they tended to visit the club less often ($p = 0.01$). Only 10 per cent of the E-girls who were members had visited their clubs within the last seven days compared with 17 per cent of the I-girls and 24 per cent of the N-girls. But this association between the level of sex activity and frequency of attendance at clubs did not apply to the boys (NSS).

Much thought has been given by youth workers to the problem of the so-called unattached (Morse, 1965; Goetshius and Tash, 1966). Experiments have been made with special types of youth clubs and social centres in an attempt to attract the type of boy who would not be interested in joining an ordinary youth club. It has been felt that the limitation of the ordinary youth club has been that it only attracts the type of boy who would keep clear of trouble in any event. But so far as sex behaviour is concerned the unattached do not stand apart.

Although youth clubs have undoubtedly had some success in other problem areas, there does not seem to be much evidence to support the view of some youth leaders that premarital sexual intercourse can be prevented by persuading the boys to join a club. There is no difference in sexual behaviour between the boys who are not in a club, and those who are in mixed clubs where it is hoped they will meet 'the right type' of girls, and those who are in segregated clubs where they will not meet any girls at all.

There are some indications that experienced girls are the first to leave youth clubs as they get older. This may be because a girl with a steady boy friend may wish to spend most of her free time with him away from the club. But in any case girls are less interested in youth clubs by the time they reach the age of eighteen and the influence of the club diminishes rapidly.

B. Other Spare-Time Activities

Most boys are interested in sport and although this interest tends to diminish after they leave school, nearly two-thirds (64 per cent) of the older boys had played some kind of sport during the four weeks before the interview; about a third (30 per cent) of them were still keen on sport and had played more than once in the week before the interview. The girls were less interested, but over half (52 per cent) the older girls had played some kind of sport in the last month and 15 per cent had played twice or more in the week before the interview.

Boys who did not play any sport at any time were more likely to be sexually experienced ($p = 0.02$); 43 per cent of the N-boys, 26 per cent of the I-boys and 43 per cent of the E-boys did not play sport at all. However, among the majority who played sport at some time, there was no difference between those who played frequently and those who hardly ever played (NSS).

Much the same tendencies are to be found among the girls. Girls who played no sports at all tended to be sexually experienced ($p = 0.05$); 37 per cent of the N-girls, 36 per cent of the I-girls and 54 per cent of the E-girls had given up sport altogether. But there seemed to be very little difference between those who played often and those who hardly ever played (NSS).

Over a third (38 per cent) of the older boys had some form of transport; 10 per cent had a motor-cycle, 9 per cent had a motor-scooter and 19 per cent either had a car of their own or the use of their parents' car. But there was no association between the level of sex activity and the boys who used any of these forms of transport (NSS). Those who had cars or motor-cycles were not more experienced than those who did not have them. Nor was there any difference between the motor-cyclists and those with scooters.

In the past audience measurements have shown that the segment of the population least interested in television is the teenage group, but since the advent of the pop music programmes especially designed to attract the teenage viewer, it seems likely that the influence of TV is growing. Everyone was asked what they had done on the evening before the interview and on the previous Saturday. Television was mentioned more than any other activity by boys and girls on both weekdays and week-ends. The other frequent activities for boys on weekdays are visiting, drinking, studying and sport; at the week-end it is a pub, a cinema, a dance or visiting friends. The most frequent activities after watching TV for girls on weekdays are visiting friends, listening to records and entertaining friends at home; at week-ends they are visiting, drinking, dancing and the cinema.

A third (31 per cent) of the boys and a quarter (27 per cent) of the girls watched television at some point of the weekday evening and even on Saturday night, when most teenagers would expect to be out of the home, 18 per cent had seen television for at least part of the evening. When they were asked how many evenings a week they watched television, 10 per cent of both boys and girls said they watched six or seven nights a week. Among the others about a third (34 per cent) watched between three and five nights a week, and about half (56 per cent) watched less often or hardly ever. But there are no indications that TV has an influence on their sexual behaviour; those who watched television most often were neither more nor less likely to be sexually experienced.

Teenagers go to the cinema more often than most people. In this sample 9 per cent went more than once a week and another 32 per cent went every week; another 27 per cent of the boys and 34 per cent of the girls went less than once a week but more than once a month. Only 31 per cent of the boys and 25 per cent of the girls went less than once a month.

Although there is little difference between the amount boys and girls went to the cinema, there is a difference in the association between this and the level of sex activity. Experienced boys go to the cinema more often ($p = 0.001$), but cinema-going and sexual experience are not related for girls (NSS).

But the person they usually accompanied to the cinema is significant for girls as well as boys. Many of the boys (46 per cent) said they usually went to the cinema with their girl friend and even more of the girls (62 per cent) went with their boy friend. There is a strong association between the level of sex activity and those who went to the cinema with their girl or boy friends ($p = 0.001$ for boys and girls). The numbers are high for I-boys and I-girls, as well as for E-boys and E-girls. The darkness inside a cinema provides one of the few semi-private places where a boy and girl can go to make love.

The last activity considered in this section is dancing. The teenagers were asked when they last went to a dance and this included dances at youth clubs and jazz clubs as well as at commercial dance halls. Although pop music and new forms of dancing are thought of as endemic to the teenage world, in fact the frequencies are not as high as might be expected. Only 4 per cent of the boys and 6 per cent of the girls went dancing three or more times a week. Among the boys a quarter (26 per cent) went dancing at least once a week, a third (37 per cent) went less often, and the rest (37 per cent) hardly ever or never went to a dance. The girls went a bit more often; 31 per cent at least once a week, 40 per cent went less often, and 29 per cent hardly ever or never went. As with the cinema, there is an association for boys ($p = 0.001$), but not for girls (NSS), between dancing and the level of sex activity.

Again as with the cinema, the person they went with to the dance was more important for the girls than the number of times they went. Although many (31 per cent) girls went to dances with other girls, and some (11 per cent) went in a mixed group, the largest proportion went with their boy friends. These girls who went dancing with their boy friends were more likely to be experienced than those who went with other people ($p = 0.05$).

This association was not found among the boys. Although 23 per cent usually took their girl friend with them when they went dancing, these boys were not likely to be more experienced than those who went with other boys (37 per cent) or in a mixed group (10 per cent). So for a boy the level of sex activity for both cinema-going and dancing is associated with the number of times he goes but for a girl it depends whether she goes with her boy friend or not. As we have already noted (Section C of Chapter 10) girls with steady boy friends tend to be more experienced whether they go to the cinema and dances or not, and this may be influencing the association which we found for girls. But the clear-cut association between sex experience and both cinema-going and dancing among the boys is unaffected by the person they went with, and can be taken as a sign of gregariousness, a characteristic which will be discussed in Chapter 13.

C. Parties

Although by no means the most frequent teenage activity, we made special and detailed inquiries about parties because it has been alleged that many of these teenage gatherings are specifically arranged to facilitate sexual activities. Those teenagers who admitted getting drunk, often said it was at a party; 32 per cent of the older teenagers said they had got drunk at a party, compared with 17 per cent at a public house, 4 per cent at their own home, 3 per cent at someone else's home; 5 per cent mentioned other places and 39 per cent had never been drunk.

In Chapter 8 it was noted that about half (52 per cent) of the boys and girls sometimes had the house to themselves, and it can be assumed that in many of these cases it was possible to throw a party. At all events teenagers who could entertain at home were often the experienced teenagers. But of course teenagers can go to many parties given by friends even if they are unable to hold a party at their own home without the supervision of their parents.

Only 11 per cent of the boys and 7 per cent of the girls said they had never been to a party. But parties vary enormously from the staid to the riotous. We tried to define what we meant by a party by asking about the age of the other people at the last party they attended. If it was obviously not a children's or a family party, and it was not supervised by parents, then by our definition it was a *teenage* party if most of the people were the same age as the interviewee, and an *adult* party if most of the people there were older.

We found that the last party attended by 57 per cent of the boys and 41 per cent of the girls was a teenage party, and for 11 per cent of the boys and 26 per cent of the girls it was an adult party. So girls were more likely than boys to go to parties where most of the other people were older. Boys who attended teenage or adult parties were as likely to be I-boys as E-boys, but were less likely to be N-boys ($p = 0.01$). Girls who went to teenage or adult parties were most often I-girls, not so often E-girls or N-girls (NSS). The teenagers were also asked how often they had been to a party when there were no parents in the house. There was an association between the level of sex activity and the number of times a boy or girl had been to a party without parental supervision ($p = 0.001$ for boys and girls).

In Chapter 8 it was noted that there was an association between the level of sex activity and the time a teenager was expected back from a party ($p = 0.02$ for boys, and $p = 0.01$ for girls). More specifically those who attended teenage or adult parties were asked how many of the parties had lasted past midnight. This is quite a common occurrence for half the E-boys, and for a quarter of the I-boys, I-girls and E-girls. There is a strong association between the level of sex activity and the number of times they went to parties which lasted past midnight ($p = 0.001$ for boys and girls).

A similar association is found between the level of sex activity and those who have been to all-night parties ($p = 0.001$ for boys and girls) although this happened much more infrequently. Among the boys 15 per cent had been to an all-night party more than twice, and nearly all of them were E-boys. Among the girls 11 per cent had been to an all-night party more than twice, half of them E-girls and half I-girls. But there were many experienced and inceptive boys and girls who had not been to this kind of party.

This detailed consideration of teenage party-going shows that it is not the number of parties attended but the type of party that appears to be associated with sexual experience. Not surprisingly parties without parental supervision tend to be more permissive. There is also a strong association between sex experience and the length of time the party goes on.

Although this section has shown that sex experience is associated with party-going and especially a particular type of party, it is possible to exaggerate the importance of this. Only 3 per cent of the older boys (10 per cent of all E-boys) met their first sexual partner at a party and only 2 per cent (7 per cent of all E-boys) had their first experience of sexual intercourse at a party; 2 per cent of the older girls (8 per cent of the E-girls) met their first sexual partner at a party and 2 per cent (7 per cent of the E-girls) had their first experience of sexual intercourse at a party.

D. Drinking and Smoking

All of the boys in the younger age group of boys were under eighteen and so legally prohibited from obtaining alcoholic drinks in a public house. In fact over a hundred (21 per cent) went to a pub at least once a week. In the older age group which we are considering in this chapter, 27 per cent were under eighteen. Over half (57 per cent) the older boys had been to a bar in the week before the interview, another 13 per cent in the previous month and another 14 per cent in the last six months; 16 per cent had never been to a bar.

Girls do not go out drinking quite so often, but the number who had been to a public house recently was not very much smaller; 43 per cent had been to a bar in the week before the interview, another 20 per cent in the previous month and another 17 per cent in the last six months; 19 per cent had never been to a bar.

According to the boys they usually went to a bar with friends of the same sex (65 per cent), less often with a mixed group (7 per cent), relatives (6 per cent) or their girl friends (5 per cent). According to the girls they usually went with their boy friends (46 per cent), in a mixed group (23 per cent) or with relatives (12 per cent). The discrepancy is probably accounted for by the fact that during a typical week the boys go with their male friends on one day and with their girl friend on another occasion.

There is a strong association between the level of sex activity and the number of times a boy or girl goes to a public house ($p = 0.001$ for both groups). E-boys went much more often and N-boys went much less often, and the same is true for girls. The usual drink for the boys was beer or stout (73 per cent) with cider (9 per cent), spirits (8 per cent) and soft drinks (6 per cent) coming a long way behind. The usual drink for the girls was spread over a wider range; 28 per cent usually had spirits, 20 per cent soft drinks, 20 per cent beer, 18 per cent cider (including champagne perry) and 13 per cent port or sherry wines.

They were asked if they had 'ever been a bit drunk'. No further definition was given and the teenager was left to answer according to his own estimation of whether he had been drunk or not. A third (33 per cent) of the boys said they had never been drunk, another third (34 per cent) said they had been drunk once or twice and the other third (33 per cent) said they had been drunk from three to ten times. No one said he had been drunk more than ten times. Fewer girls admitted to being drunk; 44 per cent had never been drunk, 38 per cent once or twice and 18 per cent three or more times.

Perhaps it will not be a surprise to find that there is a strong association between the level of sex activity and the number of times a person has been drunk ($p = 0.001$ for boys and girls), but the extent of the association may be surprising. Only a few N-boys (14 per cent) or N-girls (6 per cent) have been drunk more than twice, but over half the E-boys (56 per cent) and nearly half the E-girls (45 per cent) have been drunk three or more times in their own estimation. Conversely only a few (11 per cent) of the E-boys or E-girls have not been drunk.

The rise of coffee bars in the last decade has been much appreciated by the teenage population as it provides one of the few indoor places where they can meet. In the previous chapter it was noted that it was one of the places where teenage groups meet. Over a third (37 per cent) of the boys and a quarter (28 per cent) of the girls had been to a coffee bar in the week before they were interviewed, and another 18 per cent of the boys and 15 per cent of the girls had visited one in the previous month. Although there is no association between the level of sex activity and the last time the girls went to a coffee bar (NSS), this association does hold for boys ($p = 0.01$). A quarter (28 per cent) of the N-boys, a third (36 per cent) of the I-boys and half (50 per cent) the E-boys had been to a coffee bar within seven days of the interview.

The number of heroin addicts under twenty on the Home Office register (which is a list of people known to be addicted to opiates) increased from none in 1959 to 395 in 1967. But in the recent public outcry about teenage drug taking, it is sometimes forgotten that the number of young people dependent on these hard drugs (heroin, morphine, cocaine and pethidine) is a very small proportion of the whole. During this research we encountered a small group of teenagers who were experimenting with cannabis and we learnt about clubs and coffee bars where drugs could be obtained. Although there are signs that some teenagers are turning to cannabis (reefers) and amphetamines (pep pills) instead of alcohol, over the whole teenage population the proportion is still small; only a few of the boys and girls had ever tried cannabis and none in our sample had tried any of the hard drugs.

These numbers are too small to relate drug taking to sex behaviour. But it is certain that the statements made by Chief Constables and others who link drug taking with wild sexual orgies are mistaken. Indeed these drugs are more likely to decrease sexual performance than to encourage it. Furthermore the teenager who becomes dependent on drugs tends to be the more inward-looking and self-centred personality type, whereas the information reported in the next chapter shows that the personality characteristics of the sexually experienced teenager is more likely to be outgoing and gregarious.

Not many teenagers seem to be interested in gambling. Among the boys 10 per cent did the pools, 9 per cent placed bets on the dogs or horses about once a week and another 9 per cent gambled with cards or dice. There was no association between gambling and the level of sex experience (NSS). Although 7 per cent of the girls did the pools, there were not enough gamblers in the sample to look for association with sex behaviour.

In this sample 45 per cent of the boys and 55 per cent of the girls did not smoke. Another 5 per cent of the boys and 8 per cent of the girls said they only had one or two cigarettes a day, and 14 per cent and 18 per cent had less than ten. So over a third (36 per cent) of the boys had more than ten cigarettes a day (5 per cent smoked over twenty) and nearly one in every five girls (19 per cent) had more than ten a day (2 per cent smoked over twenty).

There is a clear association between the level of sex activity and the number of cigarettes smoked in a day ($p = 0.001$ for boys and girls). The experienced teenagers were likely to smoke more than the inceptives, and the inceptives more than the non-experienced. Practically all the girls who smoked over twenty a day were experienced, and so were half the boys who smoked this amount.

E. Delinquency

Our results confirmed the well-known fact that boys are much more likely to get into trouble than girls. Only 7 per cent of the girls had got into trouble with the police and only in 3 per cent did this involve a court appearance. On the other hand nearly half (47 per cent) the boys said they had been in trouble with the police and nearly a quarter (24 per cent) had made an appearance before a court. Most (16 per cent) of them had made only one court appearance, but a few (3 per cent) had appeared twice and one in twenty (5 per cent) had made more than two appearances.

Boys who have made an appearance in court are more likely to be sexually experienced ($p = 0.001$). A third (39 per cent) of the E-boys compared with a tenth (11 per cent) of the N-boys had appeared before a court. There is also an association between the number of court appearances and the level of sex activity ($p = 0.001$). Those who made one appearance only are as likely to be I-boys as E-boys. But those who make two or more court appearances are much more likely to be E-boys. The same tendency can be seen among the girls although the numbers are much smaller.

Of course there are all sorts of reasons why a boy might be charged with committing an offence, some more serious than others. In this sample 12 per cent were charged with traffic offences and 6 per cent with other relatively unimportant offences; but 9 per cent were on charges of stealing property and 2 per cent on charges involving violence against other people; less than 1 per cent were charged with a sexual offence.* We added the stealing, violence and sexual offences together and compared them with the other offences, but we found no association between these two groups of offences and the level of sex activity (NSS).

We made a note of the court action for each offence committed. We were aware that the sentence given by the juvenile magistrates depended on a wide variety of factors, not least the attitudes of the magistrates themselves. But for the purposes of this research we assumed that those who were sent to approved schools, detention centres, remand homes, borstals and put on probation had committed more serious offences than those who were fined, bound over, given an absolute or conditional discharge. However, we found no association between these two groups of sentences and the level of sex activity (NSS). This seems to confirm the previous finding that the type of offence is less important than the number of offences of all kinds.

But a large number of offences committed by young people do not come to the notice of the police. After we had asked these questions about delinquency we added a more general question: Have you ever done anything which might have got you into trouble if you had been found out? We defined trouble as anything that could have led to being charged by the police. We have no way of testing the validity of a question like this, but a large number of boys and girls seemed ready to admit one or more misdeeds.

Altogether 55 per cent of the boys and 20 per cent of the girls admitted breaking the law in some way. For both boys and girls the admitted offence was most often stealing, and traffic offences were also mentioned frequently by boys.

Although these answers are the spontaneous disclosures of the teenagers without being pressed, even so we found a clear association between the level of sex activity and the number of offences

* As some boys committed more than one type of offence, the percentages add up to more than the 24 per cent who had made court appearances.

admitted for boys ($p = 0.001$) and for girls ($p = 0.01$). Most of the N-boys said they had not done anything which might have got them into trouble, and most of the E-boys said they had. The girls show much the same kind of pattern and this is the only time that it has been possible to show a statistical association with female delinquency and sex activity. This may be because the figures for female delinquency are too small in our sample to show tendencies which are similar to those of the boys. But offences committed by girls are not only much less frequent, but are usually of a different type.

This chapter has indicated that sex experience in boys is often associated with 'outgoing' activities such as dancing, cinemas, coffee bars, drinking in public houses, parties; even the association with delinquency might be accounted for by high spirits, among the first offenders at any rate; the main exception is sport, and even so there are many sexually experienced boys who take an active interest in sport.

For girls it depends less upon where they go, more upon whom they go with. Most girls go to cinemas, dances, clubs, coffee bars whatever their level of sex activity; this is because they go to these places with other girls if they do not go with boy friends. It is note-worthy that the number of visits to public houses is the only one associated with sex experience, because this is an exception to the previous list of places, for girls rarely go into a bar with other girls and almost always go with boy friends. Therefore the really impor-tant factor so far as a girl's sexual experience is concerned is whether she has a steady boy friend or not. Sexually experienced girls are inclined to be romantic; sexually experienced boys tend to be cavalier.

12. Personal Factors

A. The Assessment of Personality

Although it was decided that the information about sexual behaviour could only be obtained by direct questions at a face-to-face interview, it was hoped that an objective picture of the personality of each individual could be obtained by some other method. Ideally what was required was a personality test:

   a. which was suitable for the age range fifteen to nineteen;
   b. which had been standardized for use in this country;
   c. which had gained a large measure of acceptance; and
   d. which could be easily administered and take less than twenty minutes.

Several pencil-and-paper tests for the assessment of personality have been constructed by clinical and social psychologists both here and in America. Most of these require the subject to indicate his agreement or disagreement with a number of statements which could be related to himself. The aim of the test is usually to give the subjects a score on a number of personality factors or traits. These factors tend to have names derived from the particular theory of personality which the test constructor supports. The total score is designed to give a 'profile' of the subject's personality.

A typical example of such a test is Cattel's High School Personality Inventory which gives an American High-School child a score on sixteen personality factors ranging from 'tough–sensitive' to 'dull–bright'. These tests can be criticized on a number of grounds but the most serious disadvantage from the point of view of this research was that they have been standardized largely in the United States. In many cases the language and subject matter of some of the test items require modification for use with an English sample and at the time when this research started, no norms for English teenagers were available for any of the established tests.*

* The results of Dr Warburton's work on the Cattel 16 P.F. test at Manchester University were not available at that time.

One of the well-standardized English tests is the Maudsley Personality Inventory (Eysenck, 1954), but it was decided not to use this because it has been primarily developed as a clinical instrument. One of the two factors it measures is 'neuroticism', and this would not be expected to reveal very interesting results in the context of this research.

It was planned to give the test immediately after the interview which took over an hour on its own. Therefore it was imperative that the test should not be of such a length as to tax the patience of the adolescents.* Most of the teenagers had much better things to do than to stay in and help out our interviewers. There was a very good chance that if the total time exceeded an hour and a half, the deterioration in response would seriously affect the results. Accordingly it was decided that any pencil-and-paper test must not exceed twenty minutes.

For these reasons it was decided not to use a personality test but to limit our assessment of personality to a study of the adolescent's attitudes on a number of topics. With some reluctance it was decided not to use any of the existing tests and to design a new social attitude inventory consisting of fifty opinion statements relating to a large number of topics. Each of these topics was one in which teenagers could be expected to have a strong interest and they were asked to indicate their agreement or disagreement with each statement. This served a dual purpose. It made it possible to obtain the responses of the teenagers on single items and therefore provided useful information on individual attitudes (already reported in Chapter 7). At the same time the tendency of certain attitudes to lie in particular directions could be revealed by the use of factor analysis. It was expected that correlations between the results of the factor analysis and sexual experience would show a relationship between aspects of personality and sexual behaviour.

* This ruled out many of the best-known American tests such as the Minnesota Multiphasic Personality Inventory which requires ninety minutes to administer in its complete form.

B. The Analysis of the Attitude Inventory*

A higher order factor analysis was carried out on the responses to the fifty statements on the attitude inventory. Thus it was possible to organize these statements into three levels of attitude dimensions. At the first-order level each factor is still specific and depends on one or two statements only. Attitude dimensions at this level approximate in their simplest form to the shades of opinion existing between two opposite views on a particular topic. An example of this is favourable and unfavourable attitudes towards religion. At the next level the factors become more generalized, and each dimension extends over a wider range of topics. In some cases the second-order dimension summarizes those at the first-order level and religion may appear as one of a number of items associated with morality. The third-order level produces even broader generalizations and the fifty statements are reduced to two or three basic attitude dimensions. This level is of interest because it may lead on to a picture of personality.

This research was primarily interested in the factors associated with sexual experience. Factor analysis condensed a large number of attitude statements into a smaller number of basic variables each of which could be studied in relation to sexual experience. At the first order level the relationship between sexual experience and attitudes to specific topics could be studied and at the third-order level ideas arise about personality and sexual experience.

The analysis produced the following factors:

Boys
15 first-order factors
5 second-order factors

* The analyses carried out for this chapter involve some complex statistical techniques only recently made possible by using the resources of a computer. For the sake of accuracy it has been necessary to use some technical terms, but the general reader will find that he can understand the results of the analyses without having to comprehend fully the statistical methods. Those who are interested in statistical techniques should refer to *Use and Abuse of Statistics* by W. J. Reichman, Penguin, 1964; the particular statistical method used here is described in *Promax* by A. Hendrickson and P. White in volume 17 of the *British Journal of Statistical Psychology*, 1964.

2 third-order factors

Girls
16 first-order factors
 6 second-order factors
 3 third-order factors

In order that the discussion of these factors and their relationship with sex experience is clear, we will define three concepts that will be used throughout the rest of this chapter.

Loading. This is a measure of the association between a factor and one of the fifty statements on the attitude inventory. A positive loading signifies agreement with the statement and a negative loading signifies disagreement.

Scores. This can be calculated for each individual on each factor. It is a measure of the extent to which the individual shows the factor in the attitudes he expresses. A high score or a low score on a particular factor will mean that the individual's opinions are predictable on all statements with high loadings in that factor.

Identification. We have identified and named each factor in terms of the statements which have the highest loadings in it. The name indicates the attitudes which are held by those teenagers who score highly on the factor. These names are printed in italics.

For example, *antipathy towards religion* is a factor which exists for boys and girls (factor II for boys and IV for girls). The two statements with the highest loadings are No. 18 in Appendix 3 ('The average man can lead a good life without religion') and No. 34 ('The Church is the best authority to decide on matters of right and wrong'). A high score* on this factor would indicate agreement with the former statement and disagreement with the latter. Thus it is identified as *antipathy towards religion*.

Analysis of variance was used to determine whether or not there was any significant variation between factor scores of teenagers of differing sexual experience. In this case the five stages of sex

---

* The score is determined from the opinion expressed on every single attitude statement although those that have the highest loading are the defining ones. A much wider measure of 'religiousness' is thus obtained than would be the case if only one statement on religion was considered in isolation.

experience were used (Section F of Chapter 3) instead of the three levels of sex activity (as used in Chapters 8–11). It was then possible to determine whether or not the mean factor score for all teenagers varied significantly across all five stages.

The main aim of this analysis was to determine whether or not sexually experienced teenagers had much higher or much lower scores on certain factors. The technique of the analysis involved calculating the variance ratio (F)* for each factor and comparing this value with the theoretical value of F in Fisher and Yates tables for the relevant number of degrees of freedom. At any particular significance level, if the calculated value of F is greater than the value of F in the tables, then one can infer that there is a significant variation in factor scores between the stages of sexual experience at that particular level of significance. This is indicated by giving the value of p, as explained in Section A of Chapter 8.†

The attitude inventory was not constructed with any view as to what basic attitude dimensions existed for teenagers. The statements were chosen for their topicality and relevance to subjects of interest to the research; so the analysis was not being used to refute or confirm hypotheses derived from a psychological theory. The aim was to place teenage attitudes in a simplified framework which could be studied in relation to sexual experience.

C. First-Order Factors

Tables 12.1 and 12.2 show the first order factors for boys and girls. Statements with loadings greater than 0.5 are given below the factor title. The numbers refer to the numbered statements of the attitude inventory to be found in Appendix 3. In addition the values for F and the significance levels are given.

In most cases only one or two statements have very high loadings (above 0·7) on each factor. All other statements have much lower loadings on the factor and in most cases the loading is very

* The variance ratio = the variance between stages of sexual experience divided by the variance within classes of sexual experience.

† Thus at the $p = 0·001$ level, the odds are 1,000 : 1 against this occurring by chance alone. Similarly at the $p = 0·01$ level the odds are 100 : 1 against the theoretical value of F being exceeded by chance alone.

Table 12.1
Boys' first-order factors giving the statement numbers and highest loadings for each factor and showing F values and significance levels (p)

No.	Factor name, statement number and loading	F value	p value
I	Belief in controls on teenagers 6 (−0·80), 39 (−0·67), 48 (−0·65)	4·46	0·01
II	Antipathy towards religion 18 (+0·79), 34 (−0·77)	11·87	0·001
III	Respect for adult standards 8 (−0·75), 40 (−0·71)	3·29	0·05
IV	Dislike of holidays with parents 4 (+0·85), 29 (−0·85)	27·10	0·001
V	I/1 50 (+0·82), 13 (−0·61)	3·48	0·01
VI	Tolerance towards foreigners 46 (−0·94), 45 (−0·93)	3·25	0·05
VII	Opposition to premarital sexual intercourse 27 (+0·89), 41 (+0·71)	8·09	0·001
VIII	I/2 26 (−0·69), 10 (−0·58)	0·60	NSS
IX	Preference for home activities 7 (+0·72), 5 (+0·52)	6·03	0·001
X	Belief in a new teenage culture 12 (+0·76), 17 (−0·64)	6·08	0·001
XI	Support for double standard of morality 38 (+0·72), 21 (+0·70)	9·67	0·001
XII	Lack of ambition 35 (−0·78), 42 (+0·57)	5·96	0·001
XIII	Moral scepticism 23 (+0·69), 3 (−0·67), 30 (−0·58)	28·36	0·001
XIV	Preference for living at home 24 (−0·79), 31 (+0·63)	0·82	NSS
XV	Support for moral standards 28 (−0·65), 22 (−0·64)	5·75	0·001

Notes: The statement number refers to those given in Appendix 3. All loadings greater than 0·5 are given in brackets after each statement number. I/1 and I/2 are incidental factors. The number of boys in each stage are:

Stage I = 117. Stage II = 285.
Stage III = 223. Stage IV = 36.
Stage V = 119.

Table 12.2

Girls' first-order factors giving the statement number and highest loadings for each factor and showing F values and significance levels (p)

No.	Factor name, statement number and loading	F value	p value
I	Dislike of adult interference 40 (+0·66), 48 (+0·63), 25 (+0·52)	5·58	0·001
II	Dislike of holidays with parents 4 (+0·82), 29 (−0·74)	20·32	0·001
III	Tolerance towards foreigners 46 (−0·89), 45 (−0·85)	1·45	NSS
IV	Antipathy towards religion 34 (−0·86), 18 (+0·84)	6·88	0·001
V	Desire for good time 9 (+0·73), 1 (+0·54)	0·76	NSS
VI	Opposition to premarital intercourse 27 (+0·75), 41 (+0·74), 43 (+0·71)	42·57	0·001
VII	I/3 35 (−0·87)	4·69	0·01
VIII	Support for teenage freedom 14 (−0·72), 49 (−0·69)	10·06	0·001
IX	Distaste for mass media 20 (+0·87), 36 (+0·67)	0·37	NSS
X	Dislike of other teenagers 5 (+0·76), 15 (+0·47), 2 (+0·46), 42 (+0·44)	2·19	NSS
XI	I/4 28 (+0·72)	6·26	0·001
XII	Belief in a moral authority 6 (−0·87), 32 (−0·47)	5·43	0·001
XIII	Antipathy towards family loyalty 16 (−0·66), 31 (−0·64)	7·86	0·001
XIV	Belief in a double standard of sexual morality 26 (+0·91), 38 (+0·55)	4·51	0·01
XV	Preference for friends' advice 10 (+0·82), 37 (−0·77)	3·61	0·01
XVI	Dislike of home restrictions 17 (+0·75), 24 (+0·66)	8·09	0·001

Notes: The statement number refers to those given in Appendix 3. All loadings greater than 0·5 are given in brackets after each statement number. I/3 and I/4 are incidental factors. The number of girls in each stage are:

Stage I = 47. Stage II = 338.

Stage III = 286. Stage IV = 58. Stage V = 32.

close to zero. In this respect simple structure is shown in a very clear form. The analysis has isolated those statements which have most in common and has eliminated the rest in varying degrees. It is thus simple to name most of the factors in terms of the high-loading statements. But four factors, two in each table, have not been named. These are factors which are loaded highly on only one statement or on two statements grouped in such a way as to make interpretation virtually impossible. We have called these *incidental factors* (Thurstone, 1949). The most probable explanation of their existence is that they are artefacts of the design of the attitude inventory and the analysis has simply made them apparent. They have been included in Tables 12.1 and 12.2 together with their high-loading statements, but no attempt has been made to label them.

Only two of the boys' first-order factors have insignificant F values. These are I/2 and *preference for living at home*. The first is an incidental factor, while the other covers the two statements concerned with the advantages and disadvantages of living at home. The result of the analysis shows that boys at all levels of sexual experience do not differ in their scores on these two factors.

For the girls four factors have insignificant F values. These are *tolerance towards foreigners*, *desire for good time*, *distaste for mass media* and *dislike of other teenagers*. Girls who are highly prejudiced against foreigners are no more or less sexually experienced than those who are free of prejudice. For boys the value of F is significant at the 0·05 level for the *tolerance towards foreigners* factor. However, the relationship between this factor and sexual experience is not a simple one. Figure 12/1 shows that stage III boys had the highest mean factor score, and this implies that they are less prejudiced towards foreigners than any other group. The most prejudiced group of boys appears to be stage V. These slight differences do not appear for the girls on this factor as shown in Figure 12/2.

For the boys one other factor has a significant F value at the 0·05 level. This is *respect for adult standards*. As Figure 12/3 shows, boys who score highly on this factor (i.e. who disagree with the belief that very few adults understand teenagers and that most of them are hypocrites) tend to be inexperienced sexually. Stage I boys score relatively highly on this factor whereas most of the others have scores which are close to the mean. Boys who have never had any physical contact with girls will tend to have more respect for adult standards.

Two of the boys' factors are significant at the 0·01 level. One is an incidental factor (I/1) and the other is *belief in controls on teenagers*. Figure 12/4 shows the stage V boys have a much lower score than the boys in the other stages who have factor scores quite

Mean scores for first-order factors at each stage of sex experience

Figure 12/1.   Figure 12/2.

BOYS   GIRLS

I   II   III IV   V   I   II   III IV   V
Tolerance towards foreigners   Tolerance towards foreigners

close to the mean. This means that stage V boys tend to agree that each person should decide for himself what is right and wrong, and that teenagers should be able to do what they want, dress as they like and go where they want without interference from adults.

Three of the girls' factors have significant associations with sex experience at the 0·01 level. One is an incidental factor (I/3). Another is *belief in double standards of morality* in which the stage IV girls score highest followed by stage III and stage V girls (Figure 12/5). These girls tend to agree that there are different sexual standards for men and women and that premarital intercourse is all right for boys but not for girls. This may seem to be a surprising result in view of the fact that these stage IV and V girls have actually had intercourse themselves. But it is clear that when an experienced girl signifies agreement with these two statements, she is in fact making a complaint (or a wry comment); she is not agreeing that this is a satisfactory state of affairs. The other factor at this level is *preference for friends' advice* and this is a factor which isolates stage I girls from the rest (Figure 12/6). Most of the groups have scores which are close to the mean with stage III this time

Mean scores for first-order factors at each stage of sex experience.

Figure 12/3.   Figure 12/4.

slightly ahead of the rest. Stage I girls on the other hand have a relatively low score; they would tend to turn for advice to their parents rather than their friends and they reject the idea that a person can learn more from friends than from parents.

All the other first-order factors for boys and girls have F values which are significant at the 0.001 level. At this stage much stronger relationships between the factors and sexual experience begin to appear and there are indications that in some cases besides varying between the stages of sexual experience the factor scores are also correlated with sexual experience as well. In one sense the size of the F value for each factor is a measure of the strength of the relationship between it and the stages of sexual intercourse. A very large *F* value indicates a considerable variation in mean factor score across the stages of sexual experience and a very high probability against this variation occurring through chance alone. This may or may not imply the existence of a strong linear correlation between the factor and sexual experience. Correlation exists when the mean factor score increases or decreases linearly as sexual experience increases.

Mean scores for first-order factors at each stage of sex experience

Figure 12/5.

GIRLS

Belief in double standard of sexual morality

Figure 12/6.

GIRLS

Preference for friends' advice

With this in mind the remaining first-order factors will be considered in groups according to the size of the *F* values (given in Tables 12.1 and 12.2). First those factors with *F* values which are not very much greater than the theoretical value at the $p = 0.001$ (i.e. 4 to 6) are considered. There are four of these for each sex. These are followed by factors with higher *F* values ranging from 7 to 11; there are three of these for each sex. Finally, the two factors having exceptionally high *F* values for boys and girls (over 20) are discussed.

The distribution of the mean factor scores between stages of sexual experience for the four boys' factors having *F* values ranging from 4 to 6 are shown in Figures 12/7 to 12/10. Figure

Mean scores for first-order factors at each stage of sex experience

Figure 12/7.

BOYS

Figure 12/8.

BOYS

I   II   III   IV   V

Lack of ambition

I   II   III   IV   V

Preference for home activities

Figure 12/9.

BOYS

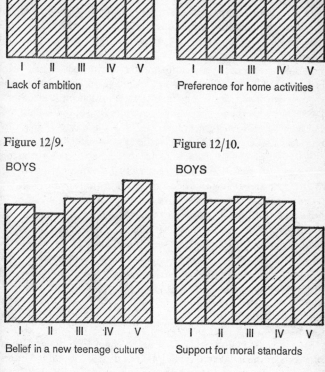

Figure 12/10.

BOYS

I   II   III   IV   V

Belief in a new teenage culture

I   II   III   IV   V

Support for moral standards

12/7 shows an unusual relationship between *lack of ambition* and sexual experience. Factor scores decrease steadily as sexual experience increases down to stage IV where it reaches its lowest level. Stage V boys, however, have a mean factor score which is comparable to that of stage II and III. High scores on this factor are associated with the belief that the average teenager expects to lead much the same kind of life as his parents. Stage IV boys appear to be most strongly opposed to this idea. One explanation of this result lies in the possibility that stage IV contains a larger proportion of boys who are having intercourse with their girl friends and fiancées than stage V. It is possible that these boys who may be actively considering marriage are determined to lead a better life than their parents. They also show more ambition when they agree with another statement, highly loaded with this factor, that they will have better jobs than their fathers when they are their age.

A different aspect of home life and the work situation is shown in Figure 12/8. Stage I boys appear to have the strongest *preference for home activities*. They tend to believe that most teenagers are bored with their jobs and that the family should spend one evening together each week. Stage III, IV and V boys all tend to oppose these views. Figure 12/9 shows the association between *belief in a new teenage culture* and sexual experience. This factor associates the view that today's teenagers are different from those in the past and that girls today believe they are on the shelf at twenty-one. Stage V boys believe this most strongly and stage II boys tend to be most opposed to the idea.

On *support for moral standards* stage V boys have the lowest scores (Figure 12/10). Most of the other classes of sexual experience seem to contain scores which are close to the mean, with tendency for stage I boys to have the highest scores. This means that stage V boys tend to believe in easier divorce, and that there is no harm in travelling without a ticket if you can get away with it. No other group has such predictable views on these topics.

Of the girls' factors with F values in the 4 to 6 range, one is probably of the incidental type (I/4). The distribution of the mean factor scores for the other three are shown in Figures 12/11 to

Mean scores for first-order factors at each stage of sex experience

Figure 12/11.

GIRLS

Dislike of adult interference

Figure 12/12.

GIRLS

Antipathy towards religion

Figure 12/13.

GIRLS

Belief in a moral authority

12/13. Stage V girls have the highest mean scores on *dislike of adult interference*, and stage I have the lowest. This means that stage V girls tend to believe that adults misunderstand teenagers and that the police are unfair to them. They also tend to think that teenagers should be free to do what they want and dress as they like.

Antipathy towards religion is related to sexual experience in the manner shown by Figure 12/12. Increasing antipathy towards religion is associated with increasing sexual experience. Thus the stage V girls are the group most antipathetic towards the Church and the stage I girls have the most favourable view of it.

On *belief in a moral authority* stage I and stage II girls have the highest scores (Figure 12/13). They tend to believe in an external moral code independent of one's own personal experience and judgement; and they disagree that each person should decide for himself what is right and wrong. Stage IV and V girls take the opposite view.

For the next range of *F* values (7 to 11) the distributions of the mean scores of the three boys' factors are shown in Figures 12/14 to 12/16. Stage V boys are less in favour of religion than other boys; they tend to believe that the average man can live a good life without religion and to disagree that the Church is the best authority on matters of right and wrong (Figure 12/14). Unlike the girls the group which follows them next in 'anti-religiousness' is the stage III boys; these boys tend to be more antipathetic in their attitudes towards religion than the boys in stage IV. For a significant proportion of stage IV boys sexual experience with one partner is not necessarily combined with antagonistic views towards religion. These are probably boys who have only had intercourse with their steady girl friends or fiancées.

The relationship between *opposition to premarital intercourse* is a simpler one (Figure 12/15). The boys who are at stages I and II are the ones who believe most strongly that most boys want to marry virgins and that girls who have sex before marriage get bad reputations.

Scores on *support for double standard of morality* increase as sexual experience increases (Figure 12/16). Thus stage V boys

Mean scores for first-order factors at each stage of sex experience

Figure 12/14.

BOYS

I II III IV V

Antipathy towards religion

Figure 12/15

BOYS

I II III IV V

Opposition to premarital intercourse

Figure 12/16.

BOYS

I II III IV V

Support for double standard of morality

tend to believe more strongly than any other group that girls look for marriage whereas boys look for sex, and that sexual intercourse before marriage is all right for boys but not for girls. This is in contrast to the previous factor *opposition to premarital intercourse*; stage V boys may not be so insistent that boys want to marry virgins but they do believe that sex before marriage is for boys, and not for girls.

Figures 12/17 to 12/19 illustrate the distributions of mean factor scores for girls in the 7–11 range of F values. *Antipathy towards family loyalty* is most strongly felt by stage V girls; they are less inclined to agree that one owes one's greatest loyalty to the family and see more disadvantages in living at home. Stage IV girls follow them on this factor and the other three groups are all fairly close to the mean. *Support for teenage freedom* (Figure 12/18) shows a similar tendency. Experienced girls tend to reject the idea that parents should advise their children about the sort of work they do, and disagree with the view that too much freedom in the early teens leads to trouble when one gets older.

A third aspect of this question is shown in *dislike of home restrictions*. This is expressed in the belief that freedom only exists away from home and that girls believe they are on the shelf at twenty-one; some girls see marriage as a means of getting away from home. There appears to be an increasing support for these views as sexual experience increases. It seems from these three results that sexual experience for girls is associated with an increasing desire for freedom and independence from the family.

The remaining first-order factors all have very high F values (over 20). One of these is common to both sexes. It is *dislike of holidays with parents*. As can be seen from Figures 12/20 and 12/21 experienced boys and girls tend to be opposed to taking their holidays with their parents. Stage IV and V girls both have high mean scores which are fairly close to each other on this factor. For boys, however, those at stage V have a high mean score, whereas those at stages IV and III are lower, with stage III very slightly ahead of stage IV. This result for boys has similarities to the earlier one for *antipathy towards religion* and suggests that in some ways stage III boys may be more like stage V than stage IV boys in their attitudes.

Mean scores for first-order factors at each stage of sex experience

Figure 12/17.

GIRLS

Antipathy towards family loyalty

Figure 12/18.

GIRLS

Support for teenage freedom

Figure 12/19.

GIRLS

Dislike of home restrictions

The desire of teenagers to take their holidays with friends rather than parents seems to be a significant turning point in their lives. It is one of the major stepping-stones to teenage independence from the family, particularly for girls. The fact that the desire is associated with the sexual experience of the teenagers who hold it shows that the move towards friends and away from the family has much wider implications than simply a desire for more freedom. This should not be interpreted to mean that once a teenager expresses a desire to have his holidays alone he is on the brink of experiencing sexual intercourse. What it does suggest is that sexually experienced teenagers tend to desire independence to a greater extent than non-experienced ones and the area of their lives where this is exemplified is in taking holidays. Not all the experienced teenagers who want to take their holidays apart from their parents do in fact go away on holiday with friends (Section D of Chapter 8). It is the desire, not the accomplishment, that is associated with sex experience.

The other factor for boys with a very high F value is *moral scepticism*. Figure 12/22 shows that experienced boys score highly on it. It suggests that experienced boys tend to take a cynical view of society. They believe that there is one law for the rich and another for the poor and they deny that it always pays to be honest. They would also rather work for an easy going boss than one who is strict and fair.

Finally the factor with the highest F value of all is the girls' factor *opposition to premarital intercourse*. Figure 12/23 shows that sexually experienced girls have very low scores on this factor. This means that they tend to reject the view that girls acquire bad reputations by having sexual experience. They also disagree that intercourse before marriage is wrong and do not believe that most boys want to marry a virgin. This result is of course the most predictable association of all.

D. Second-Order Factors

At the second-order level the difference between high and low loadings is less marked and there are a larger number of statements with relatively high loadings (0·35–0·5) for each factor. This makes

Mean scores for first-order factors at each stage of sex experience

Figure 12/20.
BOYS

Figure 12/21.
GIRLS

I   II   III   IV   V
Dislike of holidays with parents

I   II   III   IV   V
Dislike of holidays with parents

Figure 12/22.
BOYS

Figure 12/23.
GIRLS

I   II   III   IV   V
Moral scepticism

I   II   III   IV   V
Opposition to premarital
intercourse

Mean scores for boys' second-order factors at each stage of sex experience

Figure 12/24.

Support for teenagers

Distaste for mass media

Respect for adults

Support for boys' sexual-freedom

Support for moral restrictions

it more difficult to identify them. However, at this stage of the
analysis broad dimensions of social attitude begin to appear and
these can be identified by the statements which are clustered within
each of them.

Tables 12.3 and 12.4 show the second-order factors for boys and
girls. Statements with loadings greater than 0·35 are given below
the factor title. The numbers refer to the numbered statements
of the attitude inventory to be found in Appendix 3. In addition
the values for F and the significance levels are given.

All the boys' and four of the girls' second-order factor scores
vary significantly across the five stages of sexual experience at the
0·001 level. Another girls' factor has an F value which is significant
at the 0·01 level and the remaining one has an F value which is
insignificant.

The second-order factors were produced by factor analysing
the matrix of correlation between the first-order factors. Because
of this most of them appear as broad summaries of the factors
on the lower level. There are two exceptions.

The first of these is the boys' factor *distaste for mass media*. This
is highly loaded on the two statements which defined the first-order
factor IX for the girls. Statements on the mass media had relatively
low loadings on the boys' first-order factors. This boys' second-
order factor covers a slightly wider range of topics than the girls'

first-order factor IX even though the defining statements are the same.

Table 12.3
Boys' second-order factors giving the statement numbers with the highest loadings for each factor and showing F values and significance levels (p).

No.	Factor name, statement number and loading	F value	p value
I	Support for teenagers		
	15 (−0·54), 49 (−0·51), 47 (−0·39),		
	2 (−0·38), 7 (−0·36)	25·47	0·001
II	Distaste for mass media		
	20 (+0·43), 36 (+0·47), 19 (+0·35)	6·28	0·001
III	Respect for adults		
	8 (−0·53), 5 (−0·39), 40 (−0·48),		
	10 (−0·36), 23 (−0·36), 37 (+0·35)	10·07	0·001
IV	Support for boys' sexual freedom		
	21 (+0·46), 38 (+0·43), 1 (+0·42),		
	32 (+0·40), 19 (+0·38), 43 (−0·35)	16·97	0·001
V	Support for moral restrictions		
	11 (+0·49), 3 (+0·39), 44 (+0·40),		
	43 (+0·36)	15·20	0·001

The only other factor which appears for the first time at the second-order level is the girls' factor *opposition to sex instruction.* Girls who score highly on it tend to express negative views on sex education and experience. They believe that there is no need to teach about sex in schools and disagree that young people should be taught all about birth control. Also highly loaded on this factor is the view that girls should not get married before twenty-one. Both these factors are associated with sex experience.

The other second-order factors are similar to the first-order factors, and they are related to sex experience in the same way. The distribution of the mean scores across the stages of sex experience for all the second-order factors are shown in Figures 12/24 and 12/25. As the results shown in these figures are similar to those found for the first order factors, it is not necessary to discuss each one in detail.

Table 12.4
Girls' second-order factors giving the statement numbers with the highest loadings for each factor and showing F values and significance levels (p)

No.	Factor name, statement number and loading	F value	p value
I	Antipathy towards family 16 (-0.59), 7 (-0.50), 31 (-0.46), 37 (-0.45), 3 (-0.42), 42 (-0.36)	28.83	0.001
II	Opposition to sex instruction 19 (-0.51), 47 ($+0.48$), 13 ($+0.39$)	14.12	0.001
III	Tolerance towards other people 46 (-0.51), 45 (-0.50), 44 (-0.47), 9 (-0.44), 1 (-0.39), 11 (-0.36)	1.54	NSS
IV	Belief in personal moral responsibility 32 ($+0.44$), 50 ($+0.40$)	22.64	0.001
V	Belief in double standards 23 ($+0.44$), 26 ($+0.43$)	3.70	0.01
VI	Opposition to girls' sexual freedom 21 ($+0.39$), 27 ($+0.39$)	14.21	0.001

The results may be summarized as follows: Boys who are sexually experienced tend to oppose restrictions on their behaviour and accept the idea that teenagers are alienated from the adult world; they also believe that different standards exist in sex for boys and girls and that nothing is so important in life as enjoyment; and they have permissive moral views which are shown in their equivocal attitude towards honesty and in their belief that a boy who makes a girl pregnant should not have to marry her. Experienced girls on the other hand tend to be against family loyalty and family activities; they feel that girls should be taught more about sex and believe in making their own decisions; they dislike the idea of a double sexual standard and believe that girls should be allowed more sexual freedom.

Mean scores for girls' second-order factors at each stage of sex experience

Figure 12/25.

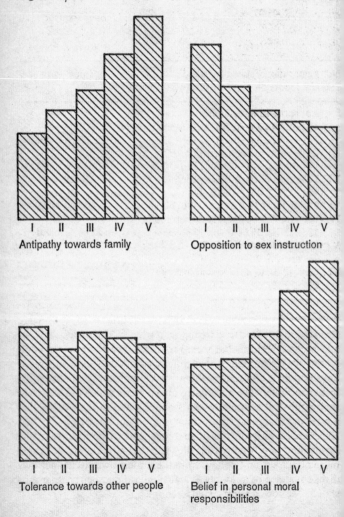

Antipathy towards family

Opposition to sex instruction

Tolerance towards other people

Belief in personal moral responsibilities

I II III IV V   I II III IV V

Belief in double standards   Opposition to girls' sexual freedom

E. Teenage Attitude Structure

Before considering the relationship between the third-order factors and sex experience, this section will describe the overall attitude structure revealed by the factor analysis. At the third-order level the difference between high loadings and low loadings becomes even smaller than for the second-order factors. Each factor has loadings over 0·3 and under 0·5 on a larger number of statements.

Two factors for the boys and two for the girls are listed in Tables 12.5 and 12.6, together with all the statements with loadings of over 0·3.

Table 12.5
Boys' third-order factors

I Teenage ethnocentrism

1 Life is so short that having a good time is more important than anything else (0·42)

48 What teenagers do and how they dress outside their homes is their business (0·40)

9 It is best to have a good time before you are married because after that life is pretty dreary (0·39)

40 Very few adults really understand teenagers (0·37)

45 Foreigners should stay in their own country (0·36)

46 It would be best to keep coloured people in their own districts to prevent too much contact with whites (0·35)

10 I learn more from friends of my own age than I do from my parents (0·35)

25 The police are unfair in their treatment of teenagers (0·35)

33 I'm usually a bit bored when I stay at home in the evenings (0·33)

44 All homosexuals should be severely punished (0·33)

39 Teenagers should be able to go out in the evening without having to tell their parents where they are going (0·31)

8   Most adults say one thing and do another (0·30)

II Restrictiveness

11 If a boy gets a girl pregnant he should be willing to marry her (0·47)

3   It always pays to be honest (0·43)

43 Sexual intercourse before marriage is wrong (0·43)

34 The Church is the best authority to decide on matters of right and wrong (0·39)

44 All homosexuals should be severely punished (0·38)

16 People should realize that their greatest loyalty is to their family (0·37)

Table 12.6
Girls' third-order factors

I Teenage ethnocentrism

46 It would be best to keep coloured people in their own districts to prevent too much contact with whites (0·42)

45 Foreigners should stay in their own country (0·40)

1   Life is so short that having a good time is more important than anything else (0·40)

9   It is best to have a good time before you are married because after that life is pretty dreary (0·39)

33 I am usually bored when I stay at home in the evenings (0·38)

12 Today's teenagers are very different from teenagers in the past (0·33)

48 What teenagers do and how they dress outside their homes is their business (0·33)

39 Teenagers should be able to go out in the evenings without telling their parents where they are going (0·31)

10 I learn more from friends of my own age than I do from my parents (0·30)

II Restrictiveness

30 I'd rather work for someone who is strict and fair than for someone who is easy going (0·38)
43 Sexual intercourse before marriage is wrong (0·37)
2 Most parents ought to be stricter with their children (0·35)
7 The family should spend one evening at home together at least once a week (0·35)
3 It always pays to be honest (0·34)
11 If a boy gets a girl pregnant he should be willing to marry her (0·33)
16 People should realize that their greatest loyalty is to their family (0·33)
49 Too much freedom in the early teens leads to trouble when one gets older (0·32)
29 I'd rather take my holidays with my parents (0·30)
44 All homosexuals should be severely punished (0·30)

A third factor for the girls was brought out by the analysis, but it is not listed with the others because only one of the statements has a loading over 0·3. This was a negative loading on the statement in favour of birth control. In addition there were four statements with loadings above 0·2. A study of these five statements will show that it is difficult to interpret this factor.

19 Young people should be taught all about birth control (−0·30).
50 There is more to sex than just having a good time (−0·28).
13 There is no need to teach about sex in schools because you can find out all you need to know yourself (0·25).
30 I'd rather work for someone who is strict and fair than for somebody who is easy-going (−0·24).
34 The Church is the best authority to decide on matters of right and wrong (0·24).

This factor is also closely correlated (0·77) with the second-order factor *opposition to sex instruction*. Most girls are in favour of sex education* and the factor analysis seems to have sorted out the few who are not, and found that they are also pro-Church, anti-birth control, anti-strictness and anti-sex. We know this applies to only a very small number of our sample and it appears to have little meaning. Consequently a detailed interpretation of this factor would be of doubtful validity and therefore it will not be discussed further.

The boys' factor with the largest number of statements with high loadings has been labelled *teenage ethnocentrism*. There is a similar factor for girls; in fact eight statements are common to both groups. *Teenage ethnocentrism* reveals the extent to which teenagers are for their own group and opposed to all other groups. There is an emphasis on enjoyment and having a good time. Adult institutions are looked upon unfavourably. Ethnocentric teenagers are against foreigners, coloured people, the police, homosexuals and marriage. They scorn advice from adults, resent interference in their affairs and take a hedonistic view of life.

The other factor common to both groups has been named *restrictiveness*. This represents the attitude dimension associated with opinions on honesty, control of teenagers and a strict moral code at one end, to permissiveness on all these topics at the other end. Both boys and girls who score highly on this factor believe that it always pays to be honest. They have strong views on sexual morality. They are opposed to premarital intercourse and think that if a boy gets a girl pregnant he should be willing to marry her. Family loyalties are also stressed by the strongly restrictive teenagers. Homosexuals are also condemned and this exemplifies the difference between ethnocentrism and this factor; in the ethnocentric context homosexuals are seen as another out-group; in terms of restrictiveness, however, homosexuality is seen as immoral behaviour.

Religious feeling is also a measure of restrictiveness for boys, but this is less strong for girls. Controls by parents over their children is important for the restrictive girls. For boys restrictive-

* Young people should be taught all about birth control: 83 per cent agree, 11 per cent don't know, 6 per cent disagree. In favour of sex education in schools: 81 per cent agree, 6 per cent don't know, 13 per cent disagree (from Appendix 3).

ness is associated with restraint and respect for a strict moral code. Girls have more statements with relatively high loadings, suggesting that morality for them covers a wider area of their lives; the restrictive girl is both moral in her views and also is strongly in favour of family life.

F. The Third Order Factors and Sex Experience

The scores of the third-order factors varied significantly between the classes of sexual experience at the $p = 0.001$ level. The F values for each of them are shown on Table 12.7 and the distribution of the mean factor scores across sexual experience are shown in Figures 12/26 and 12/27.

Table 12.7

F values and significance levels (p) for the third-order factor scores classified by sex experience

Group	No.	Factor Name	F value	p value
Boys	I	Ethnocentrism	16·00	0·001
	II	Restrictiveness	35·61	0·001
Girls	I	Ethnocentrism	6·23	0·001
	II	Restrictiveness	42·27	0·001

For both boys and girls the highest F value was obtained for *restrictiveness*. As boys and girls increase their sexual experience they tend to become more permissive in their attitudes. For the girls restrictiveness decreases steadily as sexual experience increases, but for boys the anomaly of the stage IV boys again appears; these boys tend to be slightly more restrictive in their attitude than those at stage III. As suggested earlier this may be due to a stronger element of steadiness in their sexual relationships than is found in boys at stage III or stage V.

For both sexes ethnocentrism is also associated with sexual experience but for the boys the value of F is higher than for the girls. Sexually experienced boys and girls tend to resent the adult world and all its institutions, and to believe that enjoying life is more important than anything else. Besides disliking the adult world they are also opposed to all groups outside their own teenage circle.

These results suggest that sexually experienced teenagers tend to be both ethnocentric and permissive in their attitudes. This is further illustrated in Figure 12/28. It shows the position which the various levels of sexual experience hold in relation to the two basic 'attitudes'. Each point on the diagram represents the mean score on each of these two factors for teenagers in the different

Mean scores for boys' third order-factors at each stage of sex experience

Figure 12/26.

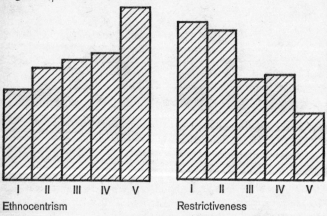

Ethnocentrism   Restrictiveness

classes of sexual experience. From the diagram it can be seen that stage V girls are the most permissive group of all in their attitudes. Stage V boys are not nearly as permissive. Stage V teenagers of both sexes are the most ethnocentric. Stage IV girls are also strongly permissive in their views; slightly more so than the stage V boys but less ethnocentric. Stage IV boys are very similar in their position to stage III girls and stage III boys. This shows the different meaning of sexual experience for boys and girls. For a girl to go as far as stage III she becomes almost as permissive in her attitudes as boys who have actually had sexual intercourse. Similarly a stage IV girl is more permissive in her attitudes than a stage V boy.

For the boys and girls who have had very little experience of sex, their positions in relation to the two dimensions are more similar. Stage I girls are the group which have the most restrictive views of all. This again illuminates the different meaning of sexual experience for boys and girls. A boy who has never had any

Mean scores for girls' third-order factors at each stage of sex experience

Figure 12/27.

Ethnocentrism   Restrictiveness

physical contact with a girl will not be so restrictive in his attitudes.

On ethnocentrism the boys and girls hardly differ at all. The more experienced they are, the farther along the ethnocentric scale they are to be found. The difference between the sexes is confined to the restrictive/permissive scale. Experienced girls are both ethnocentric and permissive; experienced boys are also ethnocentric, but not so permissive; in fact boys may be relatively restrictive in their attitudes in comparison with girls and yet still have had experience of premarital intercourse with one partner.

*Mean factor scores for boys and girls at
different levels of sex experience.*

Figure 12/28.

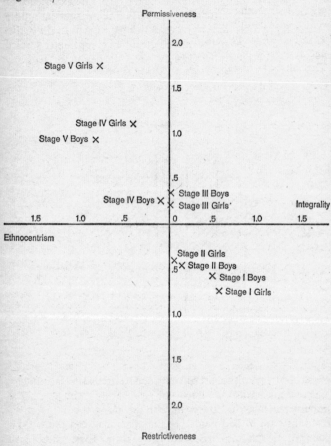

G. The Exclusion of Age

Product moment correlation coefficients were calculated between all the factors and sex experience. They were also calculated for sex experience and age because it was known that the older teenagers tended to be more experienced. The correlation between age and sexual experience is 0·393 for boys and 0·243 for girls. The influence of age on the correlation coefficient between sex experience and any one of the factors can be removed by calculating the partial correlation coefficient; this is a measure of the association between two variables holding a third variable constant. So it was possible to measure the strength of the relationship between sex experience and a factor, and at the same time exclude the influence of age. Tables 12.8 for boys and 12.9 for girls show:

a. The correlation coefficients between sex experience and each of the factors (r_1). When the correlation is plus, those with sex experience score high on the factor; when the correlation is minus, those with sex experience score low on the factor.

b. The correlation coefficients between age and each of the factors (r_2).

c. The partial correlation coefficient between sex experience and each of the factors excluding age (r_3).

If the attitudes of the teenagers varied according to age, then what might be mistaken for an association with sex experience in reality may be merely a change in attitudes as these adolescents grew up. In fact most of the factors in Tables 12.8 and 12.9 have a low correlation with age (r_2); consequently the correlation is only slightly changed when the effect of age is excluded (r_3). Therefore it is reasonable to suppose that the associations found in previous sections between most of these factors and sexual experience is not due to the effect of age.

In only eight cases among the boys and five cases among the girls is the correlation between the factor and age over 0·1. In no case is it over 0·2. In three of these cases it applies to situations where no association between sexual experience and the factor has been found. In another case the correlation is increased by removing the effects of age. In the remaining nine cases the

Table 12.8
The partial correlation of each of the boys' factors with sex experience excluding the influence of age

Order	No.	Factor	r_1	r_2	r_3
First	I	Belief in controls on teenagers	−0·140	+0·012	−0·157
	II	Antipathy towards religion	+0·205	+0·118	+0·174
	III	Respect for adult standards	−0·072	+0·020	−0·087
	IV	Dislike of holidays with parents	+0·344	+0·123	+0·324
	V	I/1	+0·015	+0·073	−0·015
	VI	Tolerance towards foreigners	−0·015	+0·044	−0·035
	VII	Opposition to premarital intercourse	−0·194	−0·095	−0·171
	VIII	I/2	−0·034	+0·128	−0·092
	IX	Preference for home activities	−0·163	−0·025	−0·167
	X	Belief in a new teenage culture	+0·143	−0·042	+0·173
	XI	Support for double standard of morality	+0·212	+0·076	+0·199
	XII	Lack of ambition	−0·105	−0·090	−0·076
	XIII	Moral scepticism	+0·342	+0·109	+0·327
	XIV	Preference for living at home	+0·061	+0·049	+0·046
	XV	Support for moral standards	−0·149	+0·146	−0·227
Second	I	Support for teenagers	+0·333	+0·094	+0·323
	II	Distaste for mass media	+0·036	+0·108	−0·007
	III	Respect for adults	−0·206	+0·011	−0·228
	IV	Support for boys' sexual freedom	+0·267	−0·008	+0·294
	V	Support for moral restrictions	−0·238	−0·116	−0·211
Third	I	Ethnocentrism	+0·264	−0·036	+0·303
	II	Restrictiveness	−0·379	−0·131	−0·359

Table 12.9

The partial correlation of each of the girls' factors with sex experience excluding the influence of age.

Order	No.	Factor	r_1	r_2	r_3
First	I	Dislike of adult interference	+0·144	−0·068	+0·166
	II	Dislike of holidays with parents	+0·304	+0·195	+0·270
	III	Tolerance towards foreigners	+0·061	+0·005	+0·062
	IV	Antipathy towards religion	+0·191	+0·013	+0·194
	V	Desire for good time	+0·002	−0·163	+0·043
	VI	Opposition to premarital intercourse	−0·397	−0·039	−0·400
	VII	I/3	+0·158	+0·087	+0·142
	VIII	Support for teenage freedom	+0·209	+0·001	+0·215
	IX	Distaste for mass media	−0·008	−0·022	−0·003
	X	Dislike of other teenagers	−0·068	+0·151	−0·109
	XI	I/4	+0·060	+0·024	+0·056
	XII	Belief in a moral authority	−0·158	−0·096	−0·139
	XIII	Antipathy to family loyalty	+0·126	+0·046	+0·118
	XIV	Belief in a double standard of sexual morality	+0·111	+0·107	+0·088
	XV	Preference for friends' advice	+0·094	−0·050	+0·110
	XVI	Dislike of home restrictions	+0·173	−0·068	+0·196
Second	I	Antipathy to family	+0·315	+0·021	+0·319
	II	Opposition to sex instruction	−0·245	+0·037	−0·262
	III	Tolerance towards other people	+0·018	+0·130	−0·015
	IV	Belief in personal moral responsibility	+0·304	+0·089	+0·292
	V	Belief in double standards	+0·121	+0·077	+0·106
	VI	Opposition to girls' freedom	−0·235	−0·003	−0·242
Third	I	Ethnocentrism	+0·162	−0·064	+0·183
	II	Restrictiveness	−0·413	−0·075	−0·408

correlation coefficients are decreased by amounts varying between 0·01 up to 0·03.

The exclusion of age reduces the correlations of *dislike of holidays with parents* for boys and girls. This is understandable as one would expect older teenagers to be keener on holidays alone, simply because of their greater independence from the family. In fact it is surprising that the association between this factor and sex experience remains so strong when age is held constant: $r_3 = 0·324$ for boys, and $r_3 = 0·270$ for girls.

Age has a much stronger association with *antipathy towards religion* for boys than for girls. As boys get older they tend to become more antipathetic towards the Church and this means the association between their views on the Church and sexual experience becomes weaker when the effect of age is excluded; removing age makes very little difference for the girls.

Age does not appear to have much effect on any of the other seven correlations and excluding it has the effect of slightly reducing the correlations, but the associations remain significant at the 0·001 level.

Of all the girls' factors for which correlation coefficients were calculated, *restrictiveness* had the highest correlation of all. As a girl's sexual experience increases there is a strong tendency for her factor score to decrease. The correlation between age and this factor is relatively low and excluding it makes little difference to the association with sexual experience. A high correlation also exists for the boys on *restrictiveness*. Here the association with age is slightly stronger. There is a greater tendency for younger boys to have high scores than for the younger girls. This has the effect of reducing r_1 when age is excluded, but it still remains very high.

For boys there is a high association between *ethnocentrism* and sexual experience demonstrating the tendency of sexually experienced boys to be more ethnocentric in their views than inexperienced ones. This factor has a small negative correlation with age. Thus younger boys tend to be slightly more ethnocentric than older ones. When age is held constant the association between sexual experience and the factor is strengthened. Girls' *ethnocentrism* is also associated with sexual experience and age acts in the same direction, so that the correlation is increased when it is excluded.

These results show that the sexual experience of boys and girls is closely associated with the restrictive-permissive dimension of their social attitude. For boys, however, sex is seen less in the context of what is right and wrong than it is for girls. It is also connected with an ethnocentric view of life – a hedonistic self-centredness associated with antagonism towards everything outside the teenage world. As the analysis of variance showed (Figure 12/28), as sexual experience increases the teenage girl gets very strongly permissive in her attitudes and fairly ethnocentric as well. The teenage boy also gets more ethnocentric and not quite as permissive.

H. The Exclusion of Other Variables

Excluding age does not radically affect the size of the correlations between these factors and sexual experience. Several of the other responses to questions asked at the interview had high correlations with sexual experience. Table 12.10 gives these correlations and it can be seen that all but three of them have high correlations for both sexes. The extent to which boys like or dislike their mothers does not appear to be strongly associated with their sexual experience (affection for mother is -0.095), whereas for girls there is an association (-0.229). Social class and type of school are included because of their importance in sociological classification. It is of interest to observe that neither of them have high correlations with sexual experience for boys or girls (see Chapter 8). Because of this they have not been included in the table of partial correlations (Table 12.11).

Table 12.11 lists the ten most important factors for boys and girls, and shows the partial correlations which were obtained when nine of the variables in Table 12.10 are removed in turn from the correlation between the factor and sexual experience. Thus Table 12.11 shows how far the correlations between these ten factors and sex experience have been influenced by nine other variables.

It can be seen that most of the correlations maintain their high

Table 12.10

Correlation of a number of variables with sexual experience

Variable	Boys, r_b	Girls, r_g
Money to spend	0·449	0·238
Church attendance	−0·202	−0·215
Time back in the evening	0·384	0·212
Proportion of time out of home	0·298	0·265
Frequency of dancing	0·330	0·119
Affection for mother	−0·095	−0·229
Wages	0·360	0·153
Cinema attendance	0·174	0·135
Enjoyment of school	−0·201	−0·142
Type of school	0·105	0·010
Social class	0·044	−0·003

Note: r_b is correlation of boys' variables with sexual experience
    r_g is correlation of girls' variables with sexual experience

level when each of the variables is excluded. The correlations which are in italics are those which are the lowest for each factor. The variables that appear to have the most influence are wages which increased the correlation five times and decreased it once and time back in the evening which increased the correlation twice and decreased it twice.

None of these partial correlations seriously weakens the association of the factor with sex experience and in many cases the result is expected. Thus the factor *support for teenagers* is most influenced by the time the boy spends out of the family home; and *antipathy to family* is most influenced by how well the girl gets on with her mother. The correlation of *dislike of holidays with parents* is decreased by all the variables, especially by the amount of spending money received in the case of the boys, and by the relationship with the mother in the case of the girls. *Moral scepticism* is most influenced by the time a boy comes back home in the evening, and *opposition to premarital intercourse* is most influenced by the number of times a girl goes to church.

When the size of the girls' wage packets are held constant, the association between *restrictiveness* and sexual experience is

Table 12.11 *Partial correlation between key factors and sexual experience excluding each variable in turn*

Factor	Correlation with sex experience	Partial correlation with sex experience after each of these variables has been excluded								
		Money	Church	Time back	Out of home	Dances	Mother	Wages	Cinema	School
Boys										
Dislike of holidays with parents	(0.344)	*0.276*	0.317	0.311	0.288	0.300	0.339	0.291	0.323	0.321
Moral scepticism	0.342	0.311	0.323	*0.293*	0.330	0.327	0.335	(0.350)	0.330	0.311
Support for teenagers	(0.333)	0.286	0.307	0.286	*0.281*	0.293	0.326	0.311	0.320	0.310
Ethnocentrism	0.264	0.203	0.218	(0.271)	0.196	0.240	0.259	*0.188*	0.239	0.234
Restrictiveness	−0.379	−0.359	−0.351	*−0.313*	−0.362	−0.361	−0.370	(−0.408)	−0.371	−0.357
Girls										
Dislike of holidays with parents	(0.304)	0.284	0.298	0.282	0.263	0.290	*0.260*	0.292	0.293	0.297
Opposition to pre-marital intercourse	−0.397	−0.387	*−0.371*	−0.380	−0.383	−0.394	−0.390	(−0.401)	−0.394	−0.390
Antipathy to family	0.315	0.315	0.290	0.305	0.275	0.302	*0.255*	(0.321)	0.311	0.301
Ethnocentrism	0.162	0.153	*0.114*	(0.170)	0.135	0.148	0.115	0.141	0.156	0.140
Restrictiveness	−0.413	−0.406	−0.390	−0.393	*−0.379*	−0.404	−0.379	(−0.421)	−0.406	−0.401

Note: Correlations shown in italics are the lowest for each factor; correlations in brackets are the highest for each factor.

slightly strengthened. Although the correlation is reduced by frequency of church attendance (as in *opposition to premarital intercourse*), the strongest influences on the restrictive factor is the time spent out of the home and the relationship with the mother. The more restrictive the girl is, the more time she spends at home, the better she gets on with her mother, and the less sexually experienced she is.

For boys the pattern is similar. The correlation between sexual experience and *restrictiveness* increases when wages are held constant, but the variable which causes the largest decrease in this correlation is the time the boy gets back in the evening. The different functions of the 'time back' for boys and 'time spent at home' for girls throw further light on differences in *restrictiveness* for the two sexes. 'Time back' can be seen as a disciplinary measure of parental control over a teenager; whereas 'time spent at home' is more a measure of independence from the family. This bears out in behavioural terms the earlier suggestion that for girls restrictive moral views are associated with family loyalties, but for boys these views are more closely associated with restraint and controls on teenage behaviour.

The factor which appears to be under a strong influence from the variables is *ethnocentrism*. For both boys and girls its correlation with sexual experience is altered considerably by excluding several of the variables. For boys the variable having the strongest influence is wages and for girls the biggest influence is church attendance. The more a boy earns the more ethnocentric he is in his views; when wages are held constant there is less likelihood of sexually experienced boys being strongly ethnocentric. The ethnocentric girl rarely attends church; when this variable is excluded, then the correlation between sexual experience and ethnocentrism drops to 0·114 which is the lowest correlation in Table 12.11, but still not insignificant.

The results given in this section show the way in which several of the basic classifying variables (obtained from questions at the interview) are related to the most important factors (obtained from the attitude inventory). Although variations do occur in the correlations between the factors and sexual experience when each of these variables is excluded, in no case is the alteration a major one, and all the correlations remain significant at the 0·01 level. From this one can conclude that these factors do have a strong association with sexual experience independently of any other influence.

I. Sexual Experience and Personality

It should be made clear that all the correlations which have been discussed in the previous sections simply indicate the association which exists between two variables, i.e. the extent to which sexual experience varies in a similar way to a factor. The existence of an association means that one can predict, at a certain level of probability, the outcome of one variable from the other one. However, these variables are all independent of each other and even though a high correlation may exist one is not justified in inferring from this that one variable is the cause of the other variable. For example, one cannot infer from the correlation coefficient alone that having sexual experience causes a teenager to dislike taking his holidays with his parents; nor can one infer the reverse, namely, that when a teenager decides that he does not want to take his holidays with his parents, this is going to cause him to become sexually experienced. But when high correlations do exist, a causal relationship is always possible. The explanation of the relationship in terms of cause and effect must be a theoretical one and it is at this point that psychological theories of personality are of value.

This study of the responses to fifty attitude statements has enabled us to identify two basic factors which are strongly related to sexual experience. One factor we have been able to plot along a *permissive-restrictive* scale; the permissive boy attempts to reject adult controls and institutions and the permissive girl tries to escape the influence of her family. The other basic factor we have called *teenage ethnocentrism* which is a rejection of the adult world.

Eysenck (1964) has suggested that two basic social attitude dimensions exist and are related to personality in different ways. One dimension is 'tough-mindedness' as opposed to 'tender-mindedness' and this is highly correlated with 'extroversion' as opposed to 'introversion'.* People who are tough-minded in their attitudes are also extroverted in their behaviour. Those who are tender-minded are introverted. In terms of Eysenck's theory these characteristics have a hereditary basis and the environment simply determines the form in which they manifest themselves.

If one can assume that there are only two basic dimensions of social attitudes, then ethnocentrism may be tough-mindedness in a teenage context. Tough-minded adults would certainly agree with the ethnocentric teenager that life is so short that having a good time is more important than anything else. They would also dislike foreigners, homosexuals and anyone who does not conform or tries to interfere. They would not, of course, share the teen-ager's antagonism to the adult world. If this suggestion is correct, then teenage ethnocentrism may be similar to extroversion. The ethnocentric teenager, besides feeling alienated from the adult world, may be highly extroverted as well.

Eysenck calls his other attitude dimension 'radicalism-conserv-atism'. This does not have such a clear association with hereditary personality characteristics, but consists largely of reactions to the influences which the individual has experienced throughout his life. Radicalism-conservatism is very similar in many ways to the permissive-restrictive dimension of our research. The difference lies mainly in the fact that the attitudes Eysenck studied in this context were largely concerned with political questions. Some of his statements on moral topics however were very similar to ours and it appears that our strongly permissive teenager would be radical in Eysenck's terms and our strongly restrictive teenager would be conservative.

Eysenck (1953, 1960) proposes that extroverts condition (in the Pavlovian sense) less easily than introverts, partly due to the nature of the nervous system they have inherited. In consequence they are less bothered by guilt and shame when they break the rules of society (on the family or community level). In other words their consciences are much weaker and they are less inhibited in

* These terms, popularized by Jung, are now used by many psychologists. The extrovert is sociable, active, outgoing, impulsive, talkative and opti-mistic. The introvert is reserved, thoughtful, unsociable, passive, quiet and careful.

their social activity. In view of this one would expect extroverts to be more sexually experienced than introverts. Sex in psychological terms is one of the basic drives motivating human behaviour. The control of this drive is one of the most elementary conditioning processes which commences very early on in a person's life. The extrovert who is less susceptible to the conditioning process will more easily abandon his inhibitions and take the opportunity to have sexual experience when it arises.

From this one can conclude that a degree of extroversion is a prerequisite for premarital sexual experience. The introverted individual would find it more difficult to lose his inhibitions as far as sex is concerned; it would be far harder for the introvert to surmount the barriers of conscience and the ensuing guilt which is associated with it.

However, extroversion alone is not sufficient to determine the extent of a teenager's sexual experience. Sex is one of the subjects which is central in the arena of controversy which exists in modern society. As with politics and religion there is a so-called radical or progressive view of it which is opposed by a conservative or reactionary one. In terms of Eysenck's theory, what determines the opinions one holds on topics which fall within the scope of this dimension are all the influences which one has encountered throughout one's life. The process by which one acquires ideas in these areas is the other form of learning, namely, the instrumental type. Most of the learning which is acquired through the mediation of language is instrumental. At the conceptual level it involves assimilating ideas, thinking about them, and accepting some and rejecting others depending on whether or not they fit in with the views which one has been developing all one's life.

In this section we are making the tentative suggestion that permissiveness-restrictiveness has many similarities with Eysenck's radical-conservative dimension. The highly permissive teenager is similar to the highly radical one, except that the topics on which he expresses his permissive opinions are mainly concerned with morality.

This chapter has shown that permissiveness is more strongly associated with sexual behaviour than any other variable, and as Figure 12/28 has shown the sexually experienced teenager also tends to be ethnocentric as well as highly permissive in his views.

In Eysenck's terms, extroversion coupled with influences which have produced a radical view of life will be the personality characteristics most likely to lead to teenage premarital sexual intercourse. The first-order factors and the second-order factors which are associated with sex experience are also manifestations of extroversion and radicalism in more specific areas of the teenager's life. They are of special interest because they reveal the extent to which the teenager desires freedom from the family and so is provided with opportunities and facilities to have sexual experience.

We have attempted to make some tentative suggestions about the personality types which are most likely to lead to sexual experience in teenagers. The suggestions are tentative because this is not the place to get involved in the controversies about theories of personality. We have used Dr Eysenck's terms, but it would have been possible to use others.

Personality is only one of the determinants of sexual behaviour. The opportunity for contact with the opposite sex and the facilities to make use of that opportunity are just as important as personality. This chapter indicates that there are probably certain personality characteristics which lead some teenagers to create the opportunities and to take advantage of the available facilities.

Part Four

Summary and Discussion

13. Profile of the Experienced Teenager

A. Rating Scales

This research concentrated upon the task of obtaining quantitative and measurable material because only a few researches on sex behaviour have provided this type of information. Up to this point of this report we have left out most of the qualitative material because many other books on teenagers have been based on general impressions. But during the course of a long interview there is little doubt that our interviewers often got a very vivid qualitative impression of the girl or boy. The difficulty is to convert this valuable information into a quantitative form which can be used statistically.

It was decided that this could best be done by making inferential assessments on a few general topics. Although this method is not free from subjective bias, it has been used successfully by Robb (1954), and Westwood (1960) as a convenient method of summarizing a battery of questions on similar subjects. After each interview the research worker was required to bring together all the answers on a particular subject and then rate each individual on a sample five-or-six-point scale. For example, the interviewer had to assess the degree of *intensity of family influence*; in this case the teenager was placed in one of these six categories:

1. Hardly ever goes out. All activities with family.
2. Spends most of time at home, but not always with family.
3. Member of other groups, but most often with family.
4. Spends some time at home, but active social life outside.
5. Usually out of home.
6. Living away from home.

These were known as 'anchor definitions'. It was unlikely that a teenager would fit exactly into one of these categories, but it was possible to learn enough about each teenager so as to feel that he was 'anchored' to one of these definitions.

The interviewers were instructed to read over the teenagers' answers to the questions relevant to the assessment under consideration. In the case of the *intensity of family influence*, they had to review the answers to 16 relevant questions.

After they had considered the answers to these questions, the interviewers took into account any other extra information obtained during the interview, and from this overall impression made their assessment.

Five of these rating scales turned out to be highly correlated with sex experience. The scale named *intensity of family influence* showed that those who were most influenced by their families were the least experienced ($p = 0.001$ for boys and girls). Similarly the *intensity of group influence* scale based on the answers to twenty-one questions was associated with sexual experience for boys ($p = 0.01$) and girls ($p = 0.001$). Another five-point scale, based on the answers to twenty questions, indicated the extent to which each individual had available the *facilities* which made sexual activities impossible, difficult or easy. This scale was strongly associated with sex experience for both boys ($p = 0.001$) and girls ($p = 0.001$).

At the end of the interview each teenager was rated on a five-point scale of appearance, ranging from handsome to ugly. There appears to be a strong association between good looks and sex experience for boys ($p = 0.001$) and, rather unexpectedly, a less strong association for girls ($p = 0.05$). A similar rating was made of the response of the teenager during the interview on a five-point scale ranging from talkative to reserved; there was no association for girls but there appears to be a strong association between sex experience and loquaciousness for boys ($p = 0.001$).

B. Undistinguishable Features

The two sections following this one will describe the characteristics which discriminate the sexually experienced teenagers from the others (as detailed in Chapters 8–12). These two sections on their own might give the impression that experienced teenagers are quite different from other boys and girls of the same age. In fact there are many more features where there is no difference between experienced and other teenagers than there are features where a difference can be detected. Consequently it is important to emphasize that it is not possible to draw a clear-cut profile of the experienced teenager, for the distinctions are often blurred and the similarities may be just as important as the differences. This is especially the case as regards the basic background features where differences might have been expected.

The boys in our sample, aged seventeen to nineteen, who had experience of premarital intercourse, came from all sections of the community and from all social classes. They were not more likely to be the sons of manual or non-manual workers. Nor did we find any difference between the two groups when we considered the social class of the mother. Their position in the family had no effect; they did not tend to be the oldest, or the youngest, or the only child in the family.

It made no difference if they came from a church-going home, and there was no difference as between those in the Church of England and Nonconformists, Roman Catholics or Jews.

The background of the boys seems to have little effect, and early experience, found to be influential in other areas of behaviour, did not appear to produce changes in sexual behaviour. Experienced boys were not more likely to come from broken homes where the father was dead or absent; the parents, marital happiness or the number of times they have moved home had no effect. Mothers who went out to work or the relations with the father were not important; only where there were poor relations with the mother were the boys more likely to be experienced.

There were only slight variations in the sexual behaviour of boys from different types of school; experienced boys were most likely to come from secondary modern schools and least likely to come from grammar schools; there was hardly any difference between state schools of all types and independent schools; there was a slight tendency for experienced boys to come from coeducational rather than segregated schools, but no difference between day and boarding schools.

Sex education did not seem to prevent premarital intercourse or to encourage it. The experienced boys, like the other boys, wished they had been told more about sex at school and by their parents. About half of each group felt they now knew all there was to know about sex. Experienced boys started work before the others and had more jobs, but they did not appear to be less contented in their work.

Youth clubs did not seem to have much effect on sexual behaviour. Neither the number of visits in a month, nor the type of club was an influencing factor. Experienced boys did not spend any less or more time watching TV, and were not less or more likely to own a motor-cycle, scooter or have the use of a car.

Thus the sexually experienced boy did not come from a deprived home, nor was he handicapped in any other way. He seems to have had much the same start in life as the others and there are no signs in early childhood which can be used to predict the later sexual behaviour of the teenager.

C. Discriminating Features

Although the early family life and background of experienced boys appear to be unexceptional, when the present family situation is considered, it is possible to detect a difference. This is particularly true of questions related to parental discipline. The parents of the less experienced boys knew where they spent their leisure and insisted that they returned home in the evenings at a definite time. Age itself is related to parental discipline; as a boy gets older he is less amenable to discipline and also more likely to be sexually experienced.

The rating scale on family influence showed a strong association with sex experience. This influence did not extend to religion as we found that the extent of parental church-going had no influence on sex behaviour. But experienced boys do not go to church and their attitudes are out of sympathy with religious thinking.

Where there is less parental discipline there are probably more opportunities for sexual behaviour. Experienced boys were more often out of the home, and when they were at home they more often had the house to themselves. They were more likely to go to parties where there was no supervision by adults and to parties that lasted after midnight, and perhaps all night. It was made clear in the factor analysis that they would prefer to take their holidays away from their parents and many of them did this.

Experienced boys either have, or create, the opportunities and facilities for more extensive sex behaviour.

The school careers of the sexually experienced boys were less satisfactory. They were more likely to be sent to a secondary modern school and they did not pass many exams; this may be more a matter of personality than intelligence because we found that the experienced boys who did take GCE 'O' level passed in just as many subjects as the other boys. But the experienced boys disliked school and had many more problems at school. And many of them left school as soon as they could.

As they left school earlier, they also went to work at an earlier age. This may partly account for the fact that they had many more jobs than the non-experienced and inceptive boys; but it is doubtful if this wholly accounts for the larger number of jobs which the experienced boys had; there are also signs of restlessness and lack of ambition (factor XII).

They received larger wages than the other boys and they had more money to spend. This is partly because they were older, but this does not fully explain the difference; the correlation between money to spend and sex experience is 0·45, and when the influence of age is excluded, it is reduced to 0·32, but this is still a high correlation. The teenagers earning very high wages were nearly all experienced boys and this may be connected in some cases with physical energy and strength. Another indication of this vigour is shown in the association with sport. Experienced boys are less likely to be interested in sport, but the few who are interested play as often as the other boys.

Their desire to leave school and go to work may also be related to physical development. It is well known that the age of puberty varies considerably (Tanner, 1961) and in the early stages of the research we tried to devise some way of recording the age at the start of puberty for each individual, but the practical difficulties were too great. So we had to be content with asking the boys if they remembered when their voice broke. Some boys had difficulty in remembering this, and in other ways it was not a very satisfactory question, but it did reveal an association with sex experience; from this slight evidence it appears that boys who reach puberty at an early age tend to have more sexual experience ($p = 0·05$).

There were other signs that physical development might be an important influence. Experienced boys found out about the facts of life before the other boys; they also started dating at an earlier age and they had their first kiss before the other boys. It is also possible that the association between parental discipline and sexual experience is related to physical maturity; the boy of seventeen who looks like an adult may resent attempts to prevent him behaving like an adult.

One of the strongest influences on a teenager's behaviour in any sphere is the desire to be like other teenagers, and sexual activities are no exception. Experienced boys spend more time in teenage groups and seek advice from friends rather than parents. They are influenced by other teenagers and by the entertainment industry and the flourishing commercial market directed towards teenage spending. Conformity with other teenagers is very important. Experienced boys are more likely to support the teenage mythology (described in Section C of Chapter 1) and are more likely to be against adult standards and outsiders of any kind. As the factor analysis showed they are the embodiment of teenage ethnocentrism.

Many boys think their friends are having more sexual experience than they are themselves. When this urgent desire to conform is combined with the fact that the most enthusiastic advocates of the teenage mythology are already sexually experienced, it becomes clear that the pressures put upon the other boys to extend the range of their sexual activities are very great indeed.

Experienced boys go out more than the others. They go to cinemas, dances, coffee bars and pubs. It is particularly the commercial premises that they like; sports clubs, youth clubs and evening institutes do not hold the same attraction. It is interesting that cinemas, dances and coffee bars are significantly associated with sexual experience for boys but not for girls. This suggests that it is not because they expect to pick up girls in these places; it is more a measure of sociability or outgoingness. (Pubs are the exception for they are significantly associated with sex for both boys and girls; this is because girls rarely go into pubs alone and are taken in by their boy friends.)

This outgoingness seems to be part of a vigorous and hedonistic search for a good time. Not only did they go to bars more often, but they also got drunk more often. They went out with a group more often and were rated as the most talkative by the interviewers. Not only did they appear before a juvenile court more often, but they were also more prepared to admit other misdeeds. It is notable that juvenile delinquency of all kinds is associated with sexual experience, but we did not find a tendency for the experienced boys to commit the more serious offences such as stealing or violence. Their transgressions often seem to be the result of thoughtless verve and liveliness.

But there is little doubt that their attitudes as well as their activities were exceedingly permissive and even indulgent. They were sceptical about adult moral standards and opposed any kind of restrictions; most of them favoured premarital intercourse for boys, but were less sure about the propriety of intercourse for unmarried girls. Although somewhat intolerant of attitudes outside the teenage world, considerable licence is allowed inside this group on most moral issues not excluding sexual behaviour.

The profile of the sexually experienced teenager falls short of the familiar image of the fast living, immoral youth with no interest in his head beyond clothes and pop music. The sexually experienced teenager can be identified in four main areas of activity:

Facilities. Although family background was not very different, lack of interest or discipline from the parents meant that the teenager found more opportunities for sex behaviour.

Physical development. The rate of human growth varies considerably and sexual behaviour seems to be connected with energy, strength and physical development, as well as with chronological age.

Conformity. The teenage mythology is now an important element in all adolescent behaviour, and those who are sexually experienced are especially liable to combine this teenage ethnocentrism with antagonism to outside adult standards.

Permissiveness. A lively gregariousness combined with a tolerant attitude to all moral questions seems to be the most universal feature of sexually experienced boys under the age of twenty.

D. Experienced Girls Compared with Boys

When the sexually experienced girls were compared with the other girls in the sample, many of the same discriminating features were found, but there were some notable differences. In general the experienced girls did not have less favourable backgrounds than the other girls, but there was a difference in family relations. There was no difference in the number who came from broken homes, who moved homes more often, whose mothers were working, whose parents went to church; nor was the religious denomination, the position in the family, or social class a discriminating feature. (Although inceptive girls tended to be higher up the social scale, there was no difference between experienced girls and the others in the social class of the father or the mother.)

But experienced girls more often reported poor relations with both the father and the mother, and there were more reports of marital difficulties among the parents. It will be remembered that there was a difference in the third-order *restrictive* factor between boys and girls (Section E of Chapter 12). Boys who scored high on this factor favoured restraints and controls without reference to family, but girls stressed the importance of family influence and loyalty. In the analysis of the attitude inventory three of the girls' first-order factors were *antipathy to family loyalty*, *dislike of home restrictions* and *preference for friends' advice*. All these factors were highly correlated with sexual experience, but did not appear at all among the boys' first-order factors.

It is clear that experienced girls have gone much farther than experienced boys in rejecting family influences. Relations with both parents were often strained and they were less likely to receive advice on sexual matters from their parents, and when they did get this advice, they were more likely to reject it.

In matters of parental discipline the experienced girls were like the experienced boys. These girls did not tell their parents where they were going, did not have to be in at a definite time, spent more time outside the home and more often entertained their friends at home when their parents were out. Like the boys, their home situation provided them with more opportunities and facilities for sexual activities.

The religious influence is the same with girls as it is with boys. The experienced girls were less likely to go to church and less likely to hold views which were favourable to religion, but they were just as likely to come from church-going homes.

The school records of the two experienced groups were very similar. Like the boys, the girls were more likely to have been to a secondary modern or comprehensive school, and were unlikely to have taken GCE; they disliked school, had more problems, and left at an earlier age. Sex education appears to have had no influence on them either way.

As with the boys, these girls had more jobs, were paid higher wages, and had more money to spend; unlike the boys they were more often discontented at work, more often unemployed, and more often in manual jobs than the other girls.

Like the boys, the school and work record of these sexually experienced girls suggests that their physical development is more advanced than it is for the other girls in the sample. They started dating and kissing at an earlier age; they were more likely than the others to have a steady boy friend; and more often they claimed to be in love, although not everyone will regard this claim as a sign of physical development.

The tendency towards teenage conformity was just as strong among the experienced girls as it was among the experienced boys. These girls were more likely than the other girls to go around in a mixed group, to spend more time with the group, and to meet on commercial premises.

More girls than boys received advice about sex from their parents, but the experienced girls like the experienced boys nearly always said they would go for advice to friends of their own age rather than parents or other adults. The experienced girls tended to hold attitudes that indicated support for teenage freedom and had a high score on teenage ethnocentrism.

The gregarious outgoingness noted among the experienced boys is not quite so apparent among the experienced girls. They did not go to the cinema, dances or coffee bars any more than the other girls. The important difference for girls is the person they go with; experienced girls were much more likely to go to these places with a boy than with another girl. Experienced girls were also less likely to play sports and they visited youth clubs less often although just as many of them were members of youth clubs.

In all other ways the experienced girls were as permissive as the experienced boys, indeed our third-order factor showed them to be more permissive. Like the boys, they went to bars more often, got drunk more often, and smoked more cigarettes. They went to more unsupervised parties, often where most of the other people there were adults, and these parties lasted past midnight and sometimes all night.

Although far fewer girls than boys had ever been in trouble with the law, those who had appeared before a court were more likely to be sexually experienced. They also admitted more misdeeds than the other girls. Not surprisingly they disagreed with the attitudes that support premarital virginity and they were not opposed to sexual intercourse before marriage. They also disputed the double standard of morality which makes premarital intercourse permissible for boys but not for girls.

The main difference between teenage girls and boys who have sexual experience is that a girl is more influenced by her family. She must overcome these family pressures and derogate her family loyalty before she can be persuaded to agree to premarital intercourse. Apart from this the discriminating factors are very similar and depend on the facilities available, the physical development, the desire to conform to the teenage mythology and the ease with which the young person can adopt a permissive attitude to moral issues; this permissiveness is essentially a personality characteristic which appears to combine with an outgoing hedonism in boys, and a rejection of family influences in girls.

14. Validity

A. Sources of Error

People who had heard about this research often asked the very relevant question: How do you know that the teenagers have been telling you the truth? The answer is that we do not know; the best we could do was to make it as easy as possible for them to tell us the truth. No social researcher can be absolutely certain that his results convey a completely accurate picture of the population he has sampled. Problems of validation are common to all researches, and are particularly pertinent to a research into sexual behaviour. No topic is more personal and private than the sexual activities of the individual, and a person who gives truthful and straightforward answers about his shopping habits or voting intentions may well hesitate before he decides to be equally frank about his sex experiences. This may seem axiomatic, but it is surprising how many surveys on sexual behaviour assume that people will answer all the questions with candour. We did not make this assumption.

From the start of this research we considered the validity of the material to be the most important problem. That is why the discussion about the validity is not part of the introduction or in the appendix, but comes here before the final chapter. As our results are the reported experiences of the individuals in the sample, ultimately their truthfulness depends upon the teenager and the interviewer. But much can be done before to ensure that the design of the research increases the validity.

Inadequate sampling is a source of error and we took considerable pains to obtain a good sample, although it is not perfect. Our sample covered several areas, but we did not visit any rural areas and we did not go to Scotland. But our interviewees were found by random sampling methods and it is likely that no particular groups or types of teenagers were left out, except possibly those girls and boys who were always on the move and did not stay in any one place long enough to get on the sampling frame:

such people may be a significant segment of the young adult population, but are a rarity among boys and girls of nineteen and younger; in only 4·4 per cent of the homes on our lists were there teenagers living away from home.

Any sample, even one taken by a production engineer from mass produced goods, is subject to sampling error, but this margin of error can be estimated statistically. Outside checks confirmed that our sample was representative; for example, the expected number of married teenagers occurred in our sample and the weighting procedure explained in Section G of Chapter 3 made hardly any change in our original results.

Indeed we are prepared to assert that no other research on sexual behaviour has used a better sample; this is not a boastful claim of assiduousness or skill, but simply the result of being provided with enough money and time to do the sampling thoroughly. But sampling is only the first step; it is also necessary to gain the cooperation of those participating in the research.

B. The Bias caused by Refusals

Every investigator dealing with human samples knows that he is very unlikely to get a 100 per cent response. It is almost inevitable that a certain percentage of those selected will not agree to an interview. The most that can be done is to keep the number of refusals down to a minimum, and to find out as much as possible about those who refuse.

Sometimes it was impossible to arrange an interview with someone in the sample for other reasons besides refusals. In some areas the sample had to be drawn from an out of date list and the family had moved out of the area. In a few cases teenagers were living away from their family during the period the research team were interviewing in that area. All those young people who were married were excluded. Teenagers who were physically handicapped or educationally subnormal were not interviewed; in a few cases the adolescent was anxious to take part and it would have been unkind to refuse to interview, but these few cases were not included in the analysis. All these reasons for not getting an interview create difficulties and add to the cost of the research, but they depend on factors having no relation to the subject matter of the research and therefore they probably do not introduce any serious bias into the results.

But refusals may well distort the results and it was essential to impress upon the interviewers the importance of minimizing the number of refusals. This was done during the training of the interviewers and during the fieldwork when the interviewers were required to persist even with the more reluctant teenagers. The attempt to arrange an interview was only abandoned if an outright refusal had been given or if it was clear that the teenager did not intend to cooperate. The interviewers were all briefed with strong arguments in favour of the research and were also taught how to justify the personal questions in the interview whenever the parents or teenagers queried them.

The result of these efforts was that the refusal rate was kept down to under 15 per cent. But three in every 20 teenagers could not be persuaded to help and this may seem a high proportion. But it is much lower than the results obtained by most researches into sexual behaviour. Only a third of the questionnaires were returned in Chesser's (1956) survey, while Bromley and Britten (1958) had a refusal rate as high as 80 per cent. Others, like Kinsey (1948, 1953), have relied entirely on volunteers and therefore are unable to estimate the effects of refusals.

The highest rate of refusals was 18 per cent in South B, while the lowest was 10 per cent in North A. The A (middle class) areas produced fewer refusals than the B (working class) areas; there were fewer refusals in the North than elsewhere, and the rate of refusals tended to rise during those periods when there was public criticism of teenage activities. Most of the outcry in the national and local papers was unfavourably disposed towards the teenagers and therefore it is not surprising that some of them were reluctant to cooperate with the Central Council for Health Education. Another increase in the number of refusals was caused by the announcement of a large increase in the VD figures in the area which led to the supposition that our interviewers were social workers looking for the source of the infection. When one girl was asked why she would not take part in the research, she said that she was afraid that we would undress her by force.

The lowest refusal rates were in North A and B; this came as no surprise to the interviewers who all remarked on the different reception they received in these areas. There seemed to be a greater degree of genuine hospitality towards visitors in the North and a greater willingness to cooperate when requested to take part in research. At that time people in the North were less aware of the activities of the market research agencies; consequently they did not suspect we were working for a commercial organization and they rather appreciated the novelty of being asked to help. It is also said that there is a more favourable response to public authority in the North, and if this is true, they might have felt obliged to help the research.

The parents of the girls refused on behalf of the teenager in about a quarter of the cases. But in two out of three refusals the interviewer actually met the teenager. Thus in many cases we were able to get full information about the reasons for refusing.

The most usual reason for refusing was lack of interest. If a teenager asked how he stood to gain from offering his cooperation, it was difficult to give an answer that he would view with satisfaction. Appeals to altruism did not carry much weight with some teenagers. Many of the girls and boys were occupied most nights of the week and there really was no good reason why they should agree to an interview. It was sometimes impossible to persuade a teenager to give up an hour of his time for a research which would not benefit him directly. The number who refuse for this reason depends on many things, none of which need necessarily be connected with the subject matter of the research. The introductory letter, time of day, and everything in the interviewer's approach were all very important, but in every survey there will usually be a residual number who cannot be persuaded to take part. Moser (1958) expects this group to be somewhere between 3 per cent and 5 per cent in most general interview surveys. In this research those who specifically said they were not interested were just under 3 per cent; if we add those who gave no particular reason for refusing, the rate is about 6 per cent. The one thing that all members of this apathetic group have in common is their lack of cooperation. This may be associated with a personality attribute, such as excessive shyness or aggressiveness, which in turn may be associated with sex experience, but any conclusions about their possible sexual behaviour based on this assumption would be very speculative. It is not unreasonable to assume that as a group their sex experiences are distributed in the same way as for the interviewed sample.

As well as those who said they were not interested, there were those who said they had no time. This was a more common reason among the boys than among the girls. The interviewers made themselves available at any time of the day or evening, and so it can be said that if the adolescents had really been interested, they could have found the time. We made it difficult for the teenagers to make this a valid excuse, but there were times when we had to accept this as the reason for not agreeing to an interview. This was also a reason given by some parents who felt they ought to protect their sons from outside distractions.

The other reason for refusing was that they guessed that questions were going to be asked about things they did not want to discuss. Many teenagers or their parents guessed that the interview would contain questions on sex experience. Some teenagers had heard distorted accounts or had picked up incorrect information about the research from misleading newspaper stories. Others had confused it with other studies on sexual behaviour reported in the press.

The teenager who felt that he was bound to be asked about his sexual behaviour would adopt an attitude towards the research which would depend largely on his attitude towards sex and his experience of it. At one end of the scale a sexually experienced teenager who felt guilty or ashamed of his sex experience might refuse to be interviewed; at the other end of the scale the immature adolescent with no sexual experience of any kind might view the prospect of answering questions about sex as too embarrassing to contemplate, and again a refusal would be the obvious solution to his difficulty. So the foreknowledge that questions about sex were to be asked would introduce a bias, but it is not certain which way this would influence the results.

It is indeed possible that knowing the interview was about sex would be an incentive to take part for some boys. It is difficult to gauge the extent to which these factors operate. It seems reasonable to guess that some experienced girls are likely to refuse because they are ashamed; at the same time it is a reasonable guess that some inexperienced girls are likely to refuse because they would be embarrassed. The younger age groups, and particularly the younger girls, were the most likely to refuse and this suggests that there is a greater tendency for the inexperienced and embarrassed to refuse rather than the experienced and ashamed.

A few parents also refused because they had heard that some of the questions were about sex; but this would have less relevance, because the fact that a parent feels he should protect his child from questions about sex is not necessarily an indication that the child is naïve or inexperienced, as our interviewers found out when some of the parents were persuaded to change their minds.

Some parents refused to allow their children to cooperate because they resented the intrusion into their private affairs. These were the most difficult refusals to deal with, for these people consider all social researches to be an incursion into their personal liberty and sometimes they were rude and unpleasant to the interviewers. Not many of the teenagers resented the intrusion, although there were a few who felt that increased knowledge about teenage activities would do more harm than good.

Whenever a refusal was recorded, the teenager was sent a refusal form and a reply-paid envelope. The form was headed by the following two paragraphs:

Although I respect any reason you may have for not taking part in this research, it would be of great help to me if you could answer the questions at the end of this letter. It will only take a minute.

As you have been selected from a random sample, no one else can act as a substitute for you. Consequently I need to know a little about the people who feel they cannot help, just so as to be sure that we are not leaving out a particular group of people.

There followed a small number of questions which were taken from the interview schedule. They were on subjects which were unlikely to cause any annoyance to the teenager and were also easy and quick to answer by ticks in the appropriate place. They covered school, job, clubs, dances, sport, church and provided enough information to give a reasonable description of the people who had refused to cooperate.

We were surprised and pleased that 78 boys and 84 girls returned these forms. Therefore exactly half those who had refused told us a little about themselves. The form was designed to give some information which could be compared directly with the answers obtained from those teenagers who had been interviewed.

This comparison showed that there were very few differences between the two groups. There was no real difference in the occupations or the number of jobs, or in church-going, or in the number of times they went out dancing. All these items are associated with sex experience. If those who had refused to be interviewed were more likely to be sexually experienced, we would have expected to find differences in these items.

The results from the refusal form suggest that it was the under-educated and uninquisitive teenager who would not agree to an interview. These boys and girls could see no point in a research of this kind and were not prepared to give up their time to help. Unless apathy is closely correlated with sex experience, and Chapter 13 leads us to believe the opposite, we doubt if these refusals have had much effect on our results.

C. External Checks

We calculated the accumulative incidence of premarital inter-course for teenage boys as reported in four American researches. All of them showed higher figures than we obtained, but it is not certain that the incidence of premarital intercourse is higher in the United States than it is here. It is possible that the different methods used in these researches might account for these higher figures.

Hardly any of the researches on the sexual behaviour of girls give enough information about the age at the time of first intercourse for us to be able to calculate the accumulative incidence. Nearly all these researches show that premarital intercourse is a fairly common phenomenon among females of all ages, but there is not much reliable information about the age when they start.

Kinsey (1953) pointed out that the first experience of premarital intercourse often takes place in the year or two before marriage, and much of it is confined to the fiancé in the period just before marriage. Consequently the incidence depends upon the age of marriage. Girls who marry at an early age tend to have premarital intercourse when they are younger than the women who marry later. Therefore there is a close correlation between age at first premarital intercourse and age at marriage.

The only large scale report on the sexual behaviour of women in Great Britain was the survey by Chesser in 1956. About 21 per cent of his youngest groups of informants had experienced premarital intercourse, and 49 per cent of all those with premarital experience had started before the age of twenty-one; so it appears that about 10 per cent of the single girls were sexually experienced at the age of twenty. This compares with our figure of 17 per cent at the age of eighteen.

We were only able to calculate the accumulative incidence for girls under nineteen from the report by Kinsey (1953). A comparison of his figures with ours at three ages (16, 17 and 18) shows that our incidence is higher than that found by Kinsey. This is surprising considering that the incidence for boys found by Kinsey was much higher than our results. This also means that the difference between boys and girls is much greater in Kinsey's research than it is in this one.

We concluded that none of the previous researches into sexual behaviour had covered the same ground; most of them are unrepresentative or study a different segment of the population; all of them are investigations carried out in different countries at different times. Consequently it is not really possible to check our results against the results of previous researches.

Nor is it possible to find much in the way of external checks from the official records. Indeed if the information on sex behaviour was available from government sources there would be no point in doing the research. But it is possible to use the small amount of official information that is available as a check on our results.

For example the official records of illegitimate births can be used as an approximate indication of the minimum incidence of premarital sexual intercourse. Wimperis (1960) found that 'unmarried mothers are far from being a psychologically average cross section of society' and in consequence it seems probable that they differ in some respects from other girls who are having premarital intercourse. But every unmarried mother has had sexual intercourse at least once and therefore the illegitimacy figures can serve as an approximate baseline for a research into the incidence of premarital sexual intercourse.

Ten of the 939 girls in our sample had given birth to an illegitimate baby or were pregnant at the time of the interview; this represents an incidence of 1·1 per cent which compares with the national average incidence for the fifteen to nineteen age group of 0·9 per cent (from the Registrar General's *Statistical Review* for 1966).

The national incidence of illegitimacy for girls aged sixteen and seventeen is 0·8 per cent and these are the ages which most nearly correspond to our younger age group, taking into account the fact that conception precedes illegitimacy by about nine months. In our sample 6 per cent of the younger girls admitted experience of sexual intercourse. The national incidence of illegitimacy for girls aged eighteen and nineteen is 1·6 per cent and these are the ages which most nearly correspond to our older age group where 16 per cent had premarital sexual intercourse. Thus our results are eight times as large as the baseline in the younger age groups and are even farther above the baseline among the older girls.

Another indication of the incidence of premarital sexual intercourse is the national figure for the number of legitimate births which occurred within the first eight months of marriage. It can be assumed that these maternities were the result of premarital sexual intercourse and so their incidence can be used as an approximate baseline in the same way as the illegitimate figures. The number of girls aged sixteen and seventeen who gave birth within eight months of marriage is 1·4 per cent which is well below the 6 per cent of our younger girls who have had premarital sexual intercourse. The average for those girls aged eighteen and nineteen is 3·9 per cent which is below the 16 per cent of our older girls who have experienced sexual intercourse.

The national figures for conceptions before marriage were used so that they could be added to the illegitimacy figures. If we add the overall average for illegitimacy (0·9 per cent) to the overall average for conceptions before marriage (1·9 per cent) we find that at least 2·8 per cent of all single girls aged fifteen to nineteen have had experience of sexual intercourse. In fact we found that 11 per cent of all such girls in our sample had experienced sexual intercourse.

Among the older girls 16 per cent of our sample had experienced sexual intercourse and the national averages for illegitimacy and conception before marriage indicate that 5·45 per cent of this age group became pregnant; this suggests that for every three girls who have premarital sexual intercourse, one becomes pregnant. Unfortunately there is very little information on the fecundity of girls under twenty. Anderson (1960) questioned 62 adolescent unmarried mothers and found that over half (58 per cent) claimed that they had conceived after less than four experiences of sexual intercourse. Gebhard (1959) found that 12·6 per cent of the girls under twenty in his sample of American women who had had premarital intercourse became pregnant; that is for every eight girls with experience of intercourse one became pregnant. So the English girls seem to run a much higher risk of pregnancy.

All illegitimacies and maternities legitimized by marriage involve a father as well as a pregnant girl, so the figures in this section are also applicable to the boys if the girls are having intercourse with boys of the same age. In the sample of younger boys 11 per cent had experienced sexual intercourse and this is more than the combined figures of illegitimacy and conceptions before marriage; 30 per cent of the older boys had experienced intercourse compared with the baseline figure of 5·45 per cent. This suggests that about one in five of the older boys who have premarital sexual intercourse will become a putative father.

The incidence figures for venereal disease do not provide a good check because only a very small proportion of the total teenage population ever get the disease. In Section E of Chapter 6 we estimated that the chances of a girl aged fifteen to nineteen getting VD were about a thousand to one; in fact one girl in our sample of 939 had been infected. It was estimated that among boys aged fifteen to nineteen only one in over 1,600 became infected by venereal disease; in our sample of 934 two boys had been infected.

The figures for premarital intercourse are always higher for boys than for girls in this research and in every other research on sexual behaviour. In this research the incidence for boys is nearly twice as high, but in the surveys by Kinsey (1948, 1953) five times as many teenage boys claimed to have had sexual intercourse. Kinsey attempted to account for this discrepancy in a number of ways and came to the conclusion that the two main factors were differences in the representativeness of his two samples for men and women, and the probability that the females have covered up some part of their premarital experience. In our sample the girls are as representative as the boys, but the social attitudes to premarital intercourse probably mean that girls tend to underestimate and boys tend to exaggerate their sexual experience. But this is unlikely to be the only explanation because there are other tendencies at work.

Most people would agree that the male is more predatory and is more likely to seek out and demand sexual conquests. Furthermore it is easier for the boy; the consequences of an unwanted pregnancy do not affect the man physically and do not damage him socially. If the boy is discovered to be having premarital intercourse, he is not often blamed, even by his parents, and his reputation in some quarters is likely to be enhanced. But a girl has to be much more careful of her reputation; indeed we have found that some boys make a clear-cut distinction between girls who will permit intercourse and girls who are a prospect for marriage.

Therefore, it is not too difficult to explain why more boys than girls have sexual intercourse. It remains true, however, that every act of heterosexual intercourse requires a girl as well as a boy. So we still have to answer the question: If more teenage boys than girls have premarital intercourse, who are their sexual partners?

The first thing to note is that for some of these experienced boys sexual intercourse is a rare occurrence. In fact 15 per cent of the experienced boys did not have intercourse in the year before they were interviewed; this was true of only 7 per cent of the experienced girls so in actual numbers more than four times as many boys than girls did not have sexual intercourse in the last year. Furthermore it has been shown that although nearly twice as many boys are experienced, in fact the girls have intercourse more often (section E of Chapter 5). Among the experienced girls 31 per cent had sexual intercourse more than 25 times in the last year, whereas only 14 per cent of the experienced boys had intercourse as often as that.

Nevertheless all the experienced boys averaged about six partners each, whereas the girls averaged only about two partners each. It is unlikely that the extra partners found by the boys are girls of twenty or older. Therefore we must assume that some of the boys' partners were extremely promiscuous teenage girls. This possibility is quite credible for in Chapter 5 we found signs that there was a small group of highly promiscuous girls not represented in our sample,* and it requires only a very few promiscuous girls to oblige many young men.

D. Evaluation of the Results

The interviewer was required to give his estimate of the truthfulness of the responses immediately after each interview. He was instructed to use the highest rating only when he had absolutely no doubts at all. In fact 6 per cent were rated as very high validity, 76 per cent as high, 26 per cent as fair and 2 per cent were rated low validity. Of course this is a subjective judgement but it should not be disregarded altogether. Every experienced interviewer will remember cases when he comes away from the interview happy and confident that he really got to know the interviewee, and he will also remember other times when he comes away perplexed and depressed with the feeling that he never got through to the other person at all.

It was also clear that in the majority of cases the teenager enjoyed the interview and this is a good indication of the validity. Nearly all (96 per cent) agreed to another interview at a later date. They were also asked if they found the interview interesting and we introduced a midway category to distinguish between people who really were interested and those who were being polite. In reply to this question, 3 per cent said they did not find it interesting, 18 per cent gave what the interviewer judged to be the polite reply and 79 per cent expressed a genuine interest.

* We met some of these very promiscuous girls when we interviewed special problem groups (girls in prison, in care and at VD clinics) outside the main random sample. These results will be published in a later report.

The five men who interviewed the boys all produced remarkably similar results, but there were some disparities between the results of the five female interviewers. For example, 11 per cent of all the girls were in stages IV and V; the two interviewers with the highest rate found 13 per cent and the two interviewers with the lowest rate found 8 per cent. It would be a mistake to make too much of this because the interviewers with the highest rates in this respect also happened to interview more older girls and so increased the chances of finding more girls in stages IV and V. However, we were left with the impression that some of our interviewers were better than others at persuading the teenage girls to be truthful about their sex experiences. But it was not a simple division; some interviewers were good with middle-class girls while others found it easier to establish rapport with working-class girls, and there were many other factors which affected the success of the interview.

As the reports from the interviewers came in, and as we checked the results, we grew more confident about the validity of the responses from the boys and less certain about the girls' replies. But the comparison with other researches shows that our results are low for boys and high for girls.

Musgrove (1963) has rightly warned researchers about the dangers of transferring American results to England. Most of the differences in the accumulative incidences for boys can probably be explained by different circumstances in different countries. But we do not rule out the possibility that other investigators have been misled by the tendency for boys to brag about their sexual adventures. There is a considerable danger that boys who volunteer to relate their sex histories are more likely to exaggerate; in this research we interviewed many boys who were not volunteers and who had to undergo considerable persuasion before they agreed to be interviewed. Furthermore the construction of our schedule of questions was specially designed to discourage boasting; the events were not taken in chronological order as we asked for a large amount of corroborative detail.

Earlier researches have shown that premarital sexual intercourse was far from rare among women of all ages, but in the two cases where we were able to get information about teenage sexual intercourse we found that our percentages were higher. We found, as others (Kinsey, 1953; Ehrmann, 1959) have found, that much of this sexual intercourse is with steady boy friends and fiancés. If the incidence of premarital intercourse among females is closely related to the age of marriage, as seems likely, and if girls are tending to marry earlier, then we must expect more premarital intercourse among teenagers. There is also the other possibility that increased sexual intercourse among teenagers has led to more early marriages.

In Section C of this chapter we found that our results were always above the rate of illegitimacy and conceptions before marriage, but we were surprised by the high risk of pregnancy that these figures revealed. On the other hand we found that girls who do have intercourse have a higher frequency rate than boys; they rarely use contraceptives and do not require their partner to take precautions; so the three to one chance of becoming pregnant is not unbelievable.

Our main concern has been to get a representative sample and to persuade the teenagers to tell us the truth. On the sampling we claim to have been reasonably successful. As far as the validity is concerned, we have found no external evidence that conflicts with our results, but we must recognize that it is very difficult to confirm that our figures are correct.

15. Questions of Public Concern

A. Premarital Sexual Intercourse

Some readers, as they approach the end of this report, may be expecting a number of definite conclusions. But the object of this report has been to provide basic factual information, not to formulate an answer to the problem of teenage immorality. In any case we doubt whether there is any one easy solution to this problem. But we hope those who are looking for answers will be able to take into account the significant facts we have been able to unearth.

Our study of inceptive behaviour has shown that girls start before boys, but gradually the boys catch up with the girls until by seventeen there are more boys than girls taking part in these activities. Fifteen to nineteen are momentous years in the sex histories of boys; during this period most of them have moved from stage I to stage III or beyond. These are also important years for the girls and over half will have moved from stage I to stage III, but there is a barrier at stage III for girls which is not apparent for boys. Once he has started, a boy will tend to move quickly from stage to stage; but the fact that a girl is at one stage does not mean that she will soon be moving on to the next.

More teenage boys than girls have experience of sexual intercourse. In our sample 11 per cent of the younger boys and 30 per cent of the older boys have had premarital intercourse; the relevant figure for the younger girls is 6 per cent and for the older girls is 16 per cent. By using the accumulative incidence concept, we estimated that at the age of eighteen 34 per cent of the boys and 17 per cent of the girls are sexually experienced.

Sexual intercourse before fourteen was rare and by sixteen 14 per cent of the boys and 5 per cent of the girls had started. The first experience of sexual intercourse was usually with someone who was already experienced; the first partner was often older and in the case of the girls was quite often an adult. It was usually with a friend and more often than not took place in the parental home of the beginner or the partner. The first experience was often unpremeditated and unplanned, and a majority said they did not enjoy it.

Boys start at an earlier age than girls because they wish to prove their masculinity to themselves, and to their friends. Although the boys start earlier, when incidence and frequency are taken together we find the total sexual outlet is very similar. Fewer girls have intercourse, but those who are experienced do it more often. The boys have more sexual partners; the girls prefer a more enduring relationship. Girls are slower to agree to intercourse, but once they have agreed they are more active sexually.

Some of the teenagers still hold attitudes which support the ancient double standard which basically states that premarital intercourse is forbidden for women but not for men. This double standard requires a minority of promiscuous and disrespected girls with whom boys are supposed to get their experience before marrying virgins.

There is another difference in attitudes between girls and boys. The girl is looking for a romantic relationship while the boy is seeking a sexual relationship. The girl is in search of security, but the boy is in search of adventure. Premarital intercourse is most likely to happen when either one modifies his or her attitude so that it comes closer to the other one's aspirations. Then if the boy gives the impression that he is in love with the girl, she is more likely to agree to intercourse; or if the girl is persuaded that sexual activities are an extension of romantic feelings, intercourse is likely to take place.

Our results have made it clear that premarital sexual relations are a long way from being universal among teenagers as over two-thirds of the boys and three-quarters of the girls in our sample have not engaged in sexual intercourse. On the other hand it is equally apparent that teenage premarital intercourse is not a minority problem confined to a few deviates. It is an activity common enough to be seen as one manifestation of teenage conformity.

B. Sex Education

This research has shown that by the age of thirteen two-thirds of the boys and three-quarters of the girls know, or think they know, about the facts of life. In fact most of them have obtained this information from their friends and much of it is inaccurate and obscene. Prejudices and misunderstandings about sex would be avoided if children first heard about it from their parents. But this research has shown that this does not happen very often.

Two-thirds of the boys and a quarter of the girls had learnt nothing about sex from their parents. Even those who had discussed sex with their parents had usually first heard about it from another source. The only exception to this was middle-class mothers who were more likely to advise their daughters. Teenagers also reported that parental advice about sex usually concentrated on moral problems, and was unspecific and vague. Furthermore we found that the young people who were most likely to have a serious sex problem were also those who were least likely to go to their parents for help.

In some countries, for example, in one state in Australia, sex education in the schools is disallowed because it is believed that the parents are the proper people to instruct the child. But our results suggest that this is unlikely to work out well. Even when special classes are instituted to help the parents to teach their children about sex, the people who attend these classes are probably the ones who would have talked to their children about sex in any case.

The best hope for those who believe that parents are the people who can do most to prepare a child for a healthy sexual life is to help the generation now at school to become the kind of parents who can speak simply and sensibly about sex to their children.

The school teacher is the second most important source of sex knowledge for boys, and the third most important source for girls. The teacher has an important role to play in sex education, especially for working-class children who are less likely to learn from their parents.

At present the adolescents who first learn about sex from teachers are those who find out later than their peers. If sex education had been given earlier, more people would have obtained correct information about sex in the first place. As the situation is at present many of those who receive sex education in schools are inattentive because they think they already know all there is to know about sex. If sex education comes too late, they will not listen because their ideas and prejudices about sex have already been formed.

Half the boys and 14 per cent of the girls did not receive any sex education at school. In all types of state schools, including grammar schools, as often as not there was no sex education for the boys. It was the working-class boys who were least likely to learn about sex from their parents and were least likely to receive sex education at school.

In view of all the discussion about sex education in recent years, it was surprising to find so many teenagers who said they were never taught about sex at school. A possible explanation is that the teachers think they are giving sex education but the adolescents do not recognize it as such. There were signs of a lack of frankness in the teaching. Sex education, when it occurred, seemed to concentrate on biological and physiological matters and seemed to be unrelated to human affairs, except when it was wholly concerned with putting across a particular moral point of view, which was often the case with the girls.

Nearly half the boys (47 per cent) and girls (43 per cent) felt they should have been told more about sex at school. The teenagers were dissatisfied with the amount of sex education they received, and with its quality. The difficulties of providing viable education about sex are immense; much of the moral code is based upon religious thinking which the teenagers do not accept and many of the arguments against premarital intercourse, when unsupported by moral exhortations, sound weak to many young people. In addition we have found a strong inclination among a large number of teenagers to reject adult advice of all kinds. But there is also plenty of evidence from this research that teenagers are anxious to be informed about sex and want sex education providing it is given with an assurance which is backed by knowledge and with a proper understanding of their particular problems.

C. Illegitimacy

It is often said that one of the consequences of premarital intercourse is illegitimacy. This is not strictly true. The birth of illegitimate children is caused by premarital sexual intercourse without
adequate precaution against an unwanted pregnancy. In this
sample 16 per cent of the boys and 18 per cent of the girls knew
nothing about birth control and many of the others had only a
slight knowledge of contraceptives.

Among those having sexual intercourse less than half the boys
always used contraceptives and a quarter never used them.
The girls having sexual intercourse usually left it to the man with
the result that the majority neither used contraceptives themselves, nor insisted that their partner used them. Ponting (1963)
interviewed a much more promiscuous group of teenagers and she
found that only 17 per cent took precautions.

Quite a large group in this sample either did not like contraceptives or could not be bothered with them. The most usual
birth-control method was either the sheath or withdrawal, but
some of the boys who possessed sheaths had not had intercourse
and had bought them as a kind of status symbol.

About half the experienced boys said they were inhibited by the
fear that their partner might become pregnant, but about 40 per
cent seemed to be unconcerned. More of the girls feared pregnancy
but they did very little about it. Many of the boys said they would
marry a girl they had made pregnant, and this is what many of
the girls hoped or expected. Others said they would want to keep
the child if they became an unmarried mother. Neither adoption
nor abortion were favoured by teenage girls, so it can be assumed
that most pregnancies will lead to a hasty marriage or an illegitimate child.

There is still a strong feeling that the boy who made the girl
pregnant has a duty to marry her, although this pressure is less
severe when both of them are young. But Greenland (1958)
found that among the 45 teenage unmarried mothers in his group,
the putative father was over nineteen in 24 (53 per cent) cases. A
study of the Registrar General's figures since 1938 on rates of
illegitimacy and premarital conceptions taken together show that

although the illegitimacy rate has gone up, the percentage of teenage brides who were pregnant on their wedding day has gone down. Therefore the social pressures on the unmarried mother to marry have declined, and this decrease in the rate of premarital conceptions 'regularized' by marriage more than accounts for the increase in illegitimate births.

Our inquiries into the use of birth-control methods among teenagers have shown that many boys are not using contraceptives and most girls who are having intercourse are at risk. This does not seem to be because teenagers have difficulty in obtaining contraceptives, but because social disapproval means that many of their sexual adventures are unpremeditated. Premarital sexual intercourse among young people is often an impulsive act; it is not planned beforehand, except in the case of an engaged couple who are regularly sleeping together. When a person is acting on impulse, it is obvious that he or she is less likely to take precautions. It can be argued that if an unmarried teenager is prepared to think far enough ahead to get advice on birth-control, then he or she is acting more responsibly than someone who allows sexual desire to override their awareness of the possible consequences.

Illegitimacy is an important social phenomenon, but it is quite fallacious to suggest that it is entirely a teenage problem. Only about a quarter of all illegitimate births were to teenage girls, about the same proportion as to women over 32 years. The incidence of illegitimate births per 1,000 unmarried women is about 9 times as great for women aged 25–29 as it is for girls aged 15–19. The belief that illegitimacy is a teenage problem is presumably based on the fact that the proportion of illegitimate births to all births is very high for the younger age groups. But this proportion is high because the number of total births to girls under twenty is much smaller (72,000) than to women aged 25–29 (263,000).*

The idea that illegitimacy is only a teenage problem has diverted attention from more important social aspects. The National Council for the Unmarried Mother and her Child in their forty-

* The statistics in this paragraph are taken from figures published by the Registrar General for England and Wales in his Statistical Reviews and in the Annual Abstract of Statistics. They are based on an analysis of Birth Certificates and can claim a high degree of accuracy.

sixth annual report stresses the need for a more sympathetic social climate 'so that individual citizens feel able to accept unmarried mothers and children in their midst, without censure, and without that hurtful comment which may have long term effects on the child'. According to one report,* the number of schoolgirls who become pregnant is small (less than one in 1,500), but one in 14 of all the children born in Britain is illegitimate. It is very important that teachers and others should not forget that in a school class of 30, there will probably be two children who will have been born out of wedlock.

D. Venereal Disease

The problem of venereal diseases among teenagers is not so great as the problem of illegitimacy. Nevertheless there has been an increase in the number of infections in the last few years, although this increase has not been so great in this age group as the rise among other sections of the community. It has been shown by the reports of the British Co-operative Clinical Group (1962, 1963) that the main increases in gonorrhoea have been among immigrants†, homosexuals and young adults. The Chief Medical Officer to the Ministry of Health wrote in his report for 1965:

It must be clearly understood that the bulk of venereal infection is among people of 25 and over, and especially in men. Only 8·6 per cent of syphilis and 13·1 per cent of gonorrhoea occurs among people aged 19 or less. The prevalence of venereal disease is not due to promiscuous teenagers . . .

This does not mean that the risks should be disregarded. Most of the teenagers in our sample had heard about VD, but not many of the experienced ones were worried about the possibility of being infected. Ponting (1963) found only 32 per cent who were

* *The Health of the School Child;* 1964–5, H.M.S.O. 1966.
† About half the increase in the VD rate is due to immigration. But over a third of these infected immigrants are not coloured, and VD is not a racialist problem. It is simply because many a young man who arrives in this country on his own without wife or girl friend is vulnerable to sexual temptations. This is nothing to do with being coloured; it is because he is lonely and unsettled.

afraid of VD and she obtained her information from a group who had visited a clinic at least once.

We found that there was still much ignorance about the venereal diseases and some of the misapprehensions and old wives' tales still persisted. About half the young people in our sample would not be able to recognize the symptoms if they were infected. Books were the best source of correct information although Dalzell-Ward (1960) has shown that some of the books on sex education do not mention the venereal diseases at all. Friends were the biggest source of misinformation and there is still some doubt whether a person who suspected that he was infected would really go to a clinic.

As the venereal diseases are sexually transmitted, the spread of the infection must involve, not two, but at least three people; one or both of the partners in the sexual act must have had intercourse with someone else. Therefore the venereal diseases must be associated with promiscuity.

It is generally considered that a stable marriage is a safeguard against promiscuity and that single people are more likely to be promiscuous. Hitchens and James (1965) investigated the amount of VD among unattached persons aged 15–50, and found that single males over the age of 20 were ten times more likely than teenagers to get VD, and single girls over the age of 20 were three times more likely to get this disease. They conclude that sexual promiscuity and recourse to prostitutes is much more widespread among older people.

This result agrees with those found in this research. In Chapter 5 we reported on the number of partners for all the experienced boys and girls, but a better indication of promiscuity is the number of sexual partners *in the last year*. It was found that less than 12 per cent of the boys had more than one partner, while 6 per cent had only one partner; in addition 3 per cent of the boys had no experience in the last year although they had previously had sexual intercourse. Therefore slightly more than half the experienced boys can be said to be promiscuous in the strictest sense of the word.*

* The Oxford dictionary definition of promiscuity uses the words 'indiscriminate mixture' and therefore it is open to doubt if sexual inter-

Less than a quarter of the experienced girls (about 2 per cent of the whole sample) had more than one sexual partner in the last year. In Chapter 5 and elsewhere in this report we have noted that the boys have more partners than the girls, but this should not hide the fact that a larger number of boys have premarital intercourse with one girl only, often with the girl they intend to marry (Section C of Chapter 10).

These results suggest that promiscuity, although it exists, is not a prominent feature of teenage sexual behaviour. Consequently the risks of venereal disease are not very great, and this conclusion is supported by the figures. Of course it is true that even the teenager who has had only one previous sexual partner may still infect another person. But the main danger of the venereal diseases is that many teenagers are ignorant about the symptoms, which are not always obvious, and may not go to a clinic if they are infected. Three-quarters of the boys who have sexual intercourse and four out of five of the girls at risk would not know if they had been infected (Section D of Chapter 8). These people are unlikely to reach diagnosis and treatment. Morton (1966) reports that about a quarter of all the new patients who attend VD clinics do not require treatment. If more people can be persuaded to go to a clinic for examination, tests and reassurance, this would help to control the spread of VD.

Only a few teenagers are restrained from having sexual intercourse by the fear of venereal disease (Section E of Chapter 7). Those people who use the rise in the VD rate in their campaign against premarital intercourse should note that teenagers are not likely to be deterred by this threat.

On the other hand the fear of pregnancy was often given as the reason for not having sexual intercourse and indeed the risks of pregnancy are greater than the risks of infection by venereal disease. Adults who comment on teenage sexual activities often bracket illegitimacy and venereal disease together, but the risks of illegitimacy are greater and the consequences more serious.

---

course with two or three people can be called promiscuity. For those who prefer a wider definition of promiscuity, it is noted that about a quarter of the experienced boys (6 per cent of the whole sample) had four or more partners in the last year.

E. Restraints and Controls

It is not one of the objects of this research to suggest ways in which premarital sexual intercourse can be prevented. But it is hoped that those who are concerned about teenage sexual behaviour will be able to make use of some of the specific facts uncovered by this research. For example, it seems to be common practice to end a criticism of adolescent sexual behaviour by adding that we all know the bad ones are an exception and that most of the youth of this country are a grand clean-living bunch of lads. But this qualification is as wrong as the criticism is inept. For the results of this research show clearly that those who are having sexual intercourse are not a tiny minority. In round figures something over 350,000 boys and girls under the age of twenty have had experience of premarital intercourse.

But although it is not a small minority, it is not a majority, and those who are concerned about this problem might begin by asking why, in view of the great strength of the sexual drive, there are not more teenagers who are sexually experienced. Young men under the age of twenty are at their highest sexual potential and social pressures are by no means all on the side of restraint.

In Chapter 7 we found that many of the teenagers gave moral reasons for not going farther, although few gave specific religious reasons. Many appeals to youth either assume Christian values or explicitly state Christian doctrines, but most of the young people we interviewed were not interested in Christianity. It is possible that many young people find their way of living incompatible with the moral teaching of Christianity and the Church's emphasis on sexual morality may make the experienced teenager feel that there is no room for him in the Christian Church.

Despite the social and physiological pressures towards sexual intercourse, many teenagers manage to resist these influences. This research has found several differences between those who do and those who do not have sexual intercourse. These are summarized in Chapter 13 and they need not be repeated here except to add that these differences do not reveal serious anti-social tendencies in those teenagers with experience of sexual intercourse. The experienced boys were gregarious and outgoing, even hedonistic, but they were not misfits. Sexual experience among teenage girls is closely associated with a desire for freedom and independence from the family, but they were not debauched.

Nor is there any evidence that premarital sexual intercourse leads to or encourages adulterous relations after marriage. Burgess and Wallin (1953) found that 90 per cent of the women who had had premarital intercourse said that it had strengthened their marital relationship. Most of the young people in this sample disapproved of extramarital relations and this is as true of the experienced teenagers as of the others.

Those who are worried about the extent of premarital sexual intercourse among teenagers must accept that these activities cannot be eliminated altogether in the foreseeable future. Murdock (1949), on the basis of evidence compiled from a worldwide sample of 158 societies, found that premarital intercourse was permitted in 70 per cent of them; in the other societies restraints reinforced by disgrace and punishments were not always effective in preventing young people from engaging in premarital intercourse. The most effective way to prevent teenage sexual activities would be to decrease the opportunities by reintroducing ideas like chaperonage of girls and further segregation of the sexes. Descriptions of a Chinese school (Huang, 1964) and of family life in the Soviet Union (Mace, 1963) make it clear that adolescent immorality can be reduced if not eliminated. But if this is what is required, we shall also have to accept a measure of Communist discipline and a reduction in personal freedom.

Many people will have noticed that this research has found an association between sex experience and lack of parental discipline. There is a danger that some people will seize upon this as if it is the most important finding in the report because it fits in with their preconceived ideas and because it appears to be easy to remedy. But it is not certain that further restrictions will be of value. Bier (1963) in the report of a symposium on adolescents warns about the dangers of 'scrupulosity' – a tendency to make an individual see evil where there is no evil, serious sin where there is no sin and obligation where there is no obligation.

In face of much of the uninformed criticism about teenage sexual activities, it is tempting to spend too much time in pointing out that many of the generalizations are without factual foundation, that there are no signs of moral collapse, that more thought should be given to adult immorality, that many teenage attitudes are refreshing and stimulating, that there are many serious young people with great intellectual curiosity and high aspirations. But these assertions of good sense are not a substitute for factual information.

Indeed a disinterested look at the teenage cult will reveal several facets which are quite depressing and many signs that the least valuable and shabbiest aspects of adult society have been adopted with enthusiasm. The flaws in teenage society have been noted in detail by several writers, particularly Fyvel (1963) and the Hechingers (1964). The particular facet which concerns this research is the pressures towards conformity within the teenage cult and the formation of a teenage mythology. A typical example is teenage fashions which may seem daringly different from adult society, but in reality they are an illustration of strict conformism within the teenage subculture.

Four out of five people in Great Britain now live in urban areas, some of immense size. This urbanism has made possible the growth of teenage subcultures which are often at variance with adult standards. The improved economic position of the teenagers have given them more independence and greater mobility. But for many it has become a confused world as they revolt against an imposed middle-class morality and at the same time lose the assurance of their own working-class environment (Bals, 1962).

Within these urban conditions has grown up the teenage mythology, built up by the press, the advertisers and the special teenage and pop music magazines. This has created an image of how the teenager is supposed to behave. Here is an organized system of behaviour expectations and attitudes, and the young person acts out his role, largely learnt from the teenage group to which he belongs.

The sexual behaviour of young people is influenced by this teenage subculture. In Chapter 4 we saw that there is a danger that a teenager may feel he is exceptional because he has not had sexual intercourse. In the same chapter we found that half the boys and two-thirds of the girls did not enjoy their first experience of sexual intercourse, but nearly all of them tried it again fairly soon. Yet at the time of the interview there were still 28 per cent of the experienced boys and 39 per cent of the experienced girls who did not always enjoy it.

In Chapter 5 we envisaged a situation in which the boy and girl engaged in sexual intercourse although neither of them wanted to do this. In Chapter 10 we found that many teenagers felt their friends were having more sex than they were and in Chapter 13 we noted that the most enthusiastic advocates of teenage conformity were the sexually experienced boys and girls.

In Chapter 12 we found that the sexually experienced were the ones who had the least respect for adult standards. Consequently the time that these people spend with adults is cut to a minimum and there is no interaction between the adult and teenage worlds. The young people no longer have what the Americans call 'corrective feedback' from adults, and youth becomes, not 'an ephemeral privilege' as Cocteau thought it ought to be, but 'a separate hardy race setting itself up in opposition to the decaying race of the old'.

Yet it is obvious that this teenage subculture has been created by the adult world, not by the young people themselves. For example, the sexually experienced went to the cinema more often than the others and therefore could see that sexual satisfaction is all important in most films, and premarital sex is acceptable in many. The teenagers with the most sexual experience were also those with the most money to spend and therefore the quarry for the very active salesmen of the teenage commercial market.

Even when we know that adult intervention may be resented, we have a social duty to help the adolescent to understand himself, and hurt himself and others as little as possible. But our ideas must be feasible if they are to be helpful. No matter what measures are taken to restrict or control or change or influence the activities of our young people, it is certain that in the immediate future a not inconsiderable number of teenagers will engage in premarital sexual intercourse. These sexually experienced teenagers are every bit as much our responsibility as the others. Whatever the long-term answer may be, there is an urgent short-term task, and that is to make youthful sex activities less harmful. This may be done by increasing the amount of knowledge and enlightenment on sexual matters, by introducing more and better sex education in the widest sense, and by providing individual counselling which on some occasions will mean making available methods of birth control to those who need them. Above all it is vital that future programmes of advice, help and restraint should be based, less on unsubstantiated impressions, and more on the demonstrable facts. It is hoped that this research has gone some way towards providing this necessary factual information.

Part Five

Appendices

Appendix 1: The Interviews

The object of the research was to obtain facts, and in particular to report on the extent of sexual experience in the fifteen to nineteen age group and, if possible, to identify any factors that seemed to be associated with sexual experience. Consequently this research did not start out with any hypothesis beyond the simple assumption that some teenagers are sexually experienced and some are not, and that there may be a difference between those who are experienced, and those who are not.

The ideal situation would be for the research team to administer some psychological test which had no apparent association with sexual behaviour, and this test would reveal the extent of sexual experience in each person. Not surprisingly no such test exists, and although there are numerous personality tests from which to choose, none of them, individually or collectively, produce results which give any indication of sexual experience.

In the present state of knowledge in the social sciences, the information could be collected in only two ways:

a. the face-to-face interview;
b. the self-administered written questionnaire.

The relative advantages of either method have often been tested and discussed (Ellis, 1948). The disadvantages of both methods are magnified when the questions refer to sexual behaviour.

The great advantage of the self-administered questionnaire is that it is possible to obtain very large numbers. For example a 1 per cent sample of the age group studied in this research would require answers from 35,000 people. Obviously it would have been prohibitively expensive to have an hour long interview with so many people, but it might have been possible to post off that number of questionnaires. But there would be a large number of refusals and the people who did answer might be a very biased sample. In fact it is possible to overestimate the value of large numbers and there is a tendency to make researches seem more important than they really are by obtaining results from hundreds of similar subjects.

In a research into sexual behaviour the actual language to be used is a big problem. In a written questionnaire it would be difficult to avoid using long words with Latin roots; it would certainly be necessary to avoid putting vernacular words into print. But in the interview situation a careful use of the vernacular often helps to make clear the meaning of a question.

Many people who can answer verbally are unable to put their thoughts down on paper. The written questionnaire would exclude a large number of people because they cannot read fluently and are not literate enough to answer the detailed questions.

Difficulties with wording are a constant source of trouble in questionnaires. In one self-administered written questionnaire given to girls the question, 'Are you a virgin?' brought the reply, 'Not yet.' Individuals often answer a question in different terms and at another level from that in the mind of the person who constructed the questionnaire.

We had the opportunity to test our questions very thoroughly before we started the field work, but there were still occasions when the purpose of the question was completely misunderstood. At one point in the interview we asked: 'Have you ever had a problem to do with sex?' On one occasion it was answered like this: 'Only a dirty joke that I heard at school and couldn't fathom. I thought about it for ages but couldn't work it out, so I asked my parents, but they couldn't see it either.' One of the leisure questions asked if there was 'any sportsman or singer or star that you particularly like?' One boy's answer was: 'Gaugin.' When a girl was asked, 'Have you ever been in love?' she replied, 'Only with my dog.' At the end of the interview each teenager was asked if there was anything else we should have asked about; one girl replied, 'Well, you didn't ask me what I thought about the Queen.'

All these and many other misunderstandings can be cleared up in the face-to-face interview situation because the research worker is able to persist until he gets the relevant answer. It is also possible to built up a friendly relationship in the early part of the interview so that by the time the questions on sex are reached, the teenager feels that he has a sympathetic and impartial listener. Sometimes the reassurances of the interviewer are better than the questionnaire as a guarantee of anonymity. The interviewer also has the opportunity to overcome an unwillingness to answer a particular question, an important advantage in researches of this kind. In an interview there is also a better chance of knowing when the teenager is covering up or avoiding the issue.

There is also the danger that the questionnaire will be filled in with others looking on, and it is obvious that this will affect the anwers given and is almost sure to make them invalid. In this research there were 234 questions on an interview schedule of 16 pages. This would be a very daunting sight for a teenager if he were asked to spend time filling in a form of this length. But in the hands of an interviewer it sometimes took less than an hour. This was because not all the questions applied to all the adolescents. For example it seemed important to ask the teenager several questions about the circumstances of and his reactions to the first experience of sexual intercourse. If a girl of fifteen has no such experience, then obviously none of these questions would be asked. But in a written questionnaire they would all have to be listed, and it is not difficult to imagine what some parents would say if they happened to see such a questionnaire.

In order to get over the embarrassment of talking to a stranger about sex, it was suggested that the questions should be recorded and the teenager left alone to record the answers. But this has the same inflexibility as the questionnaire and thus the same disadvantages, such as difficulties with vocabulary, dissimilar experiences, no chance to clear up misunderstandings, no opportunity to probe on a question, or to gauge the extent of embarrassment or cover-up in an answer.

Group interviews would not allow for individual variation and inevitably the stronger personalities would set the pace. Such a discussion might well be very informative and instructive for the less forward member of the group, but as a method of obtaining information about individuals it is not very useful.

Sexual activities are surrounded by strong social conventions and privacy is essential. The written questionnaire presents too great a temptation for the teenagers to mislead, understate or exaggerate. The interview situation is still the best method of obtaining information about sexual behaviour providing careful training is given to the interviewers and the schedule of questions is elaborately tested.

During the exploratory stage visits were made to a well-known jazz club where we expected to find sexually experienced teenagers, to a suburban youth club to find the more conforming type of adolescent, to schools so that we could interview younger boys and girls, to a Day Continuation College for a cross section of teenagers educated at secondary modern schools and to university students (some of whom were social scientists) so that we could obtain an articulate and detailed reaction to the research team's methods and techniques.

During this pilot research each teenager was asked to criticize the schedule of questions after the interview. Sometimes an interviewee would show quite clearly that he had not understood the questions even when he made no comment. After a series of interviews those who had volunteered were persuaded to meet together as a group with the research team. This group was then encouraged to criticize the questions on the schedule and tape-recordings of these group discussions revealed extra information on the right approach and the best wording to use. Here are a few examples of the kind of remarks made during these discussions:

Boy: 'Nearly everything you've said we don't use the same word for.'
Boy about masturbation: 'It's all right to ask but change the word.'
Boy about having the interview in a church hall: 'You couldn't *say* anything there.'
Girl about the interview: 'I would have felt funny at home.'
Boy on not wanting to be interviewed in a consulting room: 'I'd think the doctor was going to examine me.'
Boy: 'You want to get us where we're not interested in anything' (i.e. not in a youth club where they could be doing something else).
Boy about interviewer calling at his home: 'If you send us a letter first with the proper paper . . .'

Experience gained during the exploratory stage revealed that many of the questions on sexual behaviour would have to be restricted or altered for the younger age group. We decided to abandon our original intention of interviewing adolescents of thirteen and fourteen because the state of physical maturity is very variable at that age and in addition there would be difficulties in vocabulary and a high rate of refusal from parents. It was also clear that the leisure activities and sexual behaviour of married teenagers would be so different that comparisons with the unmarried adolescents would be meaningless. Accordingly it was decided to concentrate on unmarried adolescents between fifteen and nineteen.

The basic purpose of the investigation was to establish the incidence of sexual activities among young people. With this aim went a hypothesis that certain types of sexual activity were concomitant with certain social and psychological variables. These two factors shaped the schedule of questions to be used at each interview. To cover social variables a large net of questions was constructed which attempted to tap all aspects of the teenager's background and leisure activities, and especially those activities where opportunities or facilities for sexual experience appeared to be a possibility. Thus reading habits were not included, but questions were asked about going to parties.

Although the questions were first compiled in sections, they were not placed in the schedule section by section. The sequence of questions was decided by a number of considerations. It was important to keep up the interest of the adolescent so the dull questions had to be kept apart; one question had to follow another without too sudden a jump from one subject to the next; sometimes it was necessary to insert waste questions in order to lead up logically and smoothly to an important question. The fact that the questions were not asked in chronological order meant that it was much more difficult for a teenager to mislead or act a fictitious role, because inconsistencies would become apparent when the questioner returned to the same subject later in the interview.

Three different drafts of the interview schedule were tested during the exploratory period before the final list of questions was standardized for the random sample. Modifications were required because the questions did not elicit the information they were designed to obtain, because some of the words were not universally understood, and because the sequence of questions appeared to interrupt the flow of the interview. Inevitably verbal responses vary in a survey covering all educational levels. Standardized questions do not always bring standardized answers, for the same question can mean different things to different people. Yet some sort of standardization is necessary if statistical analysis is to be used. The difficulty is to find words and phrases that are both exact and understood.

For example, a number of adolescents thought that the term 'birth control' meant controlling the delivery of a baby at birth. Some of the younger adolescents had not heard about venereal disease. When one of the grammar schools boys was asked what he knew about VD he replied: 'Nothing, unless you mean vapour density.' One of the early questions in the first draft was: 'Do you think contraceptives are 100 per cent reliable?' It was hoped that this would indicate a difference in attitude between the experienced and inexperienced boys. Unfortunately the word 'contraceptive' was not always understood, and so when the answer was 'I don't know', as was usually the case, it was not clear if the answer referred to the reliability of contraceptives, or merely meant that the question had not been understood.

The design of the schedule was planned so that comparatively impersonal information was obtained in the first part of the interview. It commenced with questions on age, place of birth, father's occupation, type of education, size of family, work and many questions on leisure interests. All questions which attempted to find out the extent of a leisure activity were asked in two ways. For example, they were first asked: 'How often do you go to the cinema?' Then they were asked: 'When did you last go?' The latter question usually gave a better record of the actual frequency of an activity (Prais and Houthakker, 1955). In this part of the interview it was possible to build up a good relationship with the teenager, especially as many of them enjoyed the chance to talk about their spare-time activities. In this way the interviewee acquired sufficient confidence to answer questions about his sexual behaviour.

Sexual behaviour was treated in the schedule as though each individual progressed through certain stages of development. This was a reasonable assumption that was reinforced during the exploratory period. If an interviewee denied a certain activity, it had to be assumed that he had not passed through the later stages of sexual experience. In this way we avoided putting unnecessary questions about sexual behaviour to inexperienced boys and girls. This sifting approach helped particularly in the interviews with immature adolescents as it was imperative that inessential sex questions should not be asked, in case we were accused of 'putting ideas into their heads'. We had constantly to bear in mind that we might offend or shock some of the interviewees, or (more probably) their parents, if we asked questions about sexual behaviour which extended beyond their experience.

The actual form of the sex questions assumed that the interviewee had engaged in the relevant activity. So the question was phrased: 'When did you first . . . ?' This was better than: 'Have you ever . . . ?' This placed the onus of denial on the interviewee. It also helped to assure the young person that the interviewer would not be surprised or shocked if he had had such an experience. Many boys and girls said this approach helped them considerably because this assumption about their experience made them feel less embarrassed; they did not have to admit something but just give a date.

It would be satisfying to say that all possible individual reactions were anticipated and allowed for in the schedule of questions. But this was not the case. People do not fit into the preconceived ideas of researchers and teenagers do not fall nicely into groups or patterns of behaviour. After nearly every interview there were discussions and queries. Even so, the long and thorough pilot research did make it possible to revise a schedule of questions so that the information about teenage sexual behaviour was collected in a systematic and consistent manner.

Appendix 2. The Interviewers

Ten interviewers were used during the course of the research. Three were full-time members of the research team and seven were employed specifically for interviewing. All of them had some experience of working with young people and all of them were young graduates with an average age of twenty-five. Although most of them had previous experience of interviewing, they were not chosen for this reason. The interviewing techniques needed for this research were rather different from those used in case work where the emphasis is placed on diagnosis and therapy. The calm collection of emotionally charged information required a detached and straightforward manner with no hint that any act was untoward or any attitude was displeasing.

The interviewer's job required four main qualities; a pleasing appearance; determination; a methodical way of working; and the ability to establish and maintain *rapport*.

A pleasing appearance was essential because the interviewer had only a few minutes on the doorstep to persuade the parent or the adolescent to agree to an interview. First impressions are very important in this kind of situation. Clothes, accent, manner and appearance were just as important as the short introductory talk given by the interviewer on the doorstep.

Determination and persistence were necessary, as many teenagers were apathetic and showed no interest in the research, while others appeared to be interested but failed to keep appointments. The interviewers also had to learn to put up with remarks from some parents who were rude or aggressive. They had to make repeated calls on cold wet nights at houses where they could not expect to be welcome.

Methodical and accurate recording was essential because it was necessary to get a large amount of information on to the schedule in a standardized form so that it could be read by other people and used statistically.

Rapport and a natural capacity for making social contact was the most important requirement of all. It was essential that the interviewer quickly established a friendly relationship so that the young person soon felt at ease and well-disposed towards the idea of answering the questions.

Each interviewer was given a two weeks course of intensive training before he was sent out into the field. This consisted of a detailed background briefing, a series of trial interviews, sessions listening to recordings of their own and other interviews, and practice of the whole routine on subjects not in the sample.

The long exploratory stage meant that many new techniques could be passed on to the interviewers. Many hours were spent on getting to know the schedule of questions almost by heart. Familiarity with the wording and order of the questions was essential so that (1) the interviewer could look at the adolescent when talking, (2) the interview could continue at a good speed without awkward pauses and (3) the interviewer could give his full attention to maintaining *rapport* and recording the answers.

The first trial interview was carried out with one of the research team taking the role of the interviewee. In each trial interview the member of the research team would play a different role – from very inexperienced sexually to very experienced. This was made more realistic by using a schedule filled in from an actual interview during the exploratory stage. Afterwards it was possible to check the new interviewer's record with the other schedule. The research team had already been interviewing for six months before the training of the additional interviewers had started and so they were able to warn the interviewers of recurring difficulties and suggest how to deal with them.

During the exploratory period some tape-recordings were made of actual interviews with teenagers. These were played over to the new interviewers as a group and they were required to record the answers on a schedule. Afterwards the schedules were compared and differences were discussed and resolved, so that a standardized form of documentation evolved. These tape-recorded interviews were particularly valuable for teaching the interviewer to hear more than what is being said; for making him alert to what is not being said; for preparing him to deal with evasions and omissions.

Tape-recordings were also made of the trial interviews so that the interviewers could then listen to their own voices. This helped the new interviewers to correct wrong inflections and emphasis in the way they asked some of the questions. Special care was taken to avoid the hushed voice or apologetic tone when asking questions on sexual behaviour.

No amount of simulated interviews could really substitute for conversations with adolescents, and so the interviewers went along with the research team to a youth club outside the sample areas and tried to persuade the boys and girls to be interviewed. This was excellent experience, and probably a more difficult situation than the one they would have to face on the doorstep of a home where at least a formal letter of introduction had paved the way. This letter was important because it was the young person's first contact with the research and the impression it made was likely to be decisive in determining whether or not he would agree to an interview. It was signed personally by the interviewer and posted so that it arrived the day before the call. This gave him very little time to write back asking our interviewer not to call and the letter was still in his mind at the time of the call.

The value of the letter was that it obviously came from an organization conducting a serious research. The underlying assumption was that the teenager would take part and it attempted to explain why he had been chosen. The letter was addressed to the teenager, not to his parents. This personal approach to the young person himself was very valuable. Our aim was to make him realize that we considered his views to be important. But the letter did suggest that arrangements for the interview should be discussed with his parents and in most cases the parents had read the letter before the interviewer had called at the house. A few parents resented this method, but in effect they always had the chance to prevent the interview from taking place, and indeed did so on several occasions. The interviewers were instructed to obtain the permission of the parents except when the teenager was living away from home.

The interviewer called at the teenager's home and if he was able to speak to the person concerned, he assumed their cooperation and simply said that he had called round to arrange a suitable time and place for the interview. The appointment was made as easy as possible for the teenager to fulfil. He was given the choice of having the interview at home or in a near-by office, and it was part of the interviewer's job to make himself available at any time and day suggested by the teenager.

At no time was the possibility of refusing suggested to the teenager, which meant that if he could not be persuaded to fix an appointment, the onus was upon him to say he would not cooperate. For some teenagers, in the situation of a doorstep discussion, such a statement is difficult to make and so sometimes the result would be either a half-fixed interview or a postponement of the decision until a later date. This usually led on to a succession of further calls before an interview or a refusal was obtained. Obviously there is a limit to the amount of pressure that can be put upon someone to agree to an interview. But as the interviewer plainly and patiently showed that he was prepared to fit in with any suggested time and place, it was difficult for the teenager to put him off because he was too busy or because he had no free time in the immediate future.

Quite often a parent would want to know more about the research before allowing his child to take part, and other parents raised objections to all types of research on principle. If the teenager was out, the interviewer was instructed to call back to the house until he got the interview, or until it became clear that he would not get it.

Part of the policy of making it as easy as possible for the teenager to attend for an interview was to provide an office within easy reach of his home. In each town a central office was set up for the administration of the research, which could also be used for interviewing, both during the day and in the evening. It was important that this office should be easy to find and should be at some central point in the town, with easy access by public transport from any part of the neighbourhood. Besides this central office other rooms were made available which were within easy walking distance of that particular sampling area. Finding suitable rooms presented a serious problem in some areas, as landlords were not interested in short leases. When we first came to the South A area, we unknowingly chose an office in a street which was alleged to contain several brothels. Although this reputation was undeserved, as far as we could tell, we had to find other rooms for interviewing because it is important that the approach to the interview room should not be disconcerting in any way. For example, teenage girls cannot be expected to walk down badly lit streets on their way to an interview. As a rule the teenagers were only free in the evening, but rooms had to be available during the day for those who preferred to be interviewed on their days off, and for schoolchildren during the holidays.

Appointments were usually made for the interview to take place in an office rather than in the home unless there was any indication that the appointment might not be kept. This was because interviews in the home were sometimes subject to interruptions and disturbances which made it difficult to obtain the right atmosphere of privacy. When noises and conversation from other members of the family in another room were clearly audible, it was obviously difficult to persuade the teenager to talk freely. Girls appeared to be more relaxed and confident in their own home whereas boys seemed more at ease in the office.

In some homes there are enough rooms so that privacy can be obtained without disturbing other members of the family, and interviews in these homes were very successful; the teenager felt at ease in his own home surroundings and the interviewer's approach was helped by this chance to observe the home background of the young person. But in a crowded home it was often better to get the teenager away; sometimes a family which has been turned out of the room with the television showed signs of impatience, or the boy friend of the girl being interviewed arrived to take her out, or the mother came in with the tea and stayed for a chat. But in an interview of this kind privacy is essential. Taietz (1962) has shown that the individual tends to modify his answers when other members of the family are present. If it was not possible to get the teenager on his own, the discussion was terminated and arrangements were made to continue the interview away from the home on another day.

Fixing interviews in the office had one major drawback; there was no guarantee that the teenager would turn up. Broken appointments were due to a variety of reasons. Sometimes it was through a misunderstanding. A few teenagers expected to find a committee of people waiting to meet them. Sometimes the prospect became so forbidding or uninteresting that the teenager changed his mind once he was away from the interviewer's persuasive influence.

The usual reason for failed appointments was lack of interest in the first place. In these cases the teenager agreed to an appointment simply to get rid of the interviewer and had no intention of turning up at the appointed time.

Of course this was very disheartening for the interviewer who had to arrive at the agreed time and wait to no avail. But it was important that no trace of annoyance was shown when the interviewer called back to inquire gently why the appointment had not been kept, and to make another one. Such persistence often impressed the teenager and in many cases it was possible to get an interview although the teenager had been apathetic at first. There were altogether 118 cases when the tact and determination of the interviewer resulted in a successful interview although the teenager had failed to keep the first appointment.

Quite often there was a series of calls and broken appointments extending sometimes over a period of several weeks. In general the interviewer was advised to keep on trying until it had become obvious that the chances of getting the interview were virtually nil. It is estimated that over 4,450 calls were made during the course of this research; that is an average of 2·4 calls per interview.

The first essential was to convince each teenager that the information was strictly confidential and his name was not put on any part of the schedule. Experience gained during the exploratory stage convinced us that our five male interviewers should interview all the boys, and our five female interviewers should interview all the girls. Benney, Reisman and Star (1956) reported that the least inhibited answers to questions on sex were obtained when respondent and interviewer were young and of the same sex.

The interviewer had to make sure that the younger boy or girl felt at ease. There was a tendency for these interviews to be serious and formal, developing into a relationship similar to schoolmaster and pupil. If the interviewer received an answer like: 'No sir, not me,' he could be sure that he had failed. With the older interviewees more stress had to be laid on the precautions taken to keep the interview anonymous, and to make it easy for them to talk about their sexual adventures.

Interviewers were encouraged to ask the questions fairly rapidly. As well as avoiding fatigue and deterioration in response, quick spontaneous answers gave less opportunity for cover up or untrue replies. If a teenager gave an answer that was inconsistent or obviously false, care was taken to give him the chance to make a correction without implying that the interviewer knew he was lying. On a few occasions the teenager offered to go back over the questions and give a second, more truthful version of his sex behaviour.

When asking questions about sex the interviewer never apologized for asking these questions but implied by his manner that such things could be talked about quite freely without embarrassment. No attempt was made to avoid vernacular words by using long Latin substitutes, and the teenager's behaviour, however unusual, was accepted without comment.

Although a standardized form of question was used in all cases, the interviewer was allowed to press for further information if the answer was unclear or unsatisfactory. One of the advantages of the interview over the questionnaire is that valuable information can be obtained if the interviewee is persuaded to add more than the simple answer to the question. Indeed one of the compensations for the interviewer's hard work was the unexpected sides to life which were revealed occasionally as a teenager elaborated upon his answer. When one girl was asked what she had done the previous evening, she explained: 'My boy friend works for a funeral director, and his boss was away, so we had to stay in the parlour in case anyone phoned.' A boy's answer to the same question: 'I had a terrible row when I got home. I forgot to get Granny's snuff. You know. "All you think of is yourself." She still hasn't got it, poor old lass. Mum forgot it today.'

The interviewers were instructed not to force an answer into an unsuitable category. Results and tables may look neater without 'other' and 'don't know' categories, but in this case they would give a false picture. As we were reporting on all types of teenagers, we had to accept that even our long list of pre-coded answers would not fit every case.

The time when the teenager was doing the attitude inventory provided a useful ten minutes for the interviewer to go over the schedule and check the whole record; then queries or inconsistencies could be settled before the interview was brought to a close. In most cases the teenager was relaxed and eager to talk by the end of the interview, and they were encouraged to add further comments and observations. Finally all of them were asked if they would agree to another interview at a later date. More than 95 per cent of the boys and 97 per cent of the girls willingly agreed and it is felt that this indicates that the full cooperation of the teenagers was obtained in most cases.

Inevitably in a research of this kind the standard of the interview varied from excellent to poor. Not surprisingly some teenagers were not interested in social research of any kind, and others felt that the subject of this research was too personal a matter to discuss with strangers. Some parents were suspicious, others rude. Our interviewers had to contend with apathy and lethargy. Sometimes an evening was set aside for a particular interview only to find that the teenager failed to keep the appointment. Most of the work had to be done in the evenings as it was part of the job for the interviewer to make himself available at the time when it best suited the young person concerned.

Sometimes there were other unexpected hazards which the interviewers had to meet. A week before our visit to North A, the local paper had printed a story about a man wearing a white raincoat who had been molesting young girls. One of our interviewers also had a white raincoat and he was hustled into the police station soon after he had made his first call in the area. Another interviewer called on a boy who lived with his grandmother and made an appointment for the week following. Meanwhile the boy had been caught in the act of breaking into a shop but managed to evade the police. When our interviewer called, the boy thought it might be the police and asked his grandmother to say he was out. On three subsequent calls our interviewer got the same reply. Eventually the police did call and questioned the grandmother about the boy's movements. She knew nothing about the shop breaking, but she told the police that a strange man kept calling and asking for the boy who seemed to be afraid of this stranger. Next time our interviewer called, the police were waiting.

Of course we always notified the Town Clerk, the Medical Officer of Health, the Chief Education Officer and the Chief Constable of the area where we were working. Some parents quite sensibly checked up to see if we were a reputable body. But there were other parents who objected to social research in general. The father of a 17 year old girl wrote: 'I consider your research objectionable and un-British.'

Sometimes the interviewer found himself in a situation where the parent was losing his authority over his child and attempted to re-establish this authority by ordering – or forbidding – his child to be interviewed. Either way it was best for the interview to be abandoned unless the teenager himself showed some interest. Persuasion from less dominant parents, like 'Go on, it will do you good,' were not likely to be of much help.

In the end even the research team felt a sense of relief when they had completed the field work without a public outcry of one kind or another. And yet the job we were trying to do was neither illegal, nor scandalous, nor shady. We were simply trying to collect some information on the sexual behaviour of young people.

Furthermore it is fair to say that the vast majority of teenagers were friendly and cooperative, happy to talk about themselves and to take the interviewer completely into their confidence. Most of them did not hesitate to answer the interviewer's questions earnestly and truthfully, even when the questions were inquiring about the intimate details of their sexual behaviour. Indeed many of them found it a relief to be able to talk about these things to a sympathetic stranger.

Appendix 3: The Attitude Inventory

Statement	Boys Agree, %	DK, %	Disagree, %	Girls Agree, %	DK, %	Disagree, %
1 Life is so short that having a good time is more important than anything else	47	10	43	50	7	43
2 Most parents ought to be stricter with their children	54	19	27	47	15	38
3 It always pays to be honest	75	9	16	84	4	12
4 Summer holidays without parents are more enjoyable	63	23	14	65	17	18
5 Most teenagers are bored with their jobs	36	29	35	30	22	48
6 Each person should decide for himself what is right and wrong	72	5	23	84	5	11
7 The family should spend an evening at home together at least once a week	64	17	19	75	11	14
8 Most adults say one thing and do another	41	21	38	44	16	40
9 It is best to have a good time before you are married because after that life is pretty dreary	28	18	54	27	8	65
10 I learn more from friends of my own age than I can learn from my parents	58	11	31	53	10	37
11 If a boy gets a girl pregnant he should be willing to marry her	66	16	18	66	15	19

Statement	Boys Agree, %	DK, %	Dis- agree, %	Girls Agree, %	DK, %	Dis- agree, %
12 Today's teenagers are very different from teenagers in the past	52	18	30	58	9	33
13 There is no need to teach about sex in schools, because you can find out all you need to know for yourself	21	9	70	13	9	78
14 Parents should advise their children about the sort of work they should do	41	8	51	44	7	49
15 Teenage boys spend too much time thinking about their clothes and hair styles	38	12	50	34	15	51
16 People should realize their greatest loyalty is to their family	79	11	10	73	14	13
17 Girls believe today that if they are not married before they are 21 they are on the shelf	28	23	49	30	10	60
18 The average man can live a good life without religion	58	15	27	53	17	30
19 Young people should be taught all about birth control	81	13	6	83	11	6
20 TV and radio programmes have a strong influence on most teenagers	55	9	36	58	8	34
21 A girl is usually looking for a man to marry, but a boy is usually looking for sex	49	15	36	53	15	32

Statement	Boys			Girls		
	Agree, %	DK, %	Disagree, %	Agree, %	DK, %	Disagree, %
22 It should be made easier for married people to get divorced if they want to	39	15	46	30	12	58
23 In this country there is one law for the rich and another for the poor	41	15	44	32	18	50
24 Young people can only really be free if they live away from home	18	10	72	16	6	78
25 The police are unfair in their treatment of teenagers	28	13	59	19	15	66
26 When it comes to sex, there is one standard for men and another for women	31	37	32	45	28	27
27 If a girl has sex before marriage she gets a bad reputation	45	18	37	58	14	28
28 There is no harm in travelling without a ticket occasionally if you can get away with it.	53	10	37	43	9	48
29 I'd rather take my holidays with my parents	19	23	58	20	23	57
30 I'd rather work for someone strict and fair, than for someone who is easy going	72	11	17	69	11	20
31 The advantages of living at home with the family outweigh the disadvantages	71	20	9	71	16	13
32 It is important for a person who gives sex education to have had some first hand experience of sex	77	14	9	66	14	20

Statement	Boys Agree, %	DK, %	Dis-agree, %	Girls Agree, %	DK, %	Dis-agree, %
33 I'm usually a bit bored when I stay at home in the evenings	49	6	45	39	5	56
34 The Church is the best authority to decide on matters of right and wrong	22	17	61	28	14	58
35 I think I'll have a better job than my father has when I am his age	59	29	12	28	38	34
36 Teenagers have sex thrown at them all the time from advertisements, films and TV	70	7	23	68	6	26
37 I would rather go to my parents for advice than to my friends	55	16	29	53	12	35
38 Sexual intercourse before marriage is all right for boys but not for girls	23	21	56	42	14	44
39 Teenagers should be able to go out in the evening without having to tell their parents where they are going	55	13	32	40	11	49
40 Very few adults really understand teenagers	54	13	33	47	14	39
41 Most boys want to marry a virgin	66	19	15	69	19	12
42 The average teenager expects to live much the same kind of life as his parents do	37	15	48	38	13	49
43 Sexual intercourse before marriage is wrong	35	20	45	62	14	24
44 All homosexuals should be severely punished	47	17	35	35	20	45

Statement	Boys Agree, %	DK, %	Dis-agree, %	Girls Agree, %	DK, %	Dis-agree, %
45 Foreigners should stay in their own country	30	11	59	24	10	66
46 It would be best to keep coloured people in their own districts in order to prevent too much contact with whites	25	11	64	24	13	63
47 Girls should not get married before they are 21	19	21	60	18	15	67
48 What teenagers do and how they dress outside their homes is their business	59	12	29	58	12	30
49 Too much freedom in the early teens leads to trouble when one gets older	50	14	36	45	12	43
50 There is more to sex than just having a good time	86	10	4	87	8	5

References

ABRAMS, MARK. *Teenager Consumer Spending in 1959*. London, London Press Exchange, 1961

ANDERSON, E. W., KENNA, J. C., and HAMILTON, M. W. 'A Study of Extra Marital Conception in Adolescence.' *Psychiatrica et Neurologia*, **139**, 313–62, 1960

BALS, CHRISTEL. *Halbstarke unter Sich*. Köln, Kiepenheuer & Witsch, 1962

BARTLETT, M. S. 'Factor Analysis as a Statistician Sees It.' *Essays on Probability and Statistics*. London, Methuen, 1962

BENNEY, M., REISMAN, D., and STAR, S. A. 'Age and Sex in the Interviewer.' *American Journal of Sociology*, **62**, 143–52, 1956

BERNSTEIN, B. 'Social Structure, Language and Learning.' *Educational Research*, 3:3, 163–76, 1961

BIER, WILLIAM C. (ed.) *The Adolescent: His Search for Understanding*. New York, Fordham University Press, 1963

BOTT, E. *Family and Social Network*. London, Tavistock Publications, 1957

BROMLEY, D. D., and BRITTEN, F. H. *Youth and Sex. A Study of 1300 College Students*. New York, Harper, 1938

BURGESS, E. W., and WALLIN, P. *Engagement and Marriage*. Philadelphia, Lippincott, 1953

CARSTAIRS, G. M. *This Island Now*. London, Hogarth, 1963

CATTEL, R. B. 'The Basis of Recognition and Interpretation of Factors.' *Educational and Psychological Measurement*, **22**:4, 667–713, 1962

CHESSER, EUSTACE. *The Sexual, Marital and Family Relationships of the English Woman*. London, Hutchinsons, 1956

CHRISTENSEN, H. T., and CARPENTER, G. R. 'Value Behaviour Discrepancies Regarding Pre-Marital Coitus in Three Western Cultures.' *American Sociology Review*, **27**:1, 1962

CLINARD, M. B. 'Areas for Research in Deviant Behaviour.' *Sociology and Social Research*, **42**:6, 416–17

COCHRAN, W. G., MOSTELLER, F., and TUKEY, J. W. 'Statistical Problems of the Kinsey Report.' *Journal of the American Statistics Association*, **48**, 673–716, 1953

COCHRAN, W. G., MOSTELLER, F., and TUKEY, J. W. 'Principles of

Sampling.' *Journal of the American Statistics Association*, **49**, 1–12, 1954

COHEN, A. K. *Delinquent Boys: The Culture of the Gang*. Glencoe, Free Press, 1955

COMFORT, ALEX. *Sex in Society*. London, Duckworth, 1963

DALZELL-WARD, A. J. 'Venereal Diseases and the Teenager – Health Education Aspects.' *Proceedings of the Royal Society of Health*, **67**, 39–41, 1960

DESCHIN, CELIA S. *Teenagers and Venereal Disease: A Sociological Study*. New York, U.S. Department of Health Education and Welfare, Public Health Service, 1961

DOUGLAS, J. W. B. *The Home and the School*. London, MacGibbon & Kee, 1964

EHRMANN, W. W. *Premarital Dating Behaviour*. New York, Henry Holt, 1959

ELLIS, ALBERT. 'Questionnaire versus Interview Methods in the Study of Human Love Relationships.' *American Sociological Review*, **12**, 61–5, 1947

EPPEL, E. M., and EPPEL, M. *Adolescents and Morality*. London, Routledge & Kegan Paul, 1966

EYSENCK, H. J. *The Structure of Human Personality*. London, Methuen, 1953

EYSENCK, H. J. *The Psychology of Politics*. London, Routledge & Kegan Paul, 1954

EYSENCK, H. J. *Experiments in Personality*. London, Routledge & Kegan Paul, 1960

FINESTONE, HAROLD. 'Narcotics and criminality.' *Law and Contemporary problems*, **22**, 69–85, 1957

FISHER, R. A. and YATES, F. *Statistical Tables (6th edn)*. Edinburgh, Oliver & Boyd, 1963

FYVEL, T. R. *The Insecure Offenders*. London, Penguin, 1963

GEBHARD, P., POMEROY, W., MARTIN C., and CHRISTENSEN, C. *Pregnancy, Birth and Abortion*. London, Heinemann, 1959

GLUECK, S., and GLUECK, E. *Delinquents in the Making*. New York, Harper, 1952

GOETSHIUS, G., and TASH, M. J. *Working with Unattached Youth*. London, Routledge & Kegan Paul, 1966

GRAY, P. G., and CARTWRIGHT, ANN. 'Choosing and Changing Doctors.' *The Lancet*, Dec. 19, 1308–9, 1953

GREENLAND, CYRIL. 'Putative fathers.' *The Medical Officer*, **99**, 281–6, 1958

HECHINGER, GRACE, and HECHINGER, FRED. *Teenage Tyranny*. London, Duckworth, 1964

HEMMING, J. *Problems of the Adolescent Girl*. London, Heinemann, 1960

HENDRICKSON, A. E., and WHITE, P. O. 'Promax: A Quick Method for Rotation to Oblique Simple Structure.' *British Journal of Statistical Psychology*, **17**, 1964

HERON, ALASTAIR (ed.) *Towards a Quaker View of Sex*. London, Friends Home Service Committee, 1963

HIMELHOCHE, JEROME, and FAVA, SYLVIA (eds.) *Sexual Behaviour in American Society*. New York, Norton, 1955

HITCHENS, R. A. N., and JAMES, E. B. 'Premarital Intercourse, Venereal Disease and Young People: Recent Trends.' *Public Health*, **79**:5, 258–70, 1965

HOLLINGSHEAD, A. B., and REDLICH, F. *Social Class and Mental Illness*. New York, Wiley, 1958

HUANG, W. 'Adolescent Problem Solved.' *Times Educational Supplement*, **2556**, 1342–3, 1964

JEPHCOTT, P., SEEAR, N., and SMITH, J. *Married Women Working*. London, Allen and Unwin, 1962

KERR, ANTHONY. *Youth of Europe*. Cambridge, Bowes and Bowes, 1964

KINSEY, A. C., POMEROY, W. B., and MARTIN, C. E. *Sexual Behaviour in the Human Male*. Philadelphia, Saunders, 1948

KINSEY, A. C., POMEROY, W. B., MARTIN, C. E., and GEBHARD, P. H. *Sexual Behaviour in the Human Female*. Philadelphia, Saunders, 1953

KIRKENDALL, L. A. *Premarital Intercourse and Interpersonal Relationships*. New York, Julian Press, 1961

KNONHAUSEN, PHYLLIS, and KNONHAUSEN, EBERHARD. *Sex Histories of American College Men*. New York, Ballantine, 1960

LEE, J. A. H. 'Motor Cycle Accidents to Male Teenagers.' *Proceedings of the Royal Society of Medicine*, **56**:5, 1963

LOLLI, GIORGIO. *Social Drinking: The Effects of Alcohol*. New York, Collier Books, 1961

MACE, DAVID, and MACE, VERA. *The Soviet Family*. New York, Doubleday, 1963

MORRIS, J. F. 'The Development of Adolescent Value Judgements.' *British Journal of Educational Psychology*, **28**:1, 1958

MORSE, MARY. *The Unattached*. London, Penguin, 1965

MORTON, R. S. *Venereal Disease*. London, Penguin, 1966

MOSER, C. A. *Survey Methods in Social Investigation*. London, Heinemann, 1958

MURDOCK, GEORGE P. *Social Structure*. New York, Macmillan, 1949

MUSGROVE, FRANK. 'Inter-generation Attitudes'. *British Journal of Social and Clinical Psychology*, **2**, 209–23, 1963

MYERS, J. K., and ROBERTS, B. H. *Family and Class Dynamics in Mental Illness*. New York, Wiley, 1959

MYRDAL, A., and KLEIN, V. *Women's Two Roles: Home and Work*. London, Routledge & Kegan Paul, 1956

NEWSON, J., and NEWSON, E. *Infant Care in an Urban Community*. London, Allen & Unwin, 1963

PONTING, L. I. 'The Social Aspects of Venereal Disease Among Young People In Leeds and London'. *British Journal of Venereal Diseases*, **39**, 273–77, 1963

PRAIS, S. J., and HOUTHAKKER, H. S. *The Analysis of Family Budgets*. Cambridge, Cambridge University Press, 1955

RECKLESS, W. C. *The Crime Problem*. New York, Appleton-Century, 1961

REISS, IRA L. *Premarital Sexual Standards in America*. Glencoe, Free Press, 1960

ROBB, JAMES. *Working Class Anti Semite*. London, Tavistock Publications, 1954

SCHOFIELD, MICHAEL. 'The sociological contribution to health education.' *Health Education Journal*, **22**, 44–8, 1964

SCHOFIELD, MICHAEL. *Sociological Aspects of Homosexuality*. London, Longmans, 1965

SPINLEY, B. M. *The Deprived and the Privileged*. London, Routledge & Kegan Paul, 1953

TAIETZ, PHILIP. 'Conflicting Group Norms and the "Third" Person in the Interview.' *American Journal of Sociology*, **68**, 97–104, 1962

TANNER, J. M. *Education and Physical Growth*. London, University of London Press, 1961

TANNER, J. M. *Growth at Adolescence*. Oxford, Blackwell, 1962

TERMAN, L. M., and MILES, C. C. *Sex and Personality*. New York, McGraw-Hill, 1936

THURSTONE, L. L. *Multiple Factor Analysis*. Chicago, University of Chicago Press, 1949

WEST, DONALD. *The Habitual Prisoner*. London, Macmillan, 1963

WESTWOOD, GORDON. *A Minority: A Report on the Life of the Male Homosexual in Great Britain*. London, Longmans, 1960

WHYTE, W. F. *Street Corner Society*. Chicago, University of Chicago Press, 1943

WILKINS, L. T. *The Adolescent in Britain*. London, Central Office of Information, 1955

WIMPERIS, V. *The Unmarried Mother and her Child*. London, Allen & Unwin, 1960

Reports

15–18: A Report of the Central Advisory Council for Education (Crowther Report). London, H.M.S.O., 1959

The Youth Service in England and Wales (Albermarle Report). London, H.M.S.O., 1960

British Co-operative Clinical Group. *British Journal of Venereal Diseases*, **38**, 1–18, 1962

British Co-operative Clinical Group. *British Journal of Venereal Diseases*, **39**, 1–18, 1963

Half our future: A Report of the Central Advisory Council for Education (Newsom Report). London, H.M.S.O., 1963

Venereal Disease and Young People. London, British Medical Association, 1964

The Annual Report of the Chief Medical Officer of the Ministry of Health for the year 1965. London, H.M.S.O., 1966

Sex and Morality: A Report to the British Council of Churches. London, S.C.M. Press, 1966

Criminal Statistics. London, H.M.S.O., 1966

The Registrar General's Statistical Review of England and Wales for the year 1966. London, H.M.S.O., 1967

Index of Names

Abrams, Mark, 25
Albemarle Report, 25, 27
Anderson, E. W., 218
Annual Report of the Chief Medical Officer of the Ministry of Health, 229

Bals, Christel, 234
Benney, M., 251
Bernstein, B., 83
Bier, William C., 233
Bott, E., 118
British Cooperative Clinical Group, 94, 229
British Medical Association, 23 99
Britten, F. H., 211
Bromley, D. D., 211
Burgess, E. W., 233

Carstairs, G. M., 19
Cartwright, Ann, 31
Cattel, R. B., 152
Chesser, Eustace, 29, 211, 216
Clinard, M. B., 119
Cochran, W. G., 21, 48
Cocteau, J., 235
Cohen, A. K., 119
Comfort, Alex, 19
Crowther Report, 27

Dalzell-Ward, A. J., 11, 82, 230
Douglas, J. W. B., 56

Ehrmann, W. W., 81, 222
Ellis, Albert, 237

Ellis, B., 11
Eppel, E. M., 24, 102
Eysenck, H. J., 99, 153, 193–6

Fava, Sylvia, 22
Finestone, H., 66
Fyvel, T. R., 234

Gebhardt, P., 218
Glueck, S., 116
Goetshius, G., 140
Gray, P. G., 31
Greenland, Cyril, 227

Hechinger, F. and G., 234
Hendrickson, A. E., 154n
Himelhoche, Jerome, 22
Hitchen, R. A. N., 94, 230
Holingshead, A. B., 119
Houthakker, H. S., 244
Huang, W., 233

Jephcott, P., 118
James, E. B., 94, 230

Kerr, A., 118
Kinsey, A. C., 21, 29–30, 48, 60, 62, 211, 216, 219
Klein, V., 118

Lee, J. A. H., 27
Lolli, Giorgio, 119

Mace, David, 233
Miles, C. C., 99
Ministry of Health, 32, 94
Morse, Mary, 140

Morton, R. S., 231
Moser, C. A., 212
Mosteller, F., 22, 48
Murdock, George, P., 233
Musgrove, Frank, 221
Myers, J. K., 119
Myrdal, A., 118

Newsom Report, 27
Newsom, J., 83
Nuffield Foundation, 11, 19

Ponting, L. I., 227, 229
Prais, S. J., 244

Reckless, W. C., 119
Redlich, F., 119
Registrar General's Statistical Review, 27, 136n, 217, 228n
Reisman, D., 251

Robb, James, 199
Robbins Report, 27
Roberts, B. H., 119

Schofield, Michael, 61, 84
Spinley, B. M., 83
Star, S. A., 251

Taetz, Philip, 250
Tanner, J. M., 27, 83, 203
Tash, M. G., 140
Terman, L. M., 99
Tukey, J. W., 22, 48

Wallin, P., 233
West, D., 119
Westwood, Gordon, 60–61, 199
White, P. O., 154n
Whyte, W. F., 119
Wimperis, V., 216

Subject Index

Abortion, 90

Accumulative frequency curves, 49–50

Accumulative incidence, 48–51, 215, 223

Adoption, 90

Age groups, 33, 36, 185–9, 214

Alcohol, *see* Drinks

Amphetamines, 66, 148

Appearance, 200

Attitude inventory, 35, 98–9, 102, 153–6, 253

Birth control, 87–93, 139, 180n, 227–8

Birth order, 118–19

Boy friends, 64, 74, 135–6, 141

Breast stimulation, 44–6, 49–53, 58–60, 70–71

Broken homes, 116, 202

Call-backs, 34–5

Cannabis, 66, 148

Cars, 60, 142

Christian teaching, 24, 232

Church attendance, *see* Religion

Cigarettes, 25, 149

Cinema, 22, 25, 57, 64, 143–4, 190

Climax, 47, 68

Clubs:
    jazz, 140, 242
    mixed, 140–41
    segregated, 140–41

Coffee bars, 133, 147–8

Conception, 82–4

Conformism, 80, 133–5, 204–5, 207, 234–5

Contraceptive pill, 88

Contraceptives, *see* Birth control

Correlations, 185–93

Dancing, 28, 57, 133, 143–4, 190

Dating, 41, 49–53, 57–8, 70–72, 76–7

Deep kissing, 42–3, 46, 49–53, 58

Delinquency, 28, 119, 149–51, 205

Drinks, 75, 144, 146–7

Drugs, 28, 66, 148

E-boys, 115

Engagements, 136

Ethnocentrism, 180–84, 188–96, 204

Evening classes, 128

Examination, 126, 203

Factor analysis, 154, 180

Factor:
    loading, 155–7, 177
    scores, 155, 160, 182

Facts of life, *see* Conception

Failed appointments, 251

Family, *see* Parents

Fiancé, *see* Boy friends

Fiancée, *see* Girl friends

Fidelity, 233

Forced marriage, 90

French kissing, *see* Deep kissing

Friends, *see* Groups

Gambling, 148–9

Genital apposition, 45–7, 107
Genital stimulation, 44, 46, 49–53, 59–60, 70–71
Girl friends, 64, 135–6
Gonorrhoea, see Venereal diseases
Gregariousness, 204–5, 232
Groups, 132–9

Hairstyle, 28, 101
Health education, 84
Holidays, 25, 122, 168
Homosexuality, 60–63, 102, 180

I-boys, 115
Illegitimacy, 23, 28, 217–18, 227–9
Immigrants, 94, 102
Incidental factors, 157–9
Inceptive activities, 43, 52, 59–60, 74–5, 77–8, 117, 223
Inferential assessments, 199–200
Interviewers, 20–21, 34, 36, 209, 246–54
Interview:
    location, see Local offices
    questions, 35, 60, 92, 107, 192, 213, 238, 243–5
    techniques, 98, 220, 237–45, 252
Introductory letter, 34, 212, 248

Juvenile delinquency, see Delinquency

Kissing, 42–3, 49–53, 57–8, 70–72
Knowledge about sex, 82–97, 138–9, 236

Local offices, 34, 249–50
Love, 73, 135–6, 207

Marriage, 102–4
Married teenagers, 136, 210
Menstruation, 27, 83

Maternities legalized by marriage, see Premarital conception
Middle class, see Social class differences
Money to spend, 130–31, 190, 207
Motor bicycles, 25, 142, 202

National Health lists, 31
N-boys, 115

Oral-genital, 45
Orgasm, see Climax

Parents:
    advice about sex, 82, 84–6, 96, 100, 133, 137–8, 206
    discipline, 48, 60, 65, 100, 120–22, 202, 233, 254
    relations with, 24, 119–20
    supervision by, 123
Parties, 60, 64, 121, 144–6, 202
Permissiveness, 182–4, 195–6, 205, 208
Personality tests, 152–3
Petting, see Inceptive activities
Physical development, 27, 70, 204–5
Pilot research, 242, 245
Pocket money, see Money to spend
Pop music, 205, 234
Posters, 96
Precautions, see Birth control
Pregnancy, 47, 80, 89–91, 106–7, 227
Premarital conception, 217–18, 222
Premarital sexual intercourse, see Sexual intercourse
Press publicity, 26, 66, 98–9, 213
Probation, 20

Promiscuity, 13, 72, 137, 220n, 224, 230–31
Prostitutes, 64
Puberty, 24, 203
Putative fathers, 62, 218

Questionnaires, 29, 33–4, 237–8, 252
Quotations, 36, 65–7, 84–9, 134

Rapport, 35, 247
Refusal form, 35, 214–15
Refusal rate, 35
Refusals, 210–15, 243
Religion, 72–3, 93, 101, 107, 124, 155, 168, 190, 201
Restrictiveness, 180–84, 188–96, 206

Sampling, 21–2, 31–3, 209–10, 222
School:
    age left, 72, 127, 131, 203
    attendance records, 32
    boarding, 61–2, 126, 201
    coeducational, 61–2, 126, 201
    types of, 54–5, 86–7, 126, 190, 201, 226
    problems at, 127–8, 203
Sex education, 86–7, 97 104–6 138–9 225–6
Sexual intercourse:
    attitudes to 104, 108–12
    first experience, 62–70, 73, 215
    frequency, 78–81
    incidence, 45–55, 136
    locations, 64–5
    reactions, 68–70, 79–80
    social pressures, 93, 232
Sexual offences, 150
Sexual partners, 63, 73, 137, 223
Sheath, 89, 92

Social class differences, 33, 43, 54–6, 59, 83–4, 117–19, 190, 201, 221
Sports, 140–42
Stages of sex definitions, 51–5
Statistical analysis, 29–31, 55, 154
Statistical tests, 115–16
Steady, *see* Boy friends and Girl friends
Stealing, 150
Syphilis, *see* Venereal disease

Teachers, 20, 82–4, 96, 104–6, 225
Teenage market, 25–6, 28
Teenage conformity, *see* Conformism
Teenage mythology, 26, 28, 204, 208, 234–5
Television, 26, 96, 142–3, 202
Trial interviews, 247–8

Unmarried mothers, 28, 62, 90, 228

Validity, 35, 209–222
Venereal disease, 13, 20, 23, 47, 80, 93–7, 138, 218, 229–31, 244
Violence, 150
Virginity, 107–112

Wages, 130–31, 190, 203, 207
Withdrawal, 88–9
Work, 100–101, 129–31, 202–3, 207
Working class, *see* Social class differences

Youth clubs, 22, 28, 57, 64, 133, 140–41
Youth workers, 20, 34